Who Is Allah?

Islamic Civilization and Muslim Networks

CARL W. ERNST AND BRUCE B. LAWRENCE, EDITORS

Highlighting themes with historical as well as contemporary significance, Islamic Civilization and Muslim Networks features works that explore Islamic societies and Muslim peoples from a fresh perspective, drawing on new interpretive frameworks or theoretical strategies in a variety of disciplines. Special emphasis is given to systems of exchange that have promoted the creation and development of Islamic identities—cultural, religious, or geopolitical. The series spans all periods and regions of Islamic civilization.

A complete list of titles published in this series appears at the end of the book.

WHO IS
Allah?

Bruce B. Lawrence

The University of North Carolina Press CHAPEL HILL

Calligraphy for chapter opening ornament by
Mohamed Zakariya, February 2014.

Jacket illustration: Painting by Mohamed Melehi (*Ha' 2*, 1984).
At its center is a receding repetition of *ha'* (the Arabic letter "h"),
framed by angular and wavy elements. *Ha'* elides with *huwa* (the pronoun
"he"); when written alone, *ha'/huwa* connotes Allah as its inner meaning.
Used by permission of the artist.

Library of Congress Cataloging-in-Publication Data
Lawrence, Bruce B.
Who is Allah? / Bruce B. Lawrence.
pages cm
Includes bibliographical references and index.
ISBN 978-1-4696-2003-9 (cloth : alk. paper)
ISBN 978-1-4696-2004-6 (ebook)
1. God (Islam) I. Title.
BP166.2.L38 2015
297.2'11—dc23
2014032689

To M. F. Husain,
an artist for the ages,
a chain of light
linking all to Allah,
past, present, and future

Contents

Figures

Preface

Who Is Allah? is the product of a lifetime engaged by Islam and subjects relating to Islamic thought and culture, society and politics, across centuries in myriad contexts. It is aimed at a popular audience, as well as regular readers of books in the Islamic Civilization and Muslim Networks series published by the University of North Carolina Press. The conventions of Arabic are kept to a minimum, with just the *hamza* and *'ayn* used to reflect the distinctive accents of Arabic—or Persian or Turkish or Urdu—names and technical terms. In many instances English translations of common words are used after their first introduction in both Arabic and English.

A major exception is the name Allah. It is not enough to say Allah=God if one seeks to acknowledge the complexity, and also explore the mystery, of Muslim performance of Allah. In this study, Allah is center stage at every level and in every chapter. And so, in order to stress the prevalence of Allah, I will occasionally parse words that combine Allah and another word into one that takes an Allah-specific form. Hence, at times *bismillah* will be written *bismi(A)llah* ("in the name of God"), and *inshallah* ("if God wills, of God willing") will appear as *insha'(A)llah*. For Arabic speakers, this convention may seem redundant, but for those who are innocent of any knowledge of Arabic, it will be a constant reminder of how Allah is implanted in the deepest recesses of the Muslim imagination—across time, space, race, gender, and geography.

You will also find sidebars. They are included to provide readers with focused information about places, persons, and issues that until now have been dimly known but are relevant to the evidence and argument of this book.

Finally, there is the ubiquitous Internet. In many instances the Internet has provided references and resources that are readily available to twenty-first-century readers. The surfeit of their presence requires judicious selection on each topic relating to Allah. I have attempted to harvest the best, while avoiding the worst. Each reader must decide for him- or herself how well, or badly, I have performed that task, but my aim in each instance is to make Allah at once more accessible and subtle as the bedrock of Muslim self-expression.

Who Is Allah?

There is the name and the thing; the name is a voice that denotes and
signifies the thing; the name is no part of the thing, nor of the substance;
it is a foreign piece joined to the thing, outside it.
—Michel de Montaigne, *Essays*

Introduction

FRAMING THE NAME ALLAH

Allah is said to be ubiquitous, all encompassing, and inescapable. Allah
is a name but more than a name. Allah is the name for one beyond limits,
including the limits of naming. How can we approach this puzzle? Can
we dare to examine, interpret, and perhaps explain the pervasive name
that supersedes all other names? Can we accept it as the thing that
eludes all efforts to appropriate, to contain, and so to restrict it?

Perhaps we must be content with traces. And so we begin by looking
at a prayer, a hymn, an aphorism, and a pop song. Later we also examine sources on the Internet, knowing that it is the reference point for
many with the same queries as ours. But first we broach Allah in prayer.

One popular Muslim prayer invokes the name Allah repeatedly:

In the name of Allah,
And through Allah,
And from Allah,
And towards Allah,

And upon Allah,
And in Allah—
There is no strength nor power except through Allah, the High, the
Most Great.[1]

Central to Jewish ritual is repetition of the refrain, "*Baruch atah Ado-nai, Eloheinu Melech ha-olam*," which might be translated as "Blessed are You, O Lord, our God, Sovereign of the universe," while for Christians the focus is on Christ, as in the popular hymn "St. Patrick's Breastplate," the next-to-last stanza of which begins with the quatrain:

Christ be with me, Christ within me,
Christ behind me, Christ before me,
Christ beside me, Christ to win me,
Christ to comfort and restore me.[2]

Nor is this a specifically Abrahamic reflex. The notion of a single name, and a singular force, that expands to become something absolute, accessible to humans yet beyond their comprehension, also resonates in other religions: Om in Hinduism, or Om Shanti Shanti Shanti in Buddhism.

With the emergence of Islam in the seventh century, however, it is one name, and one name alone, that is said to embody all that defines life—human, animal, animate, inanimate, this world, the universe—while itself exceeding definition: Allah. Allah is a name unlike other names. Allah is *the* Name and *the* Referent beyond all other names, first for those who are Muslim, but also for those who relate to Islam and the Muslim community, such as Arab Christians. Though Christianity predates Islam by six centuries, Allah becomes the God of the Arabic Bible as well as the Arabic Qur'an. For both Arab Christians and *all* Muslims, whether Arab or non-Arab, Allah comes to embody the beauty, but also the paradox, of naming the Absolute.

In Allah Muslims confront the universal human dilemma: what does it mean to identify and name, and by so naming also to claim, the absolute? It was the paradox of naming the absolute that occupied Michel de Montaigne (d. 1592), an erudite, influential humanist of the sixteenth-century Renaissance. Montaigne probed the paradox of naming the thing. The name and the thing, he asserted, are related yet separate. In the brief aphorism cited above, Montaigne, a devoutly skeptical Christian, went on to observe: "God, who is all fullness in Himself and the height of all perfection, cannot augment or add anything to Himself *within*"; and yet there is the part of Him without, beyond His interior self, and that hinges on His name. "His name," continues Montaigne, "may be augmented and increased by the blessing and praise we attribute to His exterior works. Since we cannot incorporate our praise in Him—for nothing can be added to His good—we attribute it to *His name, the part of Him nearest to us.*"[3]

In other words, while we can praise God, we cannot add anything to His inner self, His unqualified good. Our praise instead attaches to His name, since the name is the part of Him most accessible, and nearest, to us. An educated Muslim in any century would agree: Allah is fullness and perfection beyond human knowing or owning. No name can, or should, or will, capture the Thing.[4] Because It is beyond us and beyond compare, Its name is the portal to the unseen, the gateway to the unknown. Allah may become the song of the heart, as also the measure of every day's activity, in mind and in body, in self and in society. Yet always and everywhere Allah remains beyond compare, beyond our ability to compare the One with anyone, the Thing with anything.

ALLAH BEYOND GENDER

Beyond compare also means beyond gender attributes. If no name captures the Thing, neither does any gender attribute. Someone might ask: Who is Allah? Another replies: Go ask Him! Still another retorts: Go ask Her! Both answers are correct, at once playful yet serious. The riddle they skirt is older than Islam or Allah. It goes back to the beginning of time, and to the notion of a single, omnipotent source of life, destiny, and universe. Every conceivable name evokes the paradox of trying to name the unknowable or to gender the absolute. In the case of Islam, Allah is both He and She, yet at the same time neither He nor She. Allah is beyond He and She, Him and Her, and even It.[5]

In the long history of Islam, the name Allah becomes the imperfect human instrument to connect with the perfect Divine Other. It is the name of the Thing but not itself the Thing. Allah is like Adonai ("Lord" in Hebrew) or Aboon ("Our Father"), familiar equivalents in Judaism and Aramaic Christianity. All three names remain the best of imperfect longings that strive to connect the human seeker with the One ever sought but never fully known. Allah, Adonai, and Our Father—each encodes a mystery. Only artists, poets, mystics, and saints can, and sometimes do, pierce this mystery, but only temporarily, evocatively, and always with humility about their own worthiness to understand. The rest of us are left watching and waiting. We hope. We pray. We read. We sing. And we also, of course, listen. Later in this book we will listen to some saints, but let us first listen to the voice, or rather the echo, of a renowned reggae musician.

OPENING ANECDOTE ON *BISMILLAH*

It was the summer of 1985. The king of Morocco was celebrating his birthday. Crowds of ordinary Moroccans gathered in the historic city of Marrakesh. My wife and I were leading a student summer program in Morocco and had been invited to participate. One evening we went to a huge soccer stadium. We wanted to see and hear the legendary reggae singer of West Africa, Alpha Blondy. We arrived at 9 PM. By midnight, Alpha Blondy had yet to appear. All were restive; some were annoyed; some—a very few—had already left. Then a murmur began. It grew and grew as the diminutive singer strode on stage, grabbed the microphone, and whispered into the now-silent stadium: "*Bismillah ar-rahman ar-rahim, Barukh ata Adonai,* Our Father who art in heaven." In Arabic, Hebrew, and English (translated from the original Aramaic), the names of God—Allah, Adonai, Our Father—tripped off the songster's tongue and rippled across the stunned audience. Alpha Blondy repeated the words—in the name of Allah (Arabic), May thou be blessed O Lord (Hebrew), Our Father who art in heaven (English). With each repetition there came a crescendo of applause, louder and louder until he whispered, "Amen," and moved on to the rest of his program. It lasted till 3 AM; far from being tired, the crowd left the stadium abuzz, clearly energized. Allah/Adonai/Our Father seemed a bit closer to those of us who heard Alpha Blondy that night in Marrakesh.

Bismillah is as common to Muslims as Adonai is to Jews or Our Father is to Christians. When Alpha Blondy opened his Marrakesh concert with the phrase *bismillah,* "in the name of Allah," he had merely done what many pious Muslims do before any action. Quietly they say *bismillah.* They invoke the name of Allah to bless a meal. They invoke His name before opening a book they are about to read. They invoke His name to anticipate an action. They invoke His name to mark a ritual slaughter. *Bismillah* is a sound, a sight, a taste, a touch, and a smell. But first, above all, *bismillah*, in the name of Allah, is the opening phrase of what Muslims recognize to be the Noble Book: the Holy Qur'an.

That night in Marrakesh, however, Alpha Blondy had added invocations from the two other Abrahamic religions. In so doing he drew popular attention to the tight bonds connecting Muslims, Jews, and Christians. The phrase "in the name of Allah" anchors Muslims' daily practices, but it also connects Allah to Abraham, to Moses, and to Jesus.

THE NAME ALLAH AS A REFLEX

What's in a name? Why do all religions put such a focus on the name of this or that deity, divinity, prophet, saint, or savior? The name moves beyond the unbounded, unspecified space that surrounds and engulfs the universe and everything in it, whether human, animal, animate, inanimate, earthly, or celestial. Naming borders the Thing without becoming the Thing, as Montaigne forcefully and clearly articulated the universal human dilemma over 400 years ago. The name reflects on the One Named but also the one naming. By naming we identify ourselves with one whose name mirrors, but also eludes, our desire to connect to what is beyond naming. The name given to any and every being is a human speech act. Cosmic in its aspiration, it remains human in its source.

For Muslims, Allah is that name beyond all names that becomes the singular, most potent name to be invoked, remembered, and repro-

> **Crucial Dates in the Life of the Prophet Muhammad**
> Born, 570 CE
> Married, 595 CE
> Called to prophesy, 610 CE
> Left Mecca for Medina, 622 CE
> Died, 632 CE
> 622 CE, known as the *hijra*, marks the first year in the Muslim calendar, which is lunar: 1600 CE, e.g., roughly equates to 1000 AH.

duced. More than the Initiator of Prophecy, Allah is also the Architect of the Universe as well as the Guiding Force of Human Destiny. Allah is there for eternity, but also in each breath we take. Precisely because Allah never ceases to act throughout history and in us, it is incumbent on individuals to invoke that name. Indeed, to invoke the name of Allah is the requisite sign of each individual's constant awareness of Allah acting in their own lives. Though only a name for Muslims, it still remains the most precious, the most precise, and the most potent of names for the Thing, the Absolute, the One beyond knowing, grasping, or changing.

My aim in this book is to open the door onto Islam in its multiple dimensions, all of which come from and return to Allah. It is a book about Muslims as seen through their performance of Allah. Mine is not an attempt to know the essence of the One praised—the Infinite Immortal beyond us finite mortals—but instead to seek to understand the motives and activities, the longings and legacies of those who praise the One as Allah. That quest leads through the trajectory of Islam over time. If Allah is the source of Islam, then Islam becomes the conduit of Allah. A religion of the seventh century, Islam remains vital, flexible, and potent in the twenty-first century. Estimated at 1.6 billion in 2010, the global Muslim community is projected to grow to 2.2 billion by 2030.[6] At its core are revelations given to an itinerant Arab merchant named Muhammad. Each revelation begins with an invocation in the name of the Sender: Allah. These revelations came intermittently over twenty-two years. Muhammad heard them; others wrote them; all remembered them. Allah is the Sender, the Reminder, and the Owner of all that was gifted through Muhammad. Allah is also the source and the cynosure, the beginning and the end, of all that became Islam.

FROM *BISMILLAH* TO *ALLAHU AKBAR*

While saying "in the name of Allah" connects each Muslim to the divine, another familiar phrase, *Allahu Akbar,* "Allah is Greater" (than anything or anyone you can imagine), signals the bonds that tie the community to their Lord. Visit any Muslim country and you will hear *Allahu Akbar* five times a day. The one appointed to call others to prayer, the muezzin, begins each call with *Allahu Akbar.* To say *Allahu Akbar* is to invoke Allah above, before, and beyond all others. *Allahu Akbar* complements and contrasts with *bismillah.* Whereas *bismillah* is often a private invocation of Allah as the Supreme Source of All That Is, Was, or Ever Will Be, *Allahu Akbar* is a public declaration. *Allahu Akbar* makes public and audible for all the pervasive presence, the inescapable and incalculable reach, of Allah.

MEDIA ACCENT ON *ALLAHU AKBAR*

It was mid-July 2013. Yet another deadly bombing in Iraq, and the first image on evening TV news announcing the tragedy was the Iraqi flag. Emblazoned on that flag were the words: *Allahu Akbar.*

Too often today the public power of *Allahu Akbar* is reduced to news clips that feature would-be terrorists or freedom fighters. In 2012 the award-winning TV series *Homeland* featured suicide bombers shouting *Allahu Akbar.* Whether you turn on the evening newscasts or you troll any online news source, you will find the clamor of *Allahu Akbar.* Those fighting to liberate Libya from Qaddafi in 2011 shouted *Allahu Akbar,* as do those who are still fighting to liberate Syria from Bashar al-Assad in 2013. Modern-day Muslim warriors, including those labeled terrorists, punctuate most victories in skirmishes, minor or major, with the same shout: *Allahu Akbar.* The suicide bombers, just before they crashed the hijacked planes into the World Trade Center in New York, shouted *Allahu Akbar.* And U.S. army psychiatrist Major Nidal Hasan was heard intoning *Allahu Akbar* before massacring thirteen fellow soldiers and wounding thirty-two others at Fort Hood, Texas, on 5 November 2009.

It was not so just thirty years ago. In 1983 newspapers from Cairo to Jakarta ran front-page stories about the late Neil Armstrong, who had been the first human on the moon in 1969. Armstrong was said to have had an unusual experience during his brief lunar walk: he heard an eerie noise. He had no idea where it came from or what caused it. Though he never reported it to his NASA monitors, it purportedly remained burned in his memory. Years later, while on a U.S.-sponsored trip to Cairo, Armstrong is said to have heard the same wailing noise echoing in the streets. When he asked what it was, his Muslim host said, "*Allahu Akbar*—God, than whom none is Greater; it is the Muslim call to prayer."

There are various reports about what happened next, and Armstrong himself later denied that either on the moon or in Cairo he had heard *Allahu Akbar.* Yet the story persisted in many corners of the global Muslim public square. It reverberates even today. Armstrong died in August 2012, and soon after his death there was a flurry of blogs arguing whether or not he had heard *Allahu Akbar.* "Had he not converted to Islam?" was the question that many asked, and still ask. A *fatwa,* or Islamic juridical opinion, has been issued denying Armstrong's conversion, and a Bangladeshi blogger posted a long analysis debunking the rumor mill, yet it churns on.[7] Less important than the hoax, the myth, and the rumor mill is their underlying premise: *Allahu Akbar* conveys enormous symbolic power as the bridge, the window, the brand name for all that is genuinely, authentically Islamic.

COMPETING DEFINITIONS OF ALLAH

And so who is the Allah of *Allahu Akbar*? I have not defined Allah because the One cannot be defined, only described. When dictionaries claim to define everything and everyone, including Allah, they end by obscuring what they attempt to define. An Islamic dictionary, for instance, offers this definition of Allah: "Allah, or God, is the only true reality. There is nothing permanent other than Him. Allah is considered eternal and uncreated, whereas everything else in the universe is created. The Qur'an describes Him in Sura 112: '*Say: He is Allah, Singular. Allah, the Absolute. He begetteth not nor was He begotten. And to Him has never been one equal.*' Can any human be His offspring? No! The Qur'an condemns and mocks the pre-Islamic Arabs for attributing daughters to Allah. (Q 53:19)."[8]

By quoting from the Qur'an and disparaging pre-Islamic notions of Allah, this definition glosses over the long historical development of Muslim belief in Allah. It also sidesteps the equally long, often-bitter controversy about the identity of Allah. Some trace the history of the name Allah from its primordial purity to a polluted middle period and then a prophetic restoration.[9] In other words, they see worship of the

How to Cite the Qur'an

The Qur'an consists of 114 *suras* (or chapters), each divided into *ayat* (or verses). All are considered by Muslims to have been revealed by Allah to Muhammad, yet not all are accorded equivalent importance. Q 1 and Q 112 are the pivotal bookends of the Noble Book, as it is known among most Muslims. Citations made from the Qur'an will indicate *sura* and *ayah* after the single capital letter Q. Hence Q 53:19 refers to the nineteenth verse of the fifty-third chapter. Also, for visual ease, direct citations from the Qur'an will be italicized.

Thing, the Absolute, the One as existing in ancient times then ignored or betrayed by later generations before being finally restored through the revelations given to the Prophet Muhammad. But such a neatly teleological history omits the pivotal role of the Qur'an. The Qur'an became the major authority guiding all subsequent use of the name Allah. It acknowledges Allah's history before Muhammad. "The Prophet's Arab contemporaries," notes one prominent scholar, "knew of a Supreme Being, but He did not dominate their minds."[10]

How then did Allah come to dominate, and continue to dominate, the language and the life as well as the mindset and outlook of Muslims? In order to understand how the familiar name of Allah became the triumphant name of Allah, one must reconsider the intervention of the one whom Allah declared to be the last prophet (Q 33:40). Muhammad shaped events. He did not merely triumph over his adversaries, or advocate return to worship of the One True God, as some sources suggest. Instead, Muhammad, responding to directives from the Archangel Gabriel, tried to replace images for all deities with the name of one who had neither a picture nor an image: Allah.

A LINGUISTIC SCRUTINY OF THE NAME ALLAH

The science of etymology deepens our insight into Muhammad's revolution. It focuses on tracing the origin of words. Who is Allah? Literally, Allah means "the God." The Arabic verb *ta'allaha* means "to be worshipped." As a noun, *ilah* means "one worthy of worship, a god." The *al-* prefix indicates the definite article, and so *al-ilah* is "the god," lowercase. During the period when the Qur'an was revealed, 610–32 CE, *al-ilah* was condensed. Following normative rules of Arabic grammar, *al-ilah* became *Allah*. Thus, there are three sequential steps. Starting with *ilah* or "a god," one must then trace the word to its definite form, *al-ilah*, "the god," and finally recognize how *al-ilah* becomes compressed into *Allah*, the "One and Only God"! But knowing how Allah became "God" does not answer the central question: Who is Allah? It only tells us how the name came into being. One also needs to note what several equally interested but clearly divergent groups mean by Allah.[11]

GABRIEL'S INTERVENTION/MUHAMMAD'S MEDIATION

In fact, Allah—as announced by the Archangel Gabriel in 610, then expanded during the twenty-two years of the Prophet Muhammad's revelation—becomes something new. While Allah had linguistic precedents and local familiarity as a divine name, in the *shahada*, or profession of faith, Allah stands alone, yet Muhammad stands next to him. The *shahada* is the entry point for membership in the Muslim community. It has two parts. The first part—"no god except God"—may have been introduced more than a thousand years before the rise of Islam. It is, for instance, resonant in the Tanakh or Hebrew scripture: Isaiah 46:9 declares, against all polytheistic rivals, a millennium before the Arabic/Muslim *shahada* is announced: "I am God, and there is no other; I am God and there is none beside me." That is, however, the clarion cry of a prophet whose people did not obey divine dictates. Nor did a disobedient Jewish community dominate the ancient world, itself the repository of multiple gods and competitive worldviews.

In short, the idea of One God, accepted by some but contested by many, long predated Islam in and beyond Arabia. Not the first part, but the second part of the *shahada* is the key element that confirms the Muslim difference in the quest for God: "and Muhammad is Allah's messenger." The only God—who can be, and must be, invoked, beseeched, and followed—is the God of Muhammad. Not only is there no god except God, but also, to underscore the Muslim claim on the Absolute Other, Muhammad has become the Arab prophet, at once the latest apostle and the final messenger, for the One True God.

In the early seventh century, before the advent of Islam, Arabia exhibited a polytheistic amalgam of demons, demigods, tribal gods, and idols, each of which were major players within their own domains. They

Who Is a Muslim?

Boundary markers for Muslim self-identity are called the *arkan*, or pillars. They number five.

1. Witness to Allah's divine sovereignty and Muhammad's prophetic authority (*shahada*)
2. Five-time daily prayer (*salat*)
3. Giving of alms (*zakat*)
4. Observance of fast during Ramadan (*sawm*)
5. Performance of the pilgrimage to Mecca (*hajj*).

were constantly invoked in different settings but always for the betterment of their devotees. To what extent was Allah just one among many? Which gods were Allah's closest competitors? How did the early Muslims secure Allah as the Real Thing, the Supreme Force for their community, and for all humankind?

These are crucial questions to which many have offered convincing, yet often conflicting, answers. As noted above, polytheism was endemic to the ancient world—and some would say it still persists in the modern world. In a polytheistic world there are many Things, and some of them are female. Three of the female deities from pre-Islamic Arabia—Allat, Uzzat, and Manat—are mentioned by name in the Qur'an (Q 53:19–20),[12] but other tribes also had local deities and some, such as the god ar-Rahman, who was worshipped throughout southern Arabia, clearly had transregional appeal. Allah prevailed as the fortunes of Islam were reversed after 622, when Muhammad, fleeing for his life, relocated to Yathrib (renamed Medina) and began to forge an independent, oppositional, and eventually dominant community in Arabia. The fortunes of the Muslims, who attributed their success to Allah, also ensured His success.

ALLAH AND MUHAMMAD: THEOLOGICALLY DISTINCT YET VISUALLY COEVAL

Although most Muslims emphasize the immortality of God and the mortality of all men (including Muhammad), in the history of Islam Allah and Muhammad have become inseparable, nowhere more so than in the

Fig. 1. Allah/Muhammad with the Four Righteous Caliphs.
Calligraphy by Fevzi Günüç.

visual imagination and everyday experience of most Muslims. Allah and Muhammad share contiguous space within the mind but also within the soul and the vision of each believer. Allah/Muhammad reflect a notion of intersecting domains, each projecting itself but always in company with the other. Consider the large, round, equal discs in figure 1, from a website on Islamic spirituality. In the central medallion Allah and Muhammad are calligraphically interwoven, the first letter of Allah ("a" on the far right) encompassing Muhammad, just as the final letter of his name ("d" on the left) slices through the "la" of Allah![13]

Step back. Take a longer view of monotheistic history. One can see both continuity and distinction between the God of Abraham and the Allah of Muhammad. Through the Qur'an, Muhammad as a prophet to the Arabs becomes the final prophet to humankind, but he is also linked to previous prophets, especially Abraham. The centerpiece of Muslim ritual is the Ka'ba, a cuboid building in Islam's most sacred mosque in Mecca. It houses a black stone, said to be a meteorite from heaven, which is linked to both Ishmael, the elder son of Abraham, and his mother, Hagar, Abraham's handmaid. Banished to Arabia, Ishmael and Hagar found solace at the site of the Ka'ba and sustenance from its environs,

> **Ka'ba, Qibla, Salat, and the Hajj**
>
> The Ka'ba rock serves as the point of orientation (*qibla*) for daily
> Muslim prayer (*salat*), but also for the circumambulation (*tawaf*)
> central to the once-in-a-lifetime pilgrimage (*hajj*). Visiting the Well
> of Zamzam is another part of the *hajj* ritual.

including the Well of Zamzam. The lineage of Abraham to Muhammad accents its Arabian branch: it is Ishmael, not Isaac, who is honored as Abraham's offspring, and it is Ishmael, not Isaac, who links Muslims to all the prophetic antecedents announced then developed in the Qur'an.

And so one must conclude that from the early seventh century, and for nearly 1,400 years since then, the name Allah has become the name of God for *all* communities where Islam has prevailed, whether they be Arabic- or non-Arabic-speaking Muslims, whether they be Muslims or non-Muslims in Arabic-speaking countries. Even today, the name Allah remains the name of God for most Christians and some Jews in the Middle East, just as those who live in predominantly Muslim cultures of Africa and Asia invoke Allah as God. Even if Arabic is not a language of everyday speech, it remains a prestigious liturgical language (e.g., in Senegal or Mali, Malaysia or Indonesia).[14]

DIVERSITY WITHIN ISLAM

Scholars, believers, journalists, and even the general populace tend to conceptually divide the Abrahamic community into Muslims and non-Muslims. Muslims chart their descent from Ishmael, the eldest son of Abraham by Hagar, his handmaid, while Jews and Christians chart their descent from Isaac, the youngest son of Abraham by Sarah. Although this dichotomy may be simple and unambiguous, is it really a pragmatic or productive distinction? It tends to make the debate about scriptural origins the major point of contemporary Abrahamic loyalty. "There has been too much focus on Muslim/non-Muslim relations," observed a South African Muslim blogger caught in the endless vortex of Christian-Muslim claims and counterclaims. "The real problem," he declared, "is [not between Muslims and others but] that Muslims themselves are actually divided. There is a dire need for better understanding of *the diversity within our own heritage.*"[15] In other words, one cannot elide Muslim to Christian to Jewish notions of God as quickly as does Alpha Blondy. Instead, one needs to look at the many, often contrasting, ways that Muslims have inherited, embraced, and adapted the notion of Allah.

Diversity *within* the Muslim community is critical not just because of sectarian differences or sociological curiosity, but rather because it demonstrates the intrinsic dynamism of Islam, the inevitable and wholesome contest *among* Muslims as they engage in multiple cultures, societies, and polities. Muslims relate to Allah through a variety of practices that they feel are effective precisely because they link local histories and sensibilities, belongings and longings to the name Allah. Allah is the marker for Muslim identity that trumps all other markers: it conceals deep divisions, even as it appears to erase all difference and coalesce all groups under the banner of Allah.

PRAGMATIC OBSERVATION VS. THEOLOGICAL JUDGMENT

There are many faith expositions of Allah written from a Muslim perspective. There are also many refutations of Islam, written mostly by Christian evangelicals but also by doctrinaire atheists such as Christopher Hitchens.[16] I avoid both. Neither creedal nor polemical, my approach to Allah is at once critical and appreciative. I am appealing to the typical non-Muslim reader or seeker or believer who has engaged Islam but not fully understood its richness and complexity. I also am writing for the average Muslim who relies on Allah but may not have considered the many levels of everyday practice, and how they have been challenged or changed over time. My inquiry will be critical insofar as it examines many perspectives, weighing their relevance in the contest for divine sanction to human existence, whether at home or abroad, in private or public, in peace or at war. At the same time, my assessment will be appreciative, drawing out the resonance of the name Allah and its symbolic power for millions of Muslims, as well as many non-Muslims, during the past 1,400 years.

I respect dialogical readings of Allah undertaken by well-intentioned non-Muslims, up to a point. While dialogue can promote engagement, it also overlooks, or downplays, its own limits. The late Anglican bishop Kenneth Cragg was perhaps the most adroit Christian interlocutor on matters Islamic in his generation. Bishop Cragg once declared: "Since both Christians and Muslims believe in One supreme sovereign Creator-God, they are obviously referring when they speak of Him, under whatever terms, to the same Being. To suppose otherwise would be confusing. . . . Those who say that Allah is not 'the God and Father of our Lord Jesus Christ' are right if they mean that He is not so described by Muslims. They are wrong if they mean that He is other than the One Christians so understand."[17] The metaphor of a cut diamond comes to mind. Each facet reflects some of the reality of the diamond (based on interior light reflections), but none is the diamond itself (the Thing). Each reflects the diamond but is not it. So Muslims see one view of Allah (from their facet) while Christians another (from theirs)—and who knows how many other facets there are, including those of other beings in the universe? The Thing, the Absolute, the One is the same, yet our views are incomplete, whether Christian, Muslim, or Martian. While such a metaphor, and the gesture of inclusiveness it offers, may be admirable, it still privileges a resolute relativism that Muslims might find at odds with, even subversive to, their own understanding of Allah.[18]

And there's the rub. Despite the generosity of Bishop Cragg's gesture, he sidesteps a crucial query: the one Christians so understand when they speak of God is the notion of the Thing, the Absolute, the One as transferred into human form, in the person of Jesus of Nazareth. For Christians, the One embodied sacrificial love by choice, the God-man dying on the cross as the obedient servant, and so becoming Jesus the Christ, the anointed, the messiah expected in Judaism. This is often cited as the Doctrine of the Incarnation, and God as Sacrificial Love Incarnate in Jesus the Christ is the Christian marker. Yet in Islam what Muslims mean by Allah is the notion of God ever vigilant, providing merciful guidance to humankind but not becoming human. Indeed, for Muslims it was, and it always will be, impossible for Allah to become human. Allah created Adam. Allah called Abraham. Allah commanded Moses. Allah also empowered Jesus. But Allah never became human.[19] He chose to reveal His Final Word(s) in Arabic to Muhammad. Though the Qur'an confirms all previous prophecies, it also supersedes them and privileges Arabic as the language of that supersession. One message, one messenger, one language prevail: the message is Mercy, the messenger Muhammad, the language Arabic. Because Allah provides His signs for each generation, up to Muhammad, then beyond Muhammad to our own, Allah abounds in Magisterial Mercy. There is no incarnation, no divine sacrifice, but mercy abounding from creation to eternity via Arabic.

God as Sacrificial Love in Hebrew, Greek, and Aramaic and God as Magisterial Mercy in Arabic are not the same. Our Father and Allah the Thing, the Absolute, the One are related yet not identical. Is it better to emphasize commonality or difference? On the one hand, it is possible to conclude that while Christian and Muslim devotions emphasize different natures of God, and also use different vocabularies, they often share certain sentiments (e.g., God offering guidance for humanity through history), even while not sharing others (e.g., God as incarnate).[20] And so the convergent approach of dialogue has merit; it does satisfy those who want to reconcile Christians and Muslims as contemporary faith communities.

On the other hand, however, one must recognize differences that persist. Even though at the most profound level all notions of the sacred, including all names for God, merge, one must still confront the stubborn insistence of each bounded, local memory and each community that marks itself by the difference, the distinctiveness of its own approach to the One beyond knowing. Boundary formation—and maintenance—is a necessary function of naming, branding, standing apart from others. Whether institutionally defined or historically driven or both, local memory denies access to others outside its circle. Its adherents claim exclusive sanction from the Thing for themselves: it is they, and they alone, who understand and worship the Thing deemed to be the Absolute, the One, the Only True God of History and the Universe.

Because universalism always wrestles with parochialism, there is never an end to the tension between them, nor can one ignore the need to acknowledge that tension. Allah and God are both the same and not the same. Therefore, before considering the practice of Allah among Muslims, we must briefly consider the relationship of Allah to God and the critical, durative role of the Arabic language.

CAN ALLAH BE DISTINGUISHED FROM GOD?

Parochialism is a two-way exchange. It marks the theological quest to separate Allah as God, but also God from Allah. It pervades the everyday register of both Allah and God in different linguistic and geographical settings. Consider first those Muslims who use Allah in *English.* "Some Muslims insist on using the word Allah when they speak English for several reasons," as a seasoned scholar of Islam has observed. "First, it is the primary name of God in the Koran, so the word itself is considered to have a special blessing. Second, for many Muslims, the word *God* as used in English refers to a false god worshipped by Jews and Christians."[21] In other words, there are Muslims who prefer the word Allah either because of the sanctity of the Arabic word or because they see all other names—and also all other approaches or appropriations of the sacred—as sacrilege.

There is, in effect, a thin and moving line between fact and faith. Nor is theological judgment about the weight of certain divine names peculiar to Muslims. There are Christians who are equally granular in their outlook; they reciprocate the same parochial reflex as their Muslim counterparts when they think that the name God mirrors the sole Truth, that is, that only when the Thing is addressed as the God and Father of our Lord and Savior Jesus Christ is the Thing or God an effective instrument, either in this world or in the next. By extension, this linguistic argument makes a judgment about the end of time: Allah is no more than the persistent face of a false god, and all who worship it are doomed. Pagans—whether ancient or modern, Arabian or American, Muslim or Wiccan—all worship a false god. By whatever name in whatever culture the pagan god remains "a moon god," and so its worshippers, according to these Christian monitors, will suffer perpetual pain, or hellfire, in the afterlife.[22]

Theological judgments do not stand isolated and alone. They are fortified by the linguistic history that combines yet separates Allah/God. Consider the issue of upper- and lowercase. Arabic has no upper or lower cases. And in English God in the uppercase did not always exist. God as the proper name for the God-man, Jesus the Christ in Christian circles, evolved over time. Its "canonical" status did not become secure till after the English translations of the Bible—first the sixteenth-century Tyndale rendition and then the early seventeenth-century King James Version. One cannot even argue that the term *Gott* in German or God in English was always the preferred name for the deity, as Allah has been for Muslims. Other words such as Yahweh/Jehovah, *dominus*/Lord also had authority as referents for the Divine Other among Jews and Christians, as also humanists. The practice of translating the Latin *deus* or Greek *theos* into French *dieu* or German *Gott* or English *God* only came later; even in medieval times there was no sense of uppercase/lowercase contrast or opposition.

For presentists, those who see only immediate antecedents to today's world and its preferential practices, deep history is irrelevant. They welcome neither the theological nor the linguistic references to change over time. They will resist a long diachronic view that encompasses and values the premodern era, extending much further back than 1600 CE or 1000 AH. Yet it is only in the modern or present era, roughly the past 400 years, that one could translate the Islamic creed: *la ilaha illa Allah* into English as "there is no god but God." Not only is God as a name for the Thing, the Absolute, the One comparatively recent, but it could even be argued that the convention of calling the deity by this one name in English, G-o-d, reduces our options and deprives our sensibilities of understanding the multiple, flexible, and subtle nuances of "God talk" in all premodern cultures, including and especially those marked by Islam and so by the Arabic Qur'an. Once again the stubborn insistence of Arabic as a language of the final divine revelation has to be examined. The popular Qur'an commentator Muhammad al-'Asi speaks for many contemporary Muslim scholars when he argues that *God* cannot be used as a direct translation for the Qur'anic *Allah*. Why? Because in its Western definition God reflects "the deification of human attributes" in an anthropocentric universe: "Never in any Western tradition," asserts al-'Asi, "do we encounter a concept of God as the sole and ultimate Authority," yet without such authority, he insists, "God ceases to be the Allah . . . of the Islamic vocabulary."[23]

USING LANGUAGE TO EXCEED THE REACH OF WORDS

And so one cannot resolve the dilemma of Allah/God at the level of etymology or ontology, theology or history. Even when words, whether Adonai, Our Father, or Allah, stretch the imagination beyond language, they approach the Thing, or the Absolute, or the One, but do not become part of it, for at the same time they remain rooted in the transient, the ephemeral, the human; they never cease to reflect their origin in time, space, culture, and history.

Instead of trying to shoehorn Allah into God or make God an inadequate equivalent of Allah, I want to look at the question that Muslims, like Christians, face when confronted with their own temporal, finite efforts at naming, and so owning, the Thing. More than a few Muslims in their life's journey confront the daunting question: Where does speech end so that Allah can communicate through silence? Deliberate silence is different from not speaking; it is an active form of listening. Can we "hear" silence, and if so, how? Concerned seekers throughout the ages have sought the nature of the divine through words while also registering the need for silence, to exploring the divine beyond the mask of words, and so beyond a human calculus of precise knowing and loving, engaging and trusting, benefitting and praising the Thing by any name.

Put differently, words may exercise their greatest power when they point beyond themselves. All names, including the name Allah, have that potential. A leading scholar of mystical discourse, Michael Sells, asks: "Can one imagine God divorced, and separated, from particular traditions and languages"?[24] For Jews, Christians, Muslims, or for any set of believers, that is a huge challenge. In linguistic usage can one ever truly separate the generic—what belongs to all—from the particular—what belongs to me/us? For Muslims, can *Allah* (the God) be fully separated from *ilah* (a god), or *aliha* (many gods) from *Allah* (the One True God)? All these endeavors play with the Arabic language, but each linguistic turn always and everywhere involves a truth claim that emerges from within the circumscribed community of believers. To imagine Allah/God on the rim of the universe or in the heart of the believer, minus all human attachments, interests, and explanations, is impossible. The best that one can do, and must do, is to survey what has motivated certain attachments, sustained particular interests, and produced enduring explanations.

That enterprise—let us call it the perspectival approach to Allah—is what I propose to pursue in the following chapters. It is as perilous as it is necessary. It requires deep exploration into the past. It also involves conjecture about the future. But it must begin in the present. And for Muslims, it begins with the continuous, unfolding, consequential performance of Allah in everyday life; it begins not with explaining Allah or relating Allah to God but with the practice of invoking His name, *bismillah*: in the name of Allah.

ALLAH: THE ONGOING QUEST

Among the many voices expressing their relation to Allah and their quest to understand Allah, the initial voice comes from Muhammad—or more accurately, in the Muslim tradition, from the voice of Gabriel mediated by Muhammad. Yet it was not Muhammad who wrote down the revelations, but others who heard his oral utterances and later codified them. These revelations have been compiled into what Muslims respect and read and recite and follow as the Qur'an. In addition to the Qur'an, there are also Muhammad's own words and actions, separate from the Qur'an. Often called *hadith*, or traditions, they reflect his divinely sanctioned mission but with a marked difference: they accent his own voice, not the divine speech that was first announced through the Archangel Gabriel, then repeated, remembered, written, and collected as the Qur'an.

And following in the footsteps of Muhammad come a host of Muslims—scholars, jurists, philosophers, theologians, mystics, and artists. Too many to list here, they will be identified at several points in the chapters that focus on Allah, whether as invoked, defined, remembered, traced in cyberspace, or debated in many places. There will also be skeptics, such as the British polemicist Christopher Hitchens; or ex-Muslims, such as the Somali-Dutch-American immigrant Ayaan Hirsi Ali; or mockers, such as the evangelist/cartoonist, Jack Chick and his emulators. They will mingle with sympathetic non-Muslims such as the fluent Arabist and Anglican bishop Kenneth Cragg, the ex-Roman Catholic nun Karen Armstrong, or American scholar of Islamic mysticism Carl Ernst and his Continental counterpart Denis Gril. One can even dare to hope that ordinary believers, Muslim and non-Muslim, will find their own voices in the din of these diverse reflections. Perhaps they may also see in them beacons of light that illumine their own quest for Allah.

Who is Allah? No one knows, yet everyone—at least everyone who is Muslim or connected to Muslims—wants to know. What cannot be known can be observed, and this book is an extended observation on the many practices of Allah within the *umma*, or global Muslim community. It is also a manifesto. It emerges out of a lifetime engaged with Islam and enjoying the company, friendship, and insight of countless Muslims from all corners of the globe, from the edges of the Atlantic Ocean in Europe and America to the breadth of the Indian Ocean beyond West Africa to the Arabian Peninsula and South and Southeast Asia.

This is not theology. I do not say: Allah must be like this, or be addressed like that. Nor is this apologetics, I do not suggest: Allah should do this, but would never condone that. Neither theology nor apologetics, my manifesto traces a pragmatic rather than a dogmatic approach to religion. I am engaged with Islam as one of the major communities of humankind. Most devout Muslims whom I have met or observed, at home or abroad, favor personal intention over book knowledge, public performance over analytic thought. They feel Allah in all that they do or say or pray or hope or want. To approach Allah in the footsteps of Islam requires attention to daily reflexes; it means listening, but also seeing, feeling, or even being touched by the divine presence. It is, above all, about a set of practices, and those practices are the heart of this book.

OVERVIEW

Chapter 1 explores the practice of the tongue: how is Allah invoked, by whom and for what purpose? Three subsets of the chapter look at Allah below, beyond, and within. Allah below is seen in the mirror of Adam, the One beyond all knowing reflected in His creature. Allah beyond is visible through the face of the universe, the One who created all discovered in the traces and treasures of His creation. Finally, Allah within is concealed beneath the secret of letters; a science of writing, counting, and discerning connects him to the discrete, and patient, believer.

Chapter 2 focuses on the practice of the mind. Rulers and their court, urban professionals and their dependents, scholars and their students— all produce an intellectual approach to Allah that complements but also competes with those who invoke Allah as daily practice. How have theologians and philosophers defined Allah? Have they promoted definitions suitable, but also exclusive, to their place, status, and interests? And if so, how does a rational engagement with Allah challenge both other views of Allah and also those who pursue alternative practices of Allah?

Chapter 3 examines the practice of the heart. Neither everyday practitioners nor intellectual gadflies, Sufi masters immerse themselves in remembrance of Allah. They direct their lives, their families, their communities, and their destinies to one goal: making the human heart attuned to its Source. It is an unending quest for the unattainable Beloved, and it is channeled in myriad creative ways through the name Allah, or one of the other Beautiful Names all linked to and echoing back to Allah.

Chapter 4 outlines a practice for the ear. It engages the complexity of hearing, or trying to hear, Allah in the hyperactive public square of the Information Age. Where is the voice of Allah amid the cacophony of those who claim to hear Him? While you can use your eyes to navigate beyond the negative images of Islam, you still have to listen carefully to discern the variant tones of Allah. Has Allah directed the Muslim *umma* toward a path of confrontation, one that elicits distrust, opposition, and violence toward non-Muslim others? Some would say yes. That is the response that echoes from extremists, Islamists, and terrorists, including Bin Laden. Yet listen carefully, look at historical moments, and note different contexts. Changes in time, place, and circumstance unravel the assumption that Allah is always and everywhere a bad Thing, a negative force. Over centuries past, Allah, or those who invoked His name, have also proposed mediation, promoted friendship, and urged commitment to the common good. Today an attentive listener will hear new voices and find fresh engagements with Islam and with Allah in the public domain. Some will include creatures from another world, not angels but their counterparts, *jinn*. From the *jinn* you will hear ambiguous, generous echoes of the One beyond knowing but not beyond perceiving or connecting. These echoes too warrant close scrutiny.

Chapter 5 features all the above practices as they have been redefined and redeployed in the Information Age. It focuses on the modern period and reviews the information revolution of the past twenty years, attentive to the visual options and challenges of cyberspace. How is Allah addressed online, whether through websites, Twitter, Facebook, or blogs? "Though largely associated with Islam," notes one astute observer, "Allah is not subject to Muslim copyright."[25] So how does one evaluate competing claims to the Thing, the Absolute, the One beyond naming or knowing?

The conclusion steps back from all the sensory explorations of preceding chapters. It surveys the global arena where non-Muslims as well as Muslims engage the practices linked to the name Allah. Allah is a name that embodies opposite traits, as we will discover in trying to trace Muslim practices focused on the Thing, the Absolute, the One. Which traits of Allah dominate, and for whom? While these questions can never be answered conclusively, there are options, and also incentives, to see beyond the obvious differences about Allah. With patience, goodwill, and humility it is possible to find in the shadows of Allah points of convergence. Always contested, they still persist. Their advocates include artists. Whether painters or photographers or writers, all support a fulcrum of balance and reciprocity, even as they project a vista of justice and hope, in the fraught twenty-first century. Anything more eludes; anything less will not satisfy.

A FINAL DISCLAIMER

The quest for Allah is unbounded. At the end of the ocean, I stand on one point of shore. My inquiry is emblematic, not exhaustive, of human efforts to engage Allah. The issues addressed, the authorities culled, and the approaches suggested are but a single drop in that vast ocean. You can read the following Qur'anic verse as my own disclaimer about the analyses to come:

> Say, "Even if the ocean were ink
> for [writing] the words of my Lord,
> the ocean would be exhausted
> before the words of my Lord were exhausted,
> even if We were to add another ocean to it." (Q 18:109)

There will always be a surfeit of meaning beyond the thought and words dedicated to probing the practices of Allah. *Bismillah*, in opening the Qur'an, beckons the reader to listen, to reflect, and to explore the pervasive tones of a god so close yet so far from human reckoning. And the choice of names does matter. Because Allah and God elide so much in everyday discourse, as also in scholarly writing about the divine, I will use both names in the pages that follow. Yet the major accent will be on Allah, for Allah is the name above all other names in an Islamic context.

SUMMARY

The name Allah is, first and foremost, a name. It embodies all the potency and limits of a name for anything but especially the Thing, the Absolute, the One, which is independent of any name. Humans relate to Adonai or Our Father or Allah as a link, the closest possible link, to the One beyond naming or knowing, but for Muslims Allah acquires special significance in performance. Performance is at once collective (the individual performs, but as part of a community), relational (the Thing is engaged as the Other), and potentially transformative (the end can/ should leave you in a new state, as in an Alpha Blondy concert). What we will examine for each successive chapter is the overarching, enduring significance of *Allah as performed*. Allah is inextricably thought and action, word and deed, but *only Allah performed attaches the Name to the Thing*. And so we will look at Allah through public performance, repeated public performance, in addition to private invocation and continuous reflection. To understand the deepest rhythms of Allah for Muslims, one must begin where Muslims begin, with the daily invocations of Allah. The Allah of everyday life is at once pervasive and evasive. Is the Thing, the Absolute, the One to be found in humankind, in the universe, or in letters? We examine all three domains in the first chapter as we survey the pervasive practice of the tongue in performing Allah.

Indeed Allah created Adam in His image.
—Sahih Muslim 4731

Allah Invoked

Practice of the Tongue

OVERVIEW

Daily engagement with Allah, by whatever name He is known, becomes a key approach to understanding the Thing, the Absolute, the One. It is where Muslims begin, with the daily, constant, and varied invocation of the name Allah, often in the phrase *Allah ta'ala*, Allah the Lofty the Exalted (lit. "Allah—may He be exalted"). To paint a tapestry as rich and varied as the inflection of Allah in everyday life, one must discern patterns. I have elected three. The first looks at the intimate link of the Thing, the One to the man, the many. It is an approach familiar to most Muslims. Let us call it the mainstream approach. Less common, but still well known, is another pattern that looks at Allah through the maze of names that specify Allah within a constellation of attributes. It locates the One in the midst of the many. Let us call it the mystical approach, since it is Sufi masters in general, and one very popular master in particular (Ibn 'Arabi), who pursues this approach. The final approach may

Where Does the Qur'an Refer to the Most Beautiful Names?

The Most Beautiful Names belong to Allah,
so call on Him with them,
And reject those who abuse Allah's names;
they will be recompensed for what they do. (Q 7:180)

Say: Call upon Allah, or call upon Rahman
[the Compassionate]; by whatever name you call
upon Him [it is acceptable], for to Him belong
the Most Beautiful Names. (Q 17:110)

Allah, there is no god but He. To Him belong
the Most Beautiful Names. (Q 20:8)

seem recondite, yet it is familiar to all who have special needs that they link to Allah, often through numbers instead of words. Let us call it the magical approach, for it opens up another dimension of the practice of invoking Allah. It is a practice at once more technical and more contested than others.

CONNECTING ALLAH TO ADAM: THE MAINSTREAM APPROACH

What does it mean to say that Allah created Adam/man in His image?[1] How does Adam reflect the image of his creator? In Islam, as in other branches of Abrahamic religion, Allah and Adam are connected intrinsically: the one mirrors the other. When Allah created Adam, He gave him attributes resembling His own. Seven attributes dominate: *life, power, knowledge, will, hearing, seeing,* and *speaking.*

Further, Allah is said to have made Adam a storehouse for many of His other names. There are said to be no less, and perhaps many more, than Ninety-nine Divine Names. They are known as *asma Allah al-husna,* the Most Beautiful Names of Allah. Consider *al-Karim* (the Generous). Some people are given the name *Karim,* for instance, the famous American basketball player Karim (Kareem) Abdul-Jabbar. According to tradition, those named Karim take on the attribute connected to the name,

> ### Why Is the Meaning of *Sadaqa* So Difficult?
> ### Because It Relates to Four Arabic Words!
> A *hadith* on the meaning of *sadaqa* (charitable donation):
>
> Verily in every *tasbih*
> (i.e., saying *SubhanAllah*) there is a *sadaqa,*
> in every *takbir*
> (i.e., saying *Allahu Akbar*) is a *sadaqa,*
> in every *tahmid*
> (i.e., saying *Alhamduli[A]llah*) is a *sadaqa,*
> and in every *tahlil*
> (i.e., saying *La ilaha illa[A]llah*) is a *sadaqa.*

demonstrating their worthiness of the name through their acts of generosity. Other people have the name *ar-Rahim* (the Ever Compassionate), and again, according to tradition, the name is expected to become manifest in them, through the mercy or compassion they show to others.[2]

CHARITY BEGINS AND ENDS WITH ALLAH

Whether linked to divine kindness or mercy, all Muslims are expected to be vigilant in their invocation of the name of Allah. How vigilant is made clear in another saying ascribed to the Prophet Muhammad. It came in response to the query: what charitable donation (*sadaqa*) should a Muslim make if he or she did not possess sufficient wealth to make a monetary donation?

The four words (*tasbih, takbir, tahmid,* and *tahlil*) related to the meaning of *sadaqa* may sound confusing to someone who does not know Arabic, and rightly so. Why does one need to bother with *tasbih, takbir, tahmid,* and *tahlil*? Just think of them in terms of a cycle. *Tasbih* begins the cycle; *takbir* continues it; *tahmid* crowns it, while *tahlil* completes it. All are essential. None can be bought or traded; each provides a spiritual capital that is deemed to be priceless. So what begins as a question about money or material means becomes something of eternal import: charity, or charitable donation, concerns more than money or material transfer of possessions; it is about constantly remembering the Creator, the Living One who gives life to all things living, and who brings all that is living back to Him for a life beyond this life. Adam is the channel for this activity; he serves as a role model for all humans.

ADAM THE SUCCESSOR TO ALLAH

After creating the angels as inhabitants of heaven, Allah created Adam. The first human, Adam became "successor" to Allah on earth, in this world (Q 2:30). Creating Adam with His own two hands (Q 38:75), Allah breathed His spirit into Adam (Q 15:29; 38:72) and asked him to name the things, a task the angels were unable to do (Q 2:31–2).

All these primordial moments of connection—the two hands, the breath of Allah, the ability to name—become central points of insight in the creation process. And creation itself has stages, plateaus, levels at which one can, and should, marvel at the wisdom of the Creator. The Qur'an mentions four stages in the creation of humans: from dust, to sperm, to man, to pairs. While Allah is said to have created the pair out of a single self (nafs)(Q 4:1), there was also a secret of the divine economy in the staging of creation: it was only at the third stage that Allah looked at the one, and then divided it into two equal parts: male and female. In other words, Allah created the first human Adam, from dust (Q 3:59), and then in the second stage through sperm, shaping them individually to their complete figure, before in the final stage making them male and female.

> [Allah] is the one who created you
> of dust, then of a sperm-drop,
> then shaped you in the form of a man (Q 18:37),
> and then made you pairs. (Q 35:11)

And Allah paid special attention not just to binary forms but also to gender parity in the primal act of creation. Adam, with his mate,[3] emerged from one soul:

> He created you of a single soul
> and from it created its mate,
> and from the pair scattered abroad many
> men and women (Q 4:1);
> [all were] called children of Adam. (Q 7:26–27)

Elsewhere in other Qur'anic verses Allah is said to have created every animate being of water (Q 24:45) and the jinn from a flame of fire

(Q 55:15). Still another pronouncement of creation focuses on the creation of humans in stages that parallel Q 18/35 but with a different twist culminating in bones and flesh:

We [Allah] created man of an extraction of clay,
then we set him, a drop, in a receptacle secure,
then we created of the drop a clot
then we created of the clot a tissue
then we created of the tissue bones
then we garmented the bones in flesh. (Q 23:12–14)

While there is no mention of gender in the above creation narrative, Allah does specify not just the gender dyad but also racial and tribal diversity in a subsequent revelation. The crucial verse is: *"We have created you male and female, and appointed you races and tribes"* (Q 49:13).

Within this embrace of divine-human affinity, there is a major distinction. Allah fashioned His creation with temporal limits: while creating the human in His image, Allah also determined for him a stated term of life:

He it is
who created you of clay
and then fixed a term
and a term is stated
in His keeping. (Q 6:2)

The One is Eternal, Immortal. The many are finite, mortal.

PERFORMING THE NAME

And so the appropriate, expected response—of the finite creature to the Eternal Creator—is surrender, the literal meaning of *islam*. Surrender is a lifelong practice, a daily engagement. And so daily engagement with Allah, by whatever name He is known, becomes the key approach to understanding Allah. It provides the reason and also the rhythm for each day: the insistent, repeated invocation of the name of Allah.

From the early seventh century Allah the Lofty the Exalted became the center-stage performance for Muslims. It is an oral performance that begins at birth and continues to death. The very first word that a Muslim child hears is Allah. The shortened call to prayer follows: *"Allahu Akbar!* I testify that there is no god but Allah, and Muhammad is the prophet of Allah. Come to prayer!" And at the time of funeral, or as death approaches, every devout Muslim hopes that s/he will have the strength to say the first half of the *shahada*: "there is no *ilaha* but Allah."

And the Qur'an also offers a pithy, poignant reminder of Allah when death comes. Death may come at the end of a long, well-lived life or by some unexpected horrible illness or violent act, but when it comes to a parent the pain of separation is always sharp. It was early July 2013 when I got a phone call from one of my former students. He was an Iranian American. His eighty-three-year-old father, who lived in North Carolina, had been in good health, when suddenly he contracted an infection. Within two weeks he was dead. The funeral had been immediate, as is Muslim custom, but now my student wanted to have a memorial service, an event for the larger circle of his father's friends to attend. He also asked me to attend and to say some words. What I said was less important than what others said. Nearly all recalled the same verse from the Qur'an: "*Inna lillahi wa inna illaihi raji'un*" (Q 2:156). It means: "We are to Allah, and to Allah we are returning." Its directness rivets everyone who reads or hears the Qur'an. The first part does not say: "We are from Allah," or, "We are with Allah." Instead, it declares: "We are to Allah"; that is, we are always inclined toward Him or moving toward Him. And the second part is even more forceful: "To Allah we are (always) returning." Sometimes it is translated: "To Allah we shall return," but that rendition misses the real point. It is not just at the time of death but during our entire span of time in this world that we are journeying, and our journey is one of return, our return to the Source, to the Thing, the Absolute, the One.

Instead of an accent solely on the moment of death ("To Allah we shall return") this verse reflects, or should reflect, from a Muslim perspective, one's entire life: "To Allah we are continually and always returning." It epitomizes the practice of remembering Allah as Owner—at once first source and final home, beginning and end. Just as it inspired many of those who remembered a remarkable Iranian American in July 2013, it also inspired the following reflection from an anonymous Muslim rapper. What follows evokes the everyday approach to Allah as custodian of human destiny, the Owner of it all:

Now, since everything belongs to Allah, then we have to include even our souls in that list. The very soul that we think of as our "self"; our "*nafs*"; our "being"—whatever you want to call it—that very thing

The Soul/Self

There are two main words in Arabic for soul/self: *nafs* and *ruh*. The first is the soul, while the second is our divine self or deepest level of our being, the spirit. In practice both get used to define human existence, but *nafs* comprises three levels of being: animal, human, and angelic.

that distinguishes you from the rest of the world, belongs to Allah. It's not YOURS. In fact, YOU are not YOURS. You belong to Allah.

Just like a friend who lends you his book. And then after a few days, he wants it back and you give it back to him . . . no regrets . . . no sorrow . . . no questions asked.

Similarly, if Allah takes back some of His blessings upon you for some reason, so be it. Say *Alhamduli(A)llah*. Don't grieve. Be patient. Submit to the will of Allah, being pleased with His decision for you. For surely He will only do what is best for you. Just think: The Owner came and took it back.[4]

Since "that very thing that distinguishes you from the rest of the world" can be, and will be, taken away, your response should not be anxiety but hope, not resignation but gratitude, and also, always, trust. The real takeaway here is trust. Again and again the one certainty is trust: trust in the Giver of all life, trust in the Owner of all that you have, trust in the outcome of your life and the life of the universe. Allah is the Judge, the Monitor of Eternal Space/Time/Truth.

This is more than a heartfelt commitment or occasional reflex; it is a trust that must be declared, repeated, and renewed each day, each hour, each moment. Allah pervades the daily life of devout Muslims. The most evident registers are prayer, especially the invocation of *Allahu Akbar* and the *shahada*, the proclamation of faith, which uses the name Allah twice and refers to *ilah* a third time, and prayer beads, or *tasbih*. Prayer beads become the reference, the reminder for many of how vital it is to keep His name ever fresh. Prayer, faith, beads—they nudge us toward the source, which is also the goal, of all life. But what is the role of beads? Why are they so important?

MAINSTREAM INVOCATION OF
ALLAH IN THE WORKPLACE

In charting mainstream Muslim approaches to Allah, we again find an echo of the practice that informs most believers on the Internet. In this case, it is a practice that is informed by awareness, and affirmation, of the practices that Muslims share with Catholics. Whether in Detroit or Dakar, Johannesburg or Jakarta, one sees the ubiquitous *tasbih* or *misbaha*, commonly called the Islamic rosary. Those who are devout Catholics would recognize a piety parallel to their own, and they would feel spiritual kinship with this description from another Muslim cybernaut:

> A couple of days ago at the office, a Catholic co-worker of mine, an older gentleman, commented on the presence of my prayer rug in my cubicle and of my *tasbih dhikr* (remembrance) beads. I usually keep a set of the 99-bead *tasbih* wrapped around my right wrist so that I have easy access to them whenever I feel like doing *dhikr* (figure 2). "That's why I like you," observed my Catholic co-worker, "because you believe. I can talk to you about stuff and you won't get offended."
>
> I swear there's something meditative, therapeutic, and nepenthean about the sensation of beads running your fingers, a feeling which I can't quite describe. Who cares if my co-worker is Catholic and I'm Muslim? We both recognize the importance of belief, and something as simple and humble as a set of prayer beads provided a link between our great faiths. People are less divided, less different than it would appear at first glance. Our commonalities trump our differences, and our similarities are the ones worth stressing, not our differences.
>
> *Say: "People of scripture, come to terms common between us and you, that we will worship only Allah, and not associate anything with Him, and that none of us will take others for lords instead of Allah." And if they turn back, then say: 'Witness that we submit to Him.'"* (Q 3:64)[5]

In this commentary on Catholic rosaries as *tasbihs*, and *tasbihs* as Muslim rosaries, repetition is the critical practice. Allah is there in the repetition of *SubhanAllah* at the beginning of the Ninety-nine Names. Though varied in practice, each recitation usually begins rather than ends with *SubhanAllah*, and it frequently includes *Allahu Akbar*. But it is more than words. The key element is intention, the intention to remember, and then, and only then, to recite the invocations of Allah. Many devout Muslims complete each of the five daily prayers by repeating these

Fig. 2. Beads on the Qur'an. Photograph by the author.

three phrases ninety-nine times, counting out each repetition either on the *tasbih* or on their fingers:

> *SubhanAllah* ("Glory be to God")
> *Alhamduli(A)llah* ("All praise be to God")
> *Allahu akbar* ("God is always greater than anyone or anything")

Whether Allah comes at the end, as in *SubhanAllah* and *Alhamduli(A)llah*, or at the beginning as in *Allahu,* each phrase accents Allah as the referent. Seldom does the phrase *Allahu Akbar* become a stand-alone accolade to Muslim triumphalism. Most often it projects a moment of surrender, the surrender of all humans, including and especially Muslims, to the One always greater than anyone or anything: *Allah ta'ala* (Allah the Lofty).

The five-time daily prayers, like the *tasbih* recitation at their conclusion, relate to the first pillar of Islam, the *shahada,* but they also expand the horizon of Allah as the goal of life. One begins with the *shahada*—connecting to Allah first by discerning the exclusive character of Allah and then by affirming the divine mandate for Muhammad, also noted by several Sufi masters as containing the *dhat* or essence of Allah in the first part (no god) and his *sifat* or qualities in the second part (but God), who sometimes describe it as the first affirmation.[6] *Salat* requires praying to Allah five times daily at prescribed moments, from sunrise to sunset, though there may also be supererogatory prayers on specific occasions.

The other four requirements punctuate the year rather than the everyday activity of devout Muslims, but they too highlight the pervasive centrality of Allah. *Zakat* entails giving for Allah a fixed percentage of one's wealth, not just one's annual income. *Ramadan* curtails the senses, and reorients the day, through fasting in gratitude for the word of Allah (i.e., the revelation of the Qur'an), one month out of every year. *Hajj* requires journeying to the rock of Allah, the black stone in the Ka'ba at Mecca, once in a lifetime; while *Jihad* prescribes fighting for Allah when the cause is clear and the need is great, but also surrendering the self to Allah in the greater struggle for self-awareness and inner peace.

It is *Insha'(A)llah* that underscores the pervasive power of the Absolute One. Whether occasionally or daily, in public or in private, it frames Allah as the source of all that is or will be or can be. Nothing can or does happen without God's will. The major instance of this invocation comes from the Qur'anic verse known as Ayat al-Kursi (Q 2:255), or the Throne

Ayat al-Kursi

Among all devotional verses in the Qur'an, the Throne Verse occupies a special place:

Allah! There is no god but He
the Living, The Self-subsisting, Eternal.
No slumber can seize Him nor sleep.
To Him belong
all things in the heavens and on earth.
Who is there can intercede in His presence
except as He permits?
Allah knows what is before them,
and what is after them.
But they do not encompass anything of His knowledge,
except as He wills.
His throne extends over
the heavens and earth,
and He feels no fatigue
in guarding and preserving them,
for He is the Most High,
the Supreme. (Q 2:255)

Verse. The second half of this widely invoked verse accents both Allah's total knowledge and His superior will.

Allah knows what is before them,
and what is after them;
but they do not encompass anything
of His knowledge,
except as He wills.

And just as Allah's will is acknowledged, His favor is also sought, and invoked, daily in the most common of social exchanges between Muslims. *As-salamu 'alaykum* evokes the echoing response from a fellow Muslim *Waalaykum as-salam*, but often with the additional words *Wa rahmatu(A)llah wa barakatuhu.* "Peace be upon you. . . . And upon you be peace and [not just peace but also] the mercy of Allah and His blessing."

> ### Prophets and Prophecy in Islam
> There are 124,000 prophets in Islam. Not all can be counted or accounted for, but Adam, the first human, is also the first prophet, while Muhammad, the perfect servant who embodies praise in his very name, is said to be the last prophet.

PRAISE FOR ALLAH AND PEACE UPON HIS PROPHET

In everyday performance Muslims do not mention the name of the Prophet without adding afterward: *"Salla (Allahu taʿala) alayhi wa-sallam (taslim)"* ("May Allah the Lofty bless him and give him greetings of peace") (Q 33:56). And that invocation assists the believer in approaching the proliferation of names linked to Allah.

Of special import are the number of names, both of persons and functions, that depend on Allah. For instance, the highest-ranking scholar in Shiʿi Islam is known as the *marjaʿ-i-taqlid*, "the one whom others seek to follow or imitate in matters of law," but he is chosen from another larger body of scholars known as ayatollahs, lit., ayat(A)llah. *Ayat(A)llah* means a verse or sign of Allah. The highest authority, or *marjaʿ-i-taqlid*, in fact, has also been known as the greatest Ayatollah, or the foremost sign of God. Similarly, one of the major Shiʿi political parties takes its name *Hizb Allah* from Q5:56, though it was not the first Muslim movement to do so: *Hizb Allah* goes back to the medieval period and to North Africa in its larger history.[7]

And then there are those prophets whose divine commission is often confirmed by an epithet that relates them to Allah. Adam is the first prophet in Islam, and hence he is *khalifat Allah*, the successor of God, while Abraham/Ibrahim is *khalil Allah* (the friend of God), Moses is *kalimu(A)llah* (the word of God), and Jesus is *ruh Allah* (the breath of God.)[8]

The Prophet Muhammad had many laudatory names, nearly all of them enshrined in the prayer manual *Dalaʾil al-Khayrat*.[9] Two of Muhammad's names related especially to Allah: *habib Allah*, the beloved of God, and *rasul Allah*, the messenger of God. Also, his name itself, as discussed above, means literally "the one who is both constantly praised and continually involved in praise (of Allah)."

Surat al-Fatiha: The First and Foremost Chapter of the 114 Chapters in the Qur'an

In the name of Allah
Full of Compassion, Ever Compassionate [the basmala]
Praise to the Lord of all Creation [the tahmid]
Full of Compassion, Ever Compassionate
Master of the Day of Determination
You alone do we worship
and from You alone do we seek alleviation
Guide us to the path of True Direction,
the path of those whom You favor,
not of those who cause You indignation,
nor of those who took to the path of deviation. (Q 1)

And the pilgrim follows in the footsteps of the Prophet. Note the abject submission that characterizes the pilgrim or *hajji*. Every pilgrim sets out for Arafat on the morning of the ninth day. After halting at the base of Arafat, the pilgrim climbs the hill crying, "*Labbayk Allahuma labbayk*" ("Here I come to Thee O Allah").[10]

The deeper resonance of Allah is daily underscored in the recitation of the Qur'an. Before a chapter is recited, the reciter seeks to be protected from evil influence: "*A'udhu bi(A)llahi min ash-shaitan ar-rajim*" ("I take refuge in Allah from the nasty Satan") (Q 16:98), and only then does the reciter utter the *basmala* [that is, *bismi(A)llah*]. Finally, at the end of the recitation, the reciter invokes Allah yet again when he or she says: "*Sadaqa Allah ul-'Azim*" ("Its truth is confirmed by God the Almighty," or literally, "God the Almighty confirms what is true").

Of all the varied and powerful invocations of Allah perhaps the most popular is "*Al hamduli(A)llah!*" ("Praise—all praise—is due to Allah!"). Known as *tahmid*, it occurs in Al-Fatiha, the very first *sura* or chapter of the Qur'an, and it occurs right after the *basmala*. In other words, the opening phrases of the Qur'an are "*Bismi(A)llah ar-rahman ar-rahim. Al-hamduli(A)llah.*"

CONNECTING ALLAH TO CREATION:
THE MYSTICAL APPROACH

Like the *bismi(A)llah*, *al-hamduli(A)llah* can be, and is, used at meals, either said silently or out loud. While *bismi(A)llah* begins a meal, *al-hamduli(A)llah* ends it. A major Muslim mystic, Ibn ʿArabi, even went so far as to say: "There is no word in the world that does not indicate His Praise." Praise is there in the beginning; praise is there again in the end; and praise punctuates all the moments in between. One begins a meal with bismi(A)llah ("In the name of God") but finishes the meal with al-hamduli(A)llah ("Praise be to God"). These two formulas, just like the meal, hold our whole existence, and to appreciate their interactive power we are invited to pursue the mystical approach.

A central question pervades: Can praise of the Supreme One function as the beginning of a deeper search into the meaning of Allah? Consider the Fatiha, the opening chapter of the Qurʾan. It is often called the chapter of praise, since its first words, after the *basmala*, are *Al-hamduli(A)llah*. Here is an extended, mystical meditation by Ibn ʿArabi on its layered meaning.

> It is provided for all who seek Allah through the Qurʾan with reference to a famous saying of the Prophet (*hadith*): "Al-hamduli(A)llah fills the Scales." All praise, whatever it may be and to whomsoever it may be addressed, can come only from Allah and must return to Him alone. Of this praise man is only an instrument, because it is uttered at the beginning and at the end by Allah, the First and the Last. In other words, Allah addresses His praise to Himself or to His creatures, and in the Qurʾan praise and glorification are closely linked:

> *Glorify through the praise of your Lord.* (Q 110:3)

> And again,

> *The seven heavens*
> *and the earth*
> *and all beings therein*
> *praise Allah.*
> *There is not a single thing*
> *that does not extol His praise,*
> *but you do not understand their praise.*
> *Allah is truly gracious, most forgiving.* (Q 17:44)

Indeed, His praise is manifest in birds as they soar through the sky:

> *Don't you see*
> *that all creatures*
> *in the skies and on earth*
> *glorify Allah,*
> *even the birds in flight?*
> *Each knows its prayer to Him*
> *Each its manner of praising Him.*
> *And Allah is fully aware*
> *of what they are doing.* (Q 24:41)

One might deduce that through praise the world speaks to Allah and Allah speaks to the world, while among men those who praise Him receive their share of praise through the world. But if Allah is transcendent how can we glorify Allah? After all, by praising Allah does man not limit Him?

Indeed, Allah can be praised only by His names. Yet there is not one of these names (except for Allah) by which man cannot be characterized. And so everything in the world glorifies Allah simultaneously in a negative and in an affirmative voice; but in the latter case, affirmation can proceed only from Him. Muhammad, at the end of his mission, which was above all a mission of praise, is given to say: "Glorify your Lord through praise and ask Him pardon. It is truly He who accepts repentance [*at-tawwab*]" (Q 110:3). And so to ask for forgiveness implies asking for effacement, the passing away of contingent being in the presence of Allah. All praise belongs to Allah, whether as word or performance: "There is no word in the universe that does not indicate His praise."[11]

THE *BARZAKH*: BOTH BARRIER AND BRIDGE
TO CONNECTING WITH ALLAH

Humans must practice praise, whether by word or by performance, but always and everywhere—that is the takeaway from the above reflection on the Prophet's dictum: "Praise to Allah fills the scales." And that act of laudation, whether verbal or physical, private or public, always recognizes the *barzakh*. At its simplest, the *barzakh* evokes the division between this life and the next, between our present world on earth and the celestial world beyond it, but *barzakh* is also used to describe the divide between salt- and freshwater. *Barzakh* is a barrier, yet it is also a bridge. It is a barrier that moves beyond the dyad either/or and instead confirms both/and as the metaphor of spiritual engagement. It might be defined as nonreductive, undiluted connection, linking two things— whether two realms of existence or two bodies of water—without reducing or diluting either. It is at once a concept and a method, central to understanding Muslim invocation of Allah as barrier and bridge, gap and gift.

Once again we see Muslims saying, performing, and feeling Allah. It is part and parcel of daily activities, but it also marks the long-term life cycle. It is only through these rhythms, influences, and meanings that one can fathom Allah, for it is in this same vast spectrum of protocol and piety that the metaphysical shadow of *barzakh* becomes at once barrier and bridge. Though *barzakh* comes from the Qur'an, it is as much method as metaphor, a delight to believers, a puzzle to scholars. The Egyptian artist Ahmed Moustafa has evoked *barzakh* in one of his several calligraphic masterpieces, making the exact letters and colors mirror each other in a deceptively simple pattern. One could conclude that *barzakh* is merely a divide between two oceans, or between man and woman, or between this world and the next, or between heaven and hell, but at the most profound level it is also the space, the thin space, at once evident yet porous, between the divine and the human, the Creator and the created, and it is therefore a bridge as well as a barrier. It is, in effect, the network of networks within the realm of Islamic spirituality.[12]

The *barzakh* informs invocation of Allah in Muslim popular and liturgical use. For some of the great spiritual giants of the Muslim past, it is especially evident in names. From Bistami to Hallaj to Ibn ʿArabi, every Muslim who invokes Allah also expresses a desire to dwell in the *barzakh*, to live simultaneously in this world and the world beyond,

Barzakh in the Qur'an

When death finally comes to one of them,
He says, "My Lord, send me back.
that I may do right
by what I neglected."
There is no way;
for that is just talk.
And before them is a barrier [barzakh] until
the day they'll be resurrected. (Q 23:99–100)

Allah is the One
who released the two waters
one fresh and sweet,
one salty and bitter,
and put a gap between them,
and a forbidden barrier [barzakh]. (Q 25:53)

[Allah is the one]
having released the two
bodies of water to meet
without overflowing
a barrier [barzakh] between them. (Q 55:19–20)

and the mark of that dual commitment begins with the common name 'AbdAllah.

IBN 'ARABI AND NAMING IN GOD'S NAME WITH GOD'S NAME

It is because of the deep resonance of Allah that one of the preferred names of children is 'AbdAllah (pronounced and often written as 'Abdullah). This name combines a key word from the opening *sura* of the Qur'an (Al-Fatiha) with the performative nature of an individual's life. In the Fatiha, there are three parts: invocation, connection, and petition. The *basmala* invokes God, and then identifies God's traits, but the very first connection to the worshipper comes in the fifth verse: "You we worship and you do we seek for help." The verb "worship" has in its unspoken nominal or subject position *'abd*, "the worshipper or servant," and so the name 'AbdAllah meaning Servant of Allah echoes the Fatiha in the person who is called by that name. Consider the fact that five times every day as part of *salat*, or prescribed prayer, every believer, no matter his or her name, says *iyyaka na'budu* ("surely you do we worship") as the first connection to Allah. The name by itself would be suggestive, but due to its central Qur'anic articulation it hearkens to the inner meaning of Sura al-Fatiha, and hence to the whole of the Qur'an, and to the spectrum of Islamic belief, ritual, and practice.

Ibn 'Arabi uses 'AbdAllah ("slave" to Allah or "worshipper" of Allah) to focus on the meaning of all the Divine Names. While there is one God, there are numerous Divine Names, and perhaps no Muslim scholar has probed more deeply into the pervasive significance of 'AbdAllah as a singular name linking all parts of Islamic spirituality back to Allah than Ibn 'Arabi. In one of the smallest of his many books he talks not only about names but also about naming. *Kitab al-'Abadila* is devoted to the name 'AbdAllah.[13]

In his book, Ibn 'Arabi reflects on mythical individuals whom he never met but imagines having met. He honors them by linking them first to the source of all wisdom, Allah, and giving them the name 'AbdAllah. But he also links them to spiritual lodestones, in the first instance to a Divine Name that echoes 'AbdAllah and in the second, to a prophetic figure who is a perfected person, that is, an individual who has placed his trust and his destiny in the hands of Allah.

The book is divided into two sections, the first consisting of five chapters with ten names each, the second consisting of forty-seven other names not further subdivided or categorized. Each of the chapter headings begins with 'AbdAllah, and then expands the name to connect to a prophet, with the same prophet often connected back to Allah, or else in a different sequence with the additional Divine Name coming first and then the name of the prophet.

Ibn 'Arabi is here playing with language and meaning. One of his favorite metaphors is the mirror. Each of us mirrors the divine, yet we mirror the divine differently depending on which of the Divine Names is linked to us. It is the same with prophets: each also mirrors the divine but with a name suited to and reflective of his distinctive character, mission, and meaning. The prophet Ilyas (Elias), for instance, appears in section one as 'AbdAllah ibn Abdur-Rahman ibn Ilyas, while in section three he is 'AbdAllah ibn Ilyas ibn Abdul-Hayy. In both instances

ʿAbdAllah is the anchor. It is always the first name, and it signals the further stages of the names linked to the prophet, in this case, the prophet Ilyas, whether through an intermediary, as in Abdur Rahman, or directly as in Ilyas qualified as ibn Abdul Hayy.

For outsiders, whether ordinary Muslims or non-Muslims who have never encountered a thinker of Ibn ʿArabi's complex subtlety, all these references to Allah and ʿAbdAllah may seem arcane, even nonsensical. But the first citation of Ilyas echoes the Qurʾanic reference: Elijah is mentioned in the Qurʾan, where his preaching is recounted in a concise manner. The Qurʾan relates that Elijah told his people to leave the worship of Baal, the primary local idol, and come to the worship of Allah. The Qurʾan declares:

> *Verily Elijah was one of the apostles.*
> *When he said to his people:*
> *"Will you not fear Allah?*
> *Will you call upon Baʿal*
> *and leave the Best of Creators,*
> *Allah, your Lord and Cherisher*
> *and the Lord and Cherisher*
> *of your fathers of old?"* (Q 37:123–12)

The Qurʾan makes it clear that the majority of Elijah's people denied the prophet and continued to follow idolatry. However, it mentions that a small number of devoted servants of Allah among them followed Elijah and believed in and worshiped the Lord. The Qurʾan states:

> *They denied him [Elijah],*
> *and will surely be brought to punishment,*

Except the sincere and devoted servants of Allah [among them].
And We left his [memory] for posterity. (Q 37:127–28)

And Allah praises Elijah by name in two places, once in a specific sense:

Peace be upon Elijah!
This is how We reward
those who do good.
He is truly among our believing servants. (Q 37:129–32)

And again, in a more general sense:

And Zachariah and John and Jesus and Elijah,
they were all from among the righteous. (Q 6:85)

Why are all four called the righteous? They are deemed to be righteous because they clustered around Jesus. Zachariah was the father of John the Baptist, who is also referenced as "Elias who is to come" (Matthew 11:14); and Elias/Elijah is said to have been present and talked to Jesus when God confirmed Jesus' mission on a mountaintop (Matthew 17:3; an event known as the Transfiguration). In other words, all four persons are suffused with divine resplendence.

A similar process takes place with citations referring to the Prophet Idris in Ibn 'Arabi's *Kitab al-'Abadila*. Idris (who is linked to Enoch and also sometimes to Hermes) is honored through 'AbdAllah, but always sequentially by occupying the middle position between 'AbdAllah and one of the other Divine Names. In section one he appears as: 'Abdallah ibn Idris ibn 'Abdul Khaliq, and then in section two as 'Abdullah ibn Idris ibn 'Abdul Malik and, again, in the same section, as 'Abdullah ibn Idris ibn 'Abdul Nur, and in chapter three as 'Abdullah ibn Idris ibn 'Abdul Kabir!

Like Ilyas, Idris is also mentioned twice in the Qur'an. Idris is described as a wise and great man. Once he is included with others in the lofty status of the righteous ones:

And [remember] Isma'il, Idris, and Dhul-Kifl,
all [men] of constancy and patience;
We admitted them to Our mercy:
for they were of the righteous ones. (Q 21:85–86)

And then, in Sura Maryam (Q 19), named after Jesus' mother, Mary, Allah singles out Idris for special consideration, as the occupant of "a lofty station":

Also mention in the Book the case of Idris:
He was a man of truth [and sincerity], [and] a prophet:
And We raised him to a lofty station. (Q 19:56–57)

Not surprisingly, we find numerous commentators linking Ilyas to Idris. Sometimes they are closely associated; at other times they are identical, heightening both their mystery and their importance for those who want to comprehend the message of Allah to Muhammad through the Qur'an. None of this would matter except that it expands the universe of possibilities—it probes the outer edges of human imagination—about 'AbdAllah as a charged carrier of the name Allah. 'AbdAllah is more than just one additional Muslim name; any one so named is deemed to be the servant of Allah, one echoing but never equaling or displacing the perfect servant, Muhammad ibn 'AbdAllah al-Hashmi, the Prophet of Islam.

CONNECTING ALLAH TO ALPHABETS: THE MAGICAL APPROACH

All Muslim scholars, like all "ordinary" Muslims, begin with the special role of humankind laid out in the divine conspectus, the Qur'an. Because of the centrality of the Qur'an in shaping a view of Allah and human destiny, some interpreters stress the quantitative approach. They focus on numbers. They assume that mathematical precision is divinely ordained but also occluded: only those with insight can discern the signs concealed in letters, but the letters themselves have to be translated into numbers before they can be decoded. This quasi-science of numerical discernment through letters is called gematria or numerology.

Of special import are the letters of the Beautiful Names of Allah, and while these total ninety-nine, Allah heads the list. But how does one count Allah as not just the source and the author but also the subject of the revelation given to Muhammad in early seventh-century Arabia? It is Allah who reveals who is Allah, but how does one make sense of Allah as the one who repeatedly refers to Himself, that is, to Allah, in the pages of the Qur'an?

No one has faced this challenge and met it more emphatically than the esteemed Pakistani scholar Maulana Muhammad Musa al-Ruhani al-Bazi (d. 1998). In a single massive book, *The Conquest of Allah through the Special Qualities of the Name Allah*, he attends to all the many issues about the name Allah that have been raised during the past 1,400 years.

On Numerology and *Abjad*

Numerology is as old as religion itself. In the Ugaritic text of Gilgamesh, the number seven recurs, as it does also in Genesis and elsewhere in the Hebrew Bible. The final book of the New Testament, Book of Revelation, is replete with numerical allusions. Those who translate letters into numbers move this fascination into the quasi-scientific endeavor called gematria. Prominent in kabbala, or Jewish mysticism, and in multiple Christian circles, with Masonic offshoots, it also appears in Islam, where it is known as *abjad*, or the science of letters (*'ilm al-huruf*).

He takes up and then examines almost every major Arab and non-Arab scholar, from the premodern to the modern period of Islamic civilization, on the subject of Allah as the supreme name for the Creator, Monitor, and Executor of the universe as we know it. Central to Maulana al-Bazi's argument is the number of times that the name Allah occurs in the Qur'an. This number is deemed to be consequential for all who are devoted to the content of Divine Revelation. Not only does he examine the significance of each of the letters of the name Allah—*alif, lam, ha*[14]—but he also notes that the name Allah occurs 2,698 times, out of the Qur'an's roughly 77,800 total words, accounting for slightly less than 3 percent of the entire Noble Book.

The first noun that comes after Allah in terms of frequency is *rabb*, or master, which is almost always linked to Allah. It occurs a "mere" 975 times! Yet if one also includes all the names that are attributed to Allah and seen as part of the divine canopy covering all aspects of human reflection on, and connection to, the Unseen world (*al-Ghayb*), then Allah may account for 5 percent of the entire Qur'an. Many who want to link Islam to modern science make much out of these connections and the numerical computations based on them.

And beyond counting, it is connecting the dots, literally figuring out correspondences between the Qur'anic dicta and the laws of nature, that matters most to many who want to understand the deepest meaning of Allah. The history of Islam is replete with numerology, matching correspondences between letters and numbers, but one of the most recent

Fig. 3. Counting to 7 with A-l-l-a-h. Illustration by Katie Cooke.

exponents of numerical exactitude as the key to divine wisdom comes from modern-day America. They are known by the practice they pursue: the Five Percenters.

THE FIVE PERCENTERS

Among contemporary Muslims in America where counting is crucial, few can rival the Five Percenters. Though they are a small minority of American Muslims, the Five Percenters teach that black people are the original people of the planet Earth, and that they are the fathers (Gods) and mothers (Earths) of civilization. The Five Percenters believe that the science of Supreme Mathematics is the key to understanding man's relationship to the universe. Eschewing belief in a traditional God, the Five Percenters instead believe that "the Afro-Asiatic black man" is God and that his proper name is Allah. Indeed A-l-l-a-h is itself a secret that only be decoded in English. It serves as an acronym for Arm, Leg, Leg, Arm, Head, A-l-l-a-h, with special significance for the number 7 (figure 3).[15]

So central is the notion that Allah is a human being, a mere mortal man, that followers of the Five Percenters accept the abuse heaped on them by other "orthodox" Muslims. Among their rising stars in the current generation is Michael Muhammad Knight. Knight founded Taqwacore, itself a form of fusion between Islam and popular culture. The Five Percenters in general, and Knight in particular, might be understood as modern-day Malamatis, accepting abuse in their fidelity to Islam as

Malamatis, Qalandars, and Dervishes

There are many terms for those who emphasize an interior pursuit and, with it, an internal purity. The key protocol is to debase, and often debunk, what other people consider good behavior, at once acceptable and ethical. Malamatis are Muslims who are extreme in their pursuit of internal purity. They act in ways that are deliberately offensive to the cultural, ethical, and creedal standards of their day. Some deride them, others respect them; no one ignores them.

they perceive and practice it. Taqwacore represents a subgenre of punk music dealing with Islam, its culture, and interpretation as conceived in Knight's 2003 novel, *The Taqwacores*. The title, however, retains its tie to the long sweep of Islamic piety. The term itself fuses a standard Arabic word for pious fear of God, *taqwa*, with the word for heavy metal, hardcore. Love and fear of God are also comingled in this group's membership. Taqwacore followers are mostly young Muslim artists living in the United States and other western countries. Many of them openly reject traditional interpretations of Islam and invite others to abuse them and their beliefs. Here is Knight's recent commentary on "The Taqwacore Version (of Allah and Islam)":

> I became Muslim just a hair under 20 years ago, and the peace is just starting to come in. I've worked long and hard to earn my flake-out time, my new golden age when all mosques are mine and no mosques are mine, when I can remain spiritually homeless but always find shelter somewhere. . . . Two weeks ago I received an email from a Muslim who has read one of my books, informing me that I do not qualify for his Muslim clubhouse, that I'm a *kafir* (unbeliever) and I don't know true Islam. I answered that I've my own Islam, and it works great, and he can have his clubhouse all to himself.[16]

Who then is a *kafir* and who a believer in the eyes of Allah? Only Allah knows, but what is clear is that Allah speaks across the divide of time in many voices, with Michael Muhammad Knight one of His devout, if unconventional, Information Age listeners.

THE SCIENCE OF *ABJAD*

The Five Percenters are a recent, specifically African American expression of the persistent influence of a science of numbers in Islam. It is called *abjad*, and it has been examined in many works.[17] Central to the science of *abjad* are multiple ways of appealing to Allah within the scheme of numbers. Here is how *abjad* works. *Abjad* letter-numerals are the letters of the Arabic alphabet given numerical values. They could thus be used in various combinations to represent any number from 1 to 1,999. It is not a place-notational system, for their value does not depend upon their position relative to one another. Thus the number 652 would be represented by the letters *kha'* (= 600), *nun* (= 50), and *ba'* (= 2), no matter in what order the letters were arranged. The name *abjad* comes from the first four letters in the sequence to which values 1, 2, 3, and 4 were assigned, that is, letters, *alif, ba', jim*, and *dal*. The symbol for zero was derived from Indian astronomical and mathematical manuscripts in which a symbol was often used as an abbreviation for the Greek word *ouden*, meaning "nothing." The letter-numerals for numbers 1 through 50 were the same throughout the Muslim world, though there were differences between the Maghrib (West) and the Mashriq (East) when it came to assigning letters to the remaining values.[18]

THE MAGIC SQUARE IN POPULAR CULTURE

There is extraordinary attention in popular culture to the magic square. It is produced in the science of letters when Arabic phrases, words, and letters from the Qur'an, especially the names or attributes of Allah, angels, prophets, or their numerological equivalents are placed in a grid of squares or other geometric shapes. Magic squares, and other number/letter talismans, were a popular expression of the learned systems of Islamic alchemy often attributed to the alchemical corpus of Jabir ibn Hayyan. Magic squares were also a part of Sufi and Shi'i texts where the cosmogonic nature of divine speech is mediated through Arabic orthography and mystical numerology.[19]

In various Muslim countries, especially but not solely in West African nations, one finds verbal performance, or incantational prayer, incorporated along with visual/physical representations of divine speech in magic squares known as *khawatim* or "seals/rings." The *khatim* serves a variety of purposes and is immediately effective upon the written execution of the square. When inscribed with Allah's names, these "seals" are said to produce an immediate effect in contrast with other Qur'anic passages, which only supplicate and hope for a divine response. In other words, there is a hierarchy of power in the different forms of divine speech. Most powerful and magically efficacious are the Beautiful Names of Allah (*Asma'Allah al-husna*, as well as the *ism akbar*, the greatest but secret name of Allah). Magic squares, using Divine Names or other Qur'anic materials, continue as vernacular healing and protection devices into the modern era and are still reported present in some contemporary Muslim healing rituals where it is both diagnostic tool and talismanic prescription.

Numbers can play a crucial role in the *ta'widh*, that is, the invocation of God's mercy and protection from the forces of evil, specifically in the creation of amulets or prescriptions of mercy that diviner/saints make to dispel the evil one. Every letter in the Arabic alphabet carries a value. Those numbers when added up can give you a total that symbolically represents the holy phrase. No phrase is deemed to be more important than the first phrase of the opening chapter of the Qur'an. Though nonsense words that are relevant solely for the numerical values they list, they tap into a reservoir of quantitative potency. Its devout practitioners presume that even someone who does not know Arabic can still count the numbers and see that they do in fact add up to a total of 786. Does it work for you? If not, the cause may be your blinkered attention to letters minus their numerical magic!

While the entire Qur'an is often thought to be summarized in the seven verses of the opening chapter or Sura al-Fatiha, for many the meaning of the opening chapter is itself summed up in its first words: "In the Name of Allah, Full of Compassion, Ever Compassionate."[20] This phrase, known as the *basmala*, has been often encountered in our reflections on Allah, but here it is written, then counted. In *abjad* it represents 786, and those numbers are thought to convey its power if ritually used. The 786 may be written on a piece of paper or voiced as a silent prayer. It may be spoken aloud as though it were a prayer. It may be written on glass and the ink washed off, then drunk as medicine. It may be affixed to some part of the body or, in the case of a corpse, it may be buried with the deceased in the ground.

Often 786 is written at the top of a paper or material conveying the *basmala* but then applied to specific words that are written out in Arabic script, in order to make the prescription of mercy effective:

- If a woman suffers from headache, she might wear around her neck a prescription of mercy that reads "O Allah" in symmetrical rows of three.
- If a baby has measles, the mother might be given an expanded diagram of sixteen "O Allah's" that encompass the first nine numbers in Arabic.
- For eye pain, the form of "O Allah" may be written as though it were the upper and lower eyelid, and on each corner within a rectangular box one of the mighty intervening angels be invoked: O Gabriel, O Michael, O Azrael, O Israfil!
- For beautiful women or women at risk because of their evident charm, the evil to ward off comes from the eye of others. It is known as the evil eye, and the defense against it is a Qur'anic prescription of mercy that numbers the *basmala* at top and then in even patterns of four invokes Allah by his pronominal referent "O He!," "O He!" sixteen times.
- And for women who cannot conceive, there is a still more elaborate formula of the pronominal invocation. After invocation of 786, "O He" has to be written thirty-five times, in five rows of seven pronouns each. Once written, preferably in vegetable ink, it is then washed off and drunk by the woman hoping to conceive.

If this list sounds strange or arbitrary, it is because it has been culled from multiple places where the practice of washing letters with water, and then using the sanctified water for healing, is rampant. Lived religion—the everyday practice of Islam at every level in Muslim societies from Dakar, Senegal, to Djakarta, Indonesia—means that these thaumaturgical, apotropaic formulae expand into still other realms. Similar formulae apply to amulets that cover a variety of distresses, from nosebleeds to labor pains, from toothaches to abscesses. Huge and varied is the inventory of Qur'anic invocations, always addressed to Allah or invoking a message to *Allah ta'ala*. They continue to be in use today throughout the Muslim world. Men may be the religious functionaries dispensing them, but many, if not most of their clients, are Muslim women. Whether literate or illiterate, privileged or poor, they place their trust in the deepest, hidden properties of Allah, seeking from Him medical relief from whatever afflicts them or those closest to them.[21]

DOUBT ON MANIPULATING ALLAH'S
NAMES THROUGH *ABJAD*

The idea of manipulating nature through numbers goes back to before the rise of Islam. Ibn Khaldun (d. 1406 CE), the noted Maghribi polymath, explains how Arab diviners assumed the existence of sixteen houses in the cosmos: twelve corresponding to the signs of the Zodiac (the ordinary houses) and four to the cardinal points. Those who practice *khatt-al-raml* (lit., writing in the sand, or sand writing) have, in his view, "invented a discipline which runs parallel to astrology and the system of astrological judgments." But Ibn Khaldun did not approve of this practice. He cast doubt on its legitimacy, as well as on the viability of its close correlate, geomancy. In his view, geomantic figures "are based upon arbitrary conventions and wishing thinking. Nothing about them is proven."[22]

Similarly, a modern-day detractor of "numerical soteriology" felt compelled to issue a warning against it on the Internet. Decrying the widespread use of numbers to reach *Allah ta'ala*, a Muslim netizen posted the following message on the Internet in 2009, with a stark diagram (figure 4):

> Almost all individuals really believe that number 786 is crucial for Muslims. In movies, TV series, the 786 in used over and over again, wanting Allah's help when in trouble. 786 in their car number, 786 in mobile number, 786 in house number. Muslims say 786 = Bismi-(A)llah al-Rahman al-Rahim. But does this number really work? Does Bismi(A)llah contain the name of God Allah? Can we get rid of "Bismi(A)llah al-Rahman al-Rahim" from the top of the Sura al-Fatiha and replace it with the number 786?
>
> The innovation of writing 786 and replacing Bismi(A)llah al-Rahman al-Rahim has gone on for a long time and most of the Islamic community still uses it without realizing its problematic nature. For anybody who uses 786 with the intention of obtaining the blessings of Allah is ignorant.
>
> More surprising is that 786 is an aggregation of the numbers for the Hindu Lord Hari Krishna! Since both Hari Krishna and Bismi-(A)llah al-Rahman al-Rahim add up to 786, one must avoid using this number to avoid the danger of falling into infidelity. The Quran warns us: "Whoever sets up a rival against Allah, Allah will not enable him to enter paradise, and his abode is hell" (Q 5:72b).[23]

Fig. 4. 786 belongs to all religions. Illustration by Katie Cooke.

In other words, there is no numerical equivalent that can be substituted for the prayerful invocation of the name Allah or any of the other sanctioned Beautiful Names. The recurrent need is to connect with Allah through informed, sincere, and persistent utterance of the Name or Names. The Beautiful Names of Allah remain the portals; all devout Muslims must enter into the Divine Presence, and seek Divine Guidance, through one of them.

SUMMARY

Allah is connected to humankind, to creation, and to arithmetic. While most mainstream Muslims invoke Allah by the name Allah, or by one of the other names linked to Allah, others see a deep resonance within the cosmos, above all, in the *h-m-d* sequence that can mean *hamid*, "praiseworthy," of Allah or *muhammad*, the one who praises, of the Prophet. Both meanings are echoed in the phrase known as the *tahmid*, "Praise be to Allah," that occurs in the opening chapter, or Sura al-Fatiha, of the Qur'an. The combination of invoking Allah and linking Allah to the Qur'an leads to examination of the popular name 'AbdAllah, developed by the mystic expositor, Ibn 'Arabi, with reference to earlier, pre-Islamic prophets. The numerical suggestiveness of the initial phrase, *basmala*, of the opening Qur'anic chapter has led still others to look at numbers, and to the science of geomancy, for a deeper connection with Allah, but whether numbers can replace names, and whether the former is as effective as the latter in forging the link with Allah sought by all Muslims, continues to be a matter of heated debate, much of it now waged on the Internet.

Remote from all these conventions and practices of connecting to the name Allah is the activity of scholars, jurists, theologians, and philosophers. While invocation is a daily discipline for the tongue, common to all believers, it was elites who engaged the intellect in trying to understand what the tongue said. Though separated from the "ordinary" Muslim by their education, status, and role, often serving in the courts of rulers or kings, the elites were no less concerned with the name Allah. They too wanted to probe its secrets and harness its benefits, yet their distinctive tool was not the tongue but the mind, and it is to their persistent reflections, the practices of the intellect, that we turn in the next chapter.

Nasruddin Hoca is a judge of high repute. One day he and Tamerlane
[the fourteenth-century Mongol conqueror and ruler of Central Asia] are
bathing in a public bath. "If I were a serf for sale," asks Tamerlane, "what price
would you be willing to pay for me?" "Two coins," replies the Hoca. "Be fair,"
retorts Tamerlane. "My towel alone is worth two coins." "Actually,"
replies the Hoca. "It was the towel's worth that I had in mind."
— *The Tales of Nasrettin Hoca*, trans. Talat Halman

CHAPTER TWO

Allah Defined

Practice of the Mind

OVERVIEW

There are two paths to knowing, and practicing, the name Allah. One is
content, the other context. Content focuses on the who and what: who
said what about Allah? Context focuses on the where and how: where
did the knower or practitioner invoke, or rely on, the name Allah? And
how did he or she share with others that knowledge or practice of Allah?

Mere mention of the pronoun "she" brings an instant qualification:
nearly all those who are cited in speaking about Allah are men. Their
musings and arguments are center stage in the vast literary corpus that
has been produced about Allah over the past 1,400 years. But they are
not just men; they are also, in most cases, privileged men. Literacy, education, social status and economic opportunity — all these shape the way
that Muslim men have recalled, invoked, and defined Allah.

And so gender, along with class and status, become pivotal markers of
the context for invoking and dwelling on the name Allah. In this chap-

> ## 'Ulama
>
> *'Ulama* (knowers; s., *'alim*) are those who are trained in Arabic and so have access to the sciences of religion: the Qur'an, *hadith*, and all branches of knowledge, especially those pertaining to worship and law. They are among the urban elites of medieval and modern Muslim society, though rural towns or peripheral areas also produce, and depend on, *'ulama*.

ter we begin in a bathhouse but travel throughout the premodern Muslim world, where reflection on Allah is central to producing knowledge that animates Muslim intellectual and religious life. It is, in fact, engagement with the One that dominates the tone, and defines the temper, of debates about Islam throughout the first millennium of Islamic civilization.

THE BROAD ARC OF NASRUDDIN HOCA

The bathhouse joke makes no reference to Allah, yet it reveals a common dimension to all god talk: class status.[1] The Hoca, as "a judge of high repute," is entitled to be in a bathhouse with the ruler because both enjoy privileged status in a fourteenth-century Central Asian Muslim city. Hoca belonged to the *'ulama* class, who are the agents of authority for much of what is classified as Islamic law or *shari'a*. Apart from their official functions, they also provide insights that guide the public profile of the entire Muslim community.

God talk presupposes devotion and loyalty to the Thing, the Absolute, the One, but it involves more than just calling on Allah or invoking Him by any of His many names. Allah must also be defined, and those who define Him are themselves defined by their social class. Along with the military, rulers, and merchants, they comprise the upper class. They are the scholars of Islam, the *'ulama*. It is not easy to relate the reflections and arguments, the judgments and decrees, of scholars to the everyday invocation of Allah, and yet the two elide at the level of intention: both seek to relate their own labor, and their own performance, to the Thing, the Absolute, the One.

THE KNOWLEDGE CLASS AND ORDINARY BELIEVERS

For ordinary believers, Allah is either a word to be invoked or a name to be revered. Not so for the knowledge class within Islam, those religious scholars labeled ʿulama. For the ʿulama Allah is more than the Absolute One; He is also the source of their social power. The ʿulama project their authority as deriving from, and relating back to, Allah. All the branches of Islamic science and their practitioners have tried to forge a collective ethos, with expectations, requirements, meditations, and arguments, that centers not just on the name Allah, but also appeals to the authority of one who is "Lord of all Domains"—rabb al-ʿalamin.

Despite the many common traits among members of the ʿulama, there was also a differentiation of labor among them. Nearly all members of the knowledge class in premodern Islam belonged to one of three groups: theologians (mutakallimun), philosophers (falasifa), and jurists (fuqaha). Sufi masters (mashaʾikh) also became major players, but only after the twelfth century. Technically speaking, neither the theologians nor the philosophers were ʿulama, nor were the Sufi masters. Yet in social and class background they often shared similar privileges. They had opportunities to learn and to travel. They lived by their wits and words more than their labor or deeds.[2] And they recognized the benefit of possessing different skills and outlooks, so much so that an exceptional scholar such as Imam Muhammad al-Ghazali (d. 1111) could and did excel in several branches of Islamic learning.

It is important, however, to mark differences in approach, outlook, and audience among the knowledge class. The task of defining Allah is blurred unless one first recognizes the distinct, overlapping, and sometimes-competitive emphases among scholarly elites. For theologians, the central query was dyadic: Can Allah be both anthropomorphic and transcendent? And what is at stake in these variant conceptions of the Source of All Life and Meaning? Their audience was educated and literate but not always sophisticated and wealthy. For philosophers, the central query was context specific, accenting the location of Islam at the end of a long revelatory cycle: Has Allah, the God of Abraham, Ishmael, and Muhammad, become just another of "Aristotle's children"? Or was there something about the Muslim experience that made Muslims much more than the latest family member in the Abrahamic lineage?[3] The philosophers' audience was highly literate and mostly upper class. How-

Fig. 5. Nasruddin Hoca and donkey.
Photograph by the author.

ever, for others, with a larger, less-privileged audience, the question was more practical. For judges, the overriding concern was: How can the law be enforced for every level of society with reference to the Book, that is, the Qur'an, while maintaining both the hierarchy of the ruling class and the equality of all believers? In other words, belief and status merged at multiple levels of everyday social practice.

The best way to examine the social privileges of the knowledge class is to look at one of their own: the Hoca or Nasruddin Hoca (figure 5). The Hoca is a protean figure, at once wise fool and everyday guide for Muslims throughout Turkey and Central and South Asia. Two aspects of the opening anecdote about him and Tamerlane are especially important. First, the elite bathe together. It was not unusual for someone with judicial status to be sharing public bathwater with the military/political ruler. Second, the banter often can be serious, even sarcastic, as in this case, when Nasruddin Hoca casts doubt on the worth of Tamerlane, even though the latter could order his execution were the Hoca to say the same thing at the ruler's court.

JUDGES AND OTHER MEMBERS OF THE KNOWLEDGE CLASS

From the time that Islam became identified with empire, from the mid-eighth century on, and interacted with other cultures from a dominant position, judges came to be crucial figures regulating the everyday exchange of their fellow Muslims, and also non-Muslim others. These judges claimed to be, and were seen by others as, surrogates of Divine Judgment. Allah functions as ultimate judge or arbiter in the celestial realm, but He needs agents in the temporal realm. The judges provided that transitional authority, so much so that the social status of judges was on a par with, or in some cases above that, of rulers.

Others who wrestled with the question of Allah were members of the knowledge class who shared with judges an urban location and elite status, but also a proclivity for literature—they were fond of texts and excellent at both interpreting old ones and often writing new ones. They were known as *adib*, or *udaba*, those grounded in *adab*. They were like the *ʿulama* in their zest for knowledge, but theirs was an arc that encompassed a range of literary and intellectual pursuits outside the domain of religion.

One must traverse a long span—in memory and in imagination— from the seventh-century Arabia of the Prophet Muhammad to the fourteenth-century world of Tamerlane and Mullah Nasruddin. The earliest period (till ca. 750 CE) produced little philosophical speculation, echoing the tribal, Arabian background of the Prophet. But then with expansion and empire came the challenge of urban society and above all, the demands of literacy, hierarchy, and new social relations.

From oral discourse to written word is the simplest way of charting the social shift in Muslim public life, but more complex and ultimately more important is the shift from open affirmation of the Qurʾan to secret accommodation with Aristotle. All the branches of urban/literary/official Islamic knowledge have to consider the Greek challenge. It is not a question of "either/or," but of "how much" and at what popular cost.

THE GREEK CHALLENGE: CREATION OUT OF NOTHING

By the early ninth century, no reflection on Allah could avoid the major exponents of Aristotle in Arabic. The philosopher al-Kindi (d. 873 CE) affirms that prophetic knowledge is akin to philosophical knowledge, only easier. Prophets, he says, grasp the same truths philosophers do, but grasp them more easily and express them more pithily. As an example he cites Q 36:81–82:

Isn't the One who created
The heavens and the earth
Able to create their like?
Certainly, being the Absolute Creator,
The Omniscient One,
Whose only command
When willing a thing
Is to say to it "Be,"
And it is.

The key line is the last: when Allah wills something to be, He says to it "Be," and it is. Al-Kindi explains that all generation involves the existence of something before which it does not exist: for example when fire is generated, it comes into being from not-fire. This is perfectly Aristotelian. Less Aristotelian is his further point that when Allah creates, He brings something to exist after complete nonexistence, that is, he produces something out of nothing—also known as *creatio ex nihilo*, or cre-

Creatio ex Nihilo

Creation from nothing is a philosophical and theological riddle: how can there be absolutely nothing before there is something? Christians, Jews, and Muslims wrestle with this issue. For Muslims, one of the crucial verses in favor of Allah creating from nothing is

[Allah is] the Creator of the heavens and the earth;
Whose only command
When willing a thing
Is to say to it "Be,"
And it is. (Q 2:117b and Q 36:82)

ation from nothing.[4] Unlike created agents, Allah can bring about generation instantaneously and without preexisting matter.

But here arises a major tension. While humans can dare to talk of the universe as divine creation, there is a simultaneous need for believers to affirm the unique character of its divine origin as creation. These tensions arise in most, if not all, philosophical approaches to creation in the Abrahamic religions: Judaism, Christianity, and Islam.

Christians, like Muslims, wished to stress the difference between divine creation and other sorts of generation or change. Thus the doctrine of *creatio ex nihilo* became a way to explain how Greek philosophers got it wrong, since God (or theos), like Allah, transcends the conceptual apparatus of philosophers, as also the constraints of natural causation. The first doctrines of *creatio ex nihilo* were motivated not by a desire to preserve divine freedom or contingency but to defend Allah as First Cause.[5] While Aristotle argued for the eternity of the world, al-Kindi asserts that Allah creates instantly without matter, unlike natural causes, which operate on preexisting matter and need time.[6]

THE ROLE OF IBN SINA

It is Ibn Sina (d. 1037 CE) who makes the production of being as such the hallmark of "metaphysical" causation. Natural causes, he argues, only produce motion. He inserts the divine/natural contrast within the fold of philosophy through a bold comparison: whereas metaphysics

Ibn Sina

Abu Ali Ibn Sina, known in Europe as Avicenna, was an eleventh-century medical lexicographer, philosopher, and mystical seeker of broad intellectual skills. Persian and central Asian in background, he mastered all the critical sciences in Arabic and became known as the "second Aristotle." He was a true *adib*, linked to the *'ulama* by class but not by outlook.

Neoplatonism

Neoplatonism is a school of mystical philosophy from the third century based on the teachings of Platonists. Their focus was on spiritual and cosmological aspects of Platonic thought. Neoplatonists closely engaged with the thinkers of other intellectual schools, e.g., Augustine, and in late Antiquity their arguments were taken seriously in the speculation of medieval Islamic and Jewish thinkers.

Neoplatonism is a form of theistic monism that incorporates elements of polytheism in its cosmology. Its proponents affirm a singular Source of Being, the One and the Infinite, as opposed to the many and the finite, which remain dependent on, yet related in stages to, the One. Though the Source is depicted as absolute causality and said to be the only real existent, it still remains elusive, beyond human reasoning or philosophical understanding.

studies Allah, the absolute cause of existence, physics only studies natural causes, which modify things that already exist. This contrast of the metaphysical to the physical seems to reflect an equally fundamental contrast between the necessary and the contingent, but it does so at the expense of naturalizing Allah, stressing the likeness of the divine precisely by following the Neoplatonists.

Like his predecessors, Ibn Sina made Allah into a divine creative force behind the natural order: what the Eternal, Immortal made could be, and should be, perceived, analyzed, studied, and applied by temporal mortals, that is, human scientists. Ibn Sina did strive to articulate the absolute dependency of all things on Allah, but at the same time he made the Thing, the Absolute, the One into an instrument of His own thingness. Some post–Ibn Sinan philosophers went so far as to make creation little more than an appearance or "theophany" of Allah (*tajalli*).

THOSE WHO CHALLENGED IBN SINA

Of course, not all Muslim thinkers were so taken with Ibn Sina's modalization of the relation between Allah and creation, slotting Allah as the Necessary-in-itself while all else is necessary-through-another. In his *Incoherence of the Philosophers*, Imam Ghazali sought to reassert the temporal origination of the world. It did not happen as a matter of course, flowing from natural elements already set in place. There needed to be a definite point, a specific moment of origin, in order to preserve the contingency of the created and also the transcendence, which is to say, the independence, of the Creator. But Al-Ghazali did something more. He attributed to philosophical argument an unspoken, ideological project: to make of the One beyond knowing a platform or source of knowledge for human inquirers. Al-Ghazali made it his own project "to expose the predisposition of philosophical thought to absolutist and authoritarian appropriation [of divine authority]."[7]

Many Abrahamic theologians, whether Jewish, Christian, or Muslim, have been disquieted at the pretensions of philosophers in domesticating divinity within the parameters of human reason and therefore subject to human manipulation. It is an intellectual game that also reflects one's sensibility, one's conduct, and one's connection to other persons.[8]

This question—the possibility of reconciling rational science and the idea of *creatio ex nihilo*—persists into today. Can the big bang theory be accommodated to theories of creation in Ibn Sina and later Aristotelians such as Mir Damad (d. 1631 CE) and Mulla Sadra (d. 1640 CE)? Not easily, and so the question of how creation might relate to the big bang is simply the most recent version of the issue: how does creation compare to the kinds of causation recognized in natural philosophy (physics)? In opposition to the entire notion of evolution à la Darwin, some Muslim creationists, such as Harun Yahya, claim that Allah alone is the instant or *ex nihilo* Creator.[9] If the whole point of *creatio ex nihilo* is to affirm a supernatural kind of causation, then how can God talk or theology be related to the causal framework of nature, including the big bang? Have science and religion grown so far apart that the two have little to say to one another? Muslim philosophers would want to argue that creation

could be, and should be, grounds for the intelligibility of the universe,
which is presupposed in science.

Leading philosophers of Judaism and Christianity—including Mai-
monides, Aquinas, and Duns Scotus—as well as later Muslim thinkers
such as Mir Damad and Mulla Sadra all confronted Ibn Sina's idea that
creation *ex nihilo* is not a one-off temporal event but an unbroken, rudi-
mentary dependence of the contingent upon the necessary for its continued existence. In other words, the process of creation, from a human
perspective, involves repeated acts of creation in time and space, all
necessarily linked to a single, and presumably divine, source.

OTHER MUSLIM RATIONALISTS: THE MUʿTAZILITES

Social factors also intrude: the ordinary folk are invoked but almost
always derided. Major exponents of rationalism, the Muʿtazilites did not
believe that ordinary folk, that is, the majority of professing Muslims,
could understand the intellective soul or ever attain self-knowledge
through exercise of the higher/active intelligence.[10]

Though the ultimate goal was to bring people closer to Allah through
the *shariʿa*, the reality was that for the masses, both the letter of the
revelation and the materialistic symbols must remain the literal truth.
In supporting their philosophical quest, the Muʿtazilites perpetually
sought verbal means, clever phrases, to make anthropomorphic expressions of Allah in the Qurʾan merely metaphoric, not literal. The best way
out of the comparison, and seeming assimilation, between human and
divine bodily parts was to invoke *bi la kayfa* (acceptance of Allah's creation without knowing how it happened).[11]

While the ordinary believer might accept disparities without asking why, philosophers wanted more, and so Ibn Sina tries to explain that *al ʿaql al-faʿal* (the active intellect) can influence bodies and even circumvent natural laws. *Khawariq al-adat* ("breaking what was customary or customarily expected," i.e., miracles) was the way that popular preachers and also Sufi masters tried to explain such miracles.[12]

Mobility was a huge social factor within the capital cities of the Muslim world. Major thinkers moved not just from place to place but also from audience to audience. On crucial issues they spoke to the expectations of their audiences, with flexible, often fluctuating arguments. Ibn ʿArabi changed over his lifetime and also wrote some treatises solely for knowers, that is, those who were among his intimate cohort of followers. Al-Ghazali changed depending on whether he was writing for an esoteric or exoteric audience. In *Tahafut al-falasifa* (aka "The Incoherence of the Philosophers"), written for the cognoscenti, he characterizes prophecy by deriding Ibn Sina as one "traveling far from the concept of Allah the Commander," but in *Miʿraj al-Salikin*, for a public audience, he tries to accommodate philosophical with "orthodox" positions.[13]

THE CHALLENGE OF INTERPRETING SYMBOLISM

There was a particularly sharp contrast between a "practical" working Sufi *shaykh* such as Ibn ʿAtaʾ Allah (d. 1309 CE) and Ibn ʿArabi on the use of metaphors. Consider a crucial metaphor such as the two hands. For Shaykh al-Akbar, even the Divine Names are not ontological terms but rather relational aspects of the world and, above all, the human self/mirror that is to be continuously and assiduously polished, often in pairs.

If all pairing, like all creation, is divinely willed, then there is special significance to the two hands. For Ibn ʿArabi, the "two hands" symbolize the mediating position of the believer, neither comparable to the divine nor divorced from Him. As the bearer of trust, s/he is the locus of divinely bestowed opposites (i.e, *tashbih* and *tanzih*). In other words, the believer at once wants to identify with the transcendent and partake of the immanent. It is a tension intrinsic to, indeed inseparable from, the human condition.[14] Ibn ʿAtaʾ Allah understands the complementarity of hands as also central to connecting with Allah. But while for him they are no less inherently human than they are for Ibn ʿArabi, he gives them an immediate, palpable focus: the "two hands" become the two dominant domains of Allah, *jalal* and *jamal*, the left (*jalal*) connoting force, while the right (*jamal*) connotes forgiveness.[15] Yet the crucial distinction is not just metaphysical but also practical. While Ibn ʿArabi is explaining the "two hands" to the cognoscenti, those educated and disposed to decode divine secrets, Ibn ʿAtaʾ Allah is reaching out to the common seeker who wants everyday guidance. Allah's "two hands" becomes an image to calm the seeker, to help him or her understand that nurture with both hands is an ongoing, unending process of power and care. Creation, rather than something achieved by divine fiat in the past, is something that we experience continuously in each moment. It is the disposition of all seekers to treat daily sustenance as incomplete, in process, at once kneaded and shaped by Allah's "two hands."[16]

ALLAH REMEMBERED AS LIGHT, THE LIGHT OF THE HEAVENS AND THE EARTH

For Ibn ʿAtaʾ Allah, as for most Sufis, the central query remained: how to be loyal to the *sunnah* or example of the Prophet Muhammad while remembering perpetually—through sincere intent and daily practice—

the Ninety-nine Beautiful Names of Allah? Despite many differences internal to their own location and outlook, most Sufis remembered Allah through the Ninety-nine Beautiful Names at the same time that they displayed humility before the Unseen, Unknowable God. The use of performance—speech, music, and dance—became inseparable from the authority of Sufi masters, crossing social and cultural borders throughout Afro-Eurasia.

Among the many examples of this approach to Allah is the fourteenth-century Maghribi saint, Ibn 'Abbad of Ronda (d. 1390 CE). In commending witness through proximity to Allah, he extolled gratitude (*shukr*) as the truest link to divine knowledge. "The very heart of all matters (*lub al-lubab*) is gratitude . . . for gratitude is to know that [a particular] grace is from Allah and [then] to use it as a means of obeying Allah." According to Ibn 'Abbad, *shukr* is the easiest and surest path to inner knowledge. It is founded upon the attitude of attachment to Allah and the contemplation of divine grace, not upon individual worth acquired through pious works or elevated spiritual states (the formal criteria of the *'ulama*). True *shukr* seeks knowledge through practice. It begins with invoking Allah through His name *al-Shakur*, the Grateful One: "O You Who are the All Grateful, make me grateful for the blessings you have bestowed upon me, mindful of your beneficence and your gifts." The fruit of this invocation is said to be a practical methodology of spiritual transformation that literally meant, "shaping the human character in conformity with the attributes of Allah" (*takhalluq bi akhlaq Allah*). *Takhalluq bi akhlaq Allah*, as a methodology, is pedagogic by its very nature. It emphasizes the need to constantly cultivate attitudes that imbue inner meaning to each and every facet of outward ethical conduct. Conformity with the Divine Attributes, that is, the Ninety-nine Names, results in total submission to Allah as embodied in an inward and outward submission to normative ethical comportment—individually and communally.

Not surprisingly, the above pedagogic approach is grounded in the Qur'an, where Allah declares:

So remember Me;
I will remember you.
And be grateful to Me
and do not neglect Me. (Q 2:152)[17]

All four groups—philosophers, theologians, jurists, and Sufi masters—extol the Qur'an and try to wrest meaning from its multiple, dazzling stretches of rhetorical invocation of the Thing, the Absolute, the One. Yet it is easier to invoke than to explain Allah, as in the following passage:

> *That is Allah your Lord.*
> *There is no god but He . . .*
> *No vision comprehends Him*
> *but He comprehends all vision;*
> *He is the Subtle, the Aware.* (Q 6:103–4)

Allah, the One who sees but cannot be seen, created Adam (man) with His two hands (Q 38:75), and at the same time breathed into him of the Divine Spirit (Q 38:72). So close yet so far, Allah is also Light, Light that precedes and illumines the entire spectrum of the universe and human existence.

> *Allah is the Light of the Heavens and the Earth.*
> *The likeness of His Light*
> *Is as of a niche with a lamp inside;*
> *The lamp is in a glass;*
> *The glass is as if a shining star,*
> *Lit from a blessed olive tree,*
> *Neither of the East nor of the West,*
> *Its oil nearly luminous*
> *Without fire touching it.* (Q 24:35a)

Allah the Lofty Light is seemingly beyond human knowing or perceiving, and yet Allah also permeates all sentient and nonsentient beings, so much so that again in the Noble Book, Allah declares: *"And We are closer to him [man] than his jugular vein"* (Q 50:16).

How to make sense of these numerous dimensions of the One who precedes, intercedes, directs, and culminates all that is known or knowable in this world or the next? Names, Names, Names. They recur throughout the Qur'an and also in the history of Islam. Myriad are the names and mysteries, above all, the mystery of the Ninety-nine Names, which will be explored at length in the next chapter.

For all members of the knowledge class, however, Allah is, first and foremost, the Absolute One, at once unique yet accessible to those possessing ʿilm or knowledge. To the extent that Allah can be known, it is in relation to informed others, those whose qualities echo the ineffable essence/quiddity/otherness of the Lofty One beyond language, experience, and cognition. How to speak of the One therefore becomes a delicate, consequential task. It requires distinctions, many distinctions that are introduced, debated, and perpetuated by scholars.

THE EMERGING SYMBIOSIS OF *SHARI'A* AND SUFISM

Judges, theologians, philosophers, and Sufi masters—all four shared roles and coexisted in premodern Islam as part of the knowledge class seeking to engage and so to echo Allah. From the ninth century on, centrifugal forms of governance prompted the search for internal cohesion and led to an expanded spectrum of religious observance. The lack of political consensus underscored the need for a consensual notion of norms and values, often marked as law. Heightened Sunni-Shi'i sensibilities emerged at this time. They emerged, in part, because cadres of rulers and religious scholars, along with modes of popular piety, developed on a broad transregional plane. Orthodoxy was not singular but plural. Loosely defined and strongly contested, it reflected a majority ideology rather than a consensus pervading all sectors of society, even within the same polity.

During the ninth and tenth centuries much happened to make law central to Muslim identity. Central Asian Buyids (940–1031) were Twelver Shi'ites, tracing themselves to twelve generations of imams, while on the far side of North Africa, the Maghribi Fatimids, were Seveners, ascribing their authority to the seventh imam, Isma'il ibn Ja'far. All had variant notions of Allah, and the Buyids were the first to sponsor an elaborate public liturgy that focused on 'Ali and his younger son, Husayn. They saw father and son as the closest to Allah in the divine pantheon. It was the first of their dynasts, Ahmad ibn Buwayh, who embraced Twelver Shi'ism just at the critical moment of its redefinition into a quiescent movement. The period of lesser occultation had begun in 874 when the twelfth or last imam is said to have disappeared, though he continued to speak through a *bab*, or agent. It was in 941 that the Hidden Imam's fourth and last *bab* died without naming a successor, and from this date begins the greater occultation, concurrent with the Buyid emergence as champions of Twelver Shi'ism. Through fervent appeal to Allah, 'Ali, Husayn, and now the Hidden Imam, Ahmad ibn Buwayh extended his authority over much of Iraq and Iran, and in 945 when he entered Baghdad he allowed the caliph to remain in nominal control, but only after blinding him. In 962 he ordered an official commemoration of the death of Husayn at Karbala, and then the next year ordered the annual, pub-

lic celebration of Ghadir Khumm, the anniversary of Muhammad's alleged appointment of ʿAli as his successor after the Farewell Pilgrimage.
Both events were seen as ordained by Allah and have been fixtures of
Twelver Shiʿi public ritual ever since. No Sunni scholar, however, could
or would accept the basic premise of Shiʿi speculation, to wit, that certain human beings, lofty, spiritually high-minded descendants of the
Prophet Muhammad became devout martyrs, sharing eternal, celestial
space with the Absolute One.

Concurrent with these developments, therefore, and in a sense mir-
roring them, was the development of the four Sunni schools of law. If
the Shiʿites were the party of ʿAli and defenders of the Prophet's family,
then their Sunni counterparts became the people upholding the example
of Muhammad (*sunna*) and its collective application to the entire Muslim community (*jamaʿa*). Their genesis lay in the crisis of legitimacy
facing the early Abbasids, who were both heirs to their predecessors,
the Umayyads, in linking themselves back to the Prophet's family and
the Quraysh clan, but also successors to them in matters of religion.
The Abbasids had massacred all Umayyad dynasts, save for ʿAbd ar-
Rahman (d. 788 CE), who escaped to found a counter-dynasty in southern Spain or al-Andalus. In effect, the Abbasids coopted the Shiʿi revolution against the Umayyads while later betraying their fellow dissidents
and keeping the imams under house arrest lest they foster an oppositional political movement.

THE CONVERGENCE OF *ADAB* AND *SHARIʿA*

The Abbasid reliance on political expediency to erase the Umayyads and
confine the Shiʿi leadership may have been unseemly, but it was justified

in part by Umayyad excesses. Their caliphs, with few exceptions, have been depicted as prone to secular indulgence and neglect of Islamic mores. Where was Allah in the expanding contours of Umayyad rule? The Islamic community (*umma*) had to be defined on a broad consensus that was beyond dispute in its basic structure. Firmly committed to Allah and His Book, the Holy Qur'an, they also had to be at once rational and flexible. For Muslim scholars in eighth- and ninth-century Iraq, that need was met by orienting collective identity to the directives of the Qur'an supplemented by prophetic dicta (*hadith/ahadith*). With textual attention to the Noble Book and doxographical preoccupation with the Prophetic example, Sunni Muslims sought a systematic review of conduct that could provide common norms applicable to the lives of individual believers. It entailed a tacit as well as explicit code of behavior (*adab*). As a social instrument it became the index of right behavior or the law (*shari'a*). It was within the framework of the law that advocates of Islamic mysticism (*tasawwuf*) vied with proponents of dialogic disputation or Islamic theology (*kalam*), who in turn engaged philosophically minded elites (*falasifa*). Each expounded their own interpretations of Allah and the norms as well as beliefs that He had ordained for the saved community, i.e., those Muslims who would be deemed loyal legatees of Muhammad's prophetic mission.

"Without the *shari'a* there is no Islam" is a popular dictum. *Shari'a* became integral to an evolving and comprehensive Muslim worldview. If personal status was an essential domain, so were commercial codes and criminal penalties. What was sought at every level was textual evidence that could be applied by independent judgment or through analogy to arrive at a consensus acceptable to the greatest number of Muslims.

This social reformation influenced the way that Allah was viewed in the Muslim world. Gradually a class of religious specialists known as the *'ulama* came to function as scholars and judges, with the *shari'a* as their common concern. The *'ulama* had already begun to form by the time of the conflict between reason and faith, between Mu'tazilites and their opponents, Ash'arites, in mid-ninth-century Baghdad; but by the end of the tenth century, the functions of religious specialists were more precisely framed and set in place. Each had a special role that collectively supported the process they upheld. The *mujtahid* was the investigating judge, and the *faqih* was the consensus seeker; while the *mufti* was the advisory judge issuing a decree, and the *qadi* was the court judge actually applying the decree to an individual case. Especially notable was

Shariʿa and *Shariʿa* Minded

There is no single school of law in Islam, but a variety of systems
(*madhhab/madhahib*), each with an eponymous founder. Shiʿites
and Sunnis alike support *shariʿa* but with variant emphases on its
influence and implementation. It is the *ʿulama*, or knowledge class,
who define and enforce the juridical provisions of *shariʿa* as either a
faqih, jurist, or *qadi*, judge. Most Muslims are *shariʿa* minded, even
though the *shariʿa* is more formal and occasional than *adab*, which
pervades as an everyday code of conduct

the power of the *qadi*. He alone could mete out punishment if an observance of the *shariʿa* was breached. The *qadi* therefore was a pillar of
stability for maintaining social order, though it was difficult for him to
resist the covert politicization of his office.

The reality was that the rulers employed the *ʿulama* as legitimizers
of their power rather than as watchdogs monitoring, and if possible
controlling, its excesses. All professed belief in Allah, His Prophet, His
Book, His law, and His community. But multiple segments of Muslim
society were not so easily or fully subsumed under the dominance of
the state, refortified as the authoritative expression of Islam. Among
the groups contesting this system were Sufis. The years 1000–1400 witnessed the emergence of an alternative mode of Islamic loyalty linked
to institutional Sufism.

SUFI ORDERS AND PRACTICES

A major objective of early Sufis was to attain a closer, even intimate,
understanding of the Qurʾan by re-creating the circumstances of what
they imagined to be the Prophet's own lifestyle—plain dress, rigorous
piety, and openness to others. They began to elaborate spiritual exercises that led the adept, or seeker, to a direct understanding of the
divine. Music, dancing, chanting, and night vigils characterized their
devotion. They confronted the *ʿulama* most directly not by their rituals but by their beliefs. Sufis elaborated a detailed notion of knowledge
that appealed directly to Allah and seemed to complement the *ʿulama*.
They frequently cited a prophetic dictum that etches the divine motive

for creation: "I was a hidden treasure, and I longed to be known, and I created humankind so that I might be known."[18] The stress on knowledge in this saying links Sufis to the knowledge specialists in Islam, the *‘ulama* or religious scholars, since both the Sufi masters and their juridical counterparts sought to know the Thing, the Absolute, the One, "a hidden treasure longing to be known."[19]

Those who love both knowledge and the knowledge specialists, according to another *hadith*, are excused from having their sins written in the book of deeds. The stress here is double: knowledge is to be esteemed and those who attain it highly esteemed, but sins are not forgiven unless one goes beyond esteem and loves both knowledge and the knowledge specialists.

One way of reflecting on these linkages of knowledge of Allah with love of the Beloved, who mirrors but is not the human beloved, is to distinguish between gradations of knowledge. Sufis ranked knowledge in three stages: sensory knowledge, cognitive knowledge, and intuitive knowledge. Since human life is not possible without sensory knowledge, Sufis, in common with other Muslims, acknowledged the importance of the senses. Cognitive knowledge related to book learning, scholarship, and teaching, and all religious specialists, including Sufis, were expected to master this kind of knowledge; the Sufi masters and the *‘ulama* share common interest in its pursuit.

Intuitive knowledge, however, is the major quest for Sufis. It is said to be reserved for prophets and saints. It grows out of the quest to know Allah as both the Creator and the deepest source of self-knowledge. It is this level of knowledge that connects Sufis to the Prophet Muhammad, the apogee of prophecy, and projects their common goal as the reflection of divine knowledge. As a *hadith* of the Prophet states, "Whoever knows himself knows his Lord."

Institutionally the Sufi quest was framed as three stages: *shariʿa* (law), *tariqa* (way), and *haqiqa* (truth). Law may be understood as an encompassing code of conduct, the way as the pursuit of intuitive knowledge, and the truth as the point of unknowing that is the only thing worth knowing and loving. This complex experience frames the central point (*haqiqa*, or truth) within a circle of *shariʿa*, or law, with the connecting line being the *tariqa*, or way. The ultimate goal of all three is Allah, but the pathways overlap without collapsing into a single approach to the Thing, the Absolute, the One.

THE CRUCIAL ROLE OF SUFI MASTERS

This threefold orientation to *shariʿa*, *tariqa*, and *haqiqa* is a useful entry point for understanding how Sufis are at once "ordinary believers" and "extraordinary seekers." For centuries, the Sufi orientation was limited to that unitary cohort defined as the community of Muhammad.[20] Sufis are Muslims in every point of ritual, practice, and belief; they too accept a web of codes called the *shariʿa*. But for Sufis the relationship of seekers to the material world via prophecy and law fulfills only part of the obligation of Islam. Outward observance is itself subordinated to an inner vision of Allah. The vision itself is not given to everyone but is attained by only a few of the Muslim community who have elected to become seekers. Their vision of the Unseen, beyond time and place (*al-ghayb*), is mediated through luminous beings, spiritual guides on the Path (*shaykhs* and *pirs*). In sum, the same hierarchy that produced the ruler and the state also had its counterpart in the master (*shaykh*) and his followers. Sufi deference to the guide could be an expression of political dissent or mere quiescence, but it bypassed the official channels of Islamic knowledge even as it seemed to ally with forms of esoteric knowledge linked to Shiʿis. The Sufi *shaykhs*, like the Shiʿi imams, professed a direct link to Allah, the Almighty. For some Sunni religious professionals, or *ʿulama*, this link was seen as not just superfluous but as outright blasphemy; yet the majority of those who were Sunni teachers and preachers, prayer callers, and even jurists approved the piety, if not the epistemic claim, of their Sufi coreligionists, at least until the reform movements of the nineteenth century.

The range of behavior that is reflected in Sufi masters actually varies

Orthodoxy and Ecstasy

The obligations of Muslim life include five-time daily prayer, and the tension for Sufis as spiritual ecstatics was to maintain that discipline while also allowing for the flood of divine favor that exceeded all rules, even those that applied to the body of the faithful. At heart was also the authority struggle between bureaucratic power (rulers and *'ulama*) and charismatic counterclaims (Sufi masters, their lodges, and their lineages).

across a broad spectrum. Sufis range from *qalandars*, ecstatic dervishes among whom cognitive knowledge is either absent or refused, to the jurists (*fuqaha*) and scholars (*'ulama*), who represent the official religious classes and are part of both the economic and political elites of their societies. It was not only possible but also desirable to be both a religious professional and a Sufi devotee, and even the ecstatic dervishes who offended "orthodox" sensibilities were often tolerated. To the extent that many of the masters could, and did, gain widespread acceptance, neither the *'ulama* nor the rulers sought to confront them, at least not directly.

The norm for Sufi masters and their disciples was to expand rather than to contract the expected duties of pious Muslims. Theirs was a continuous tension between the routinization of truth through law and practice (*shari'a*) and the creative expression of human longing (*tariqa*). The goal of both was *haqiqa*, but that was, and still is, an elusive goal. Imam Ghazali has often been considered to be one of the few who has achieved that goal. He wrote extensively about the puzzlement of belief and reason, the pursuit of truth from the heart as well as the mind. He was also a bilingual advocate of Sunni Islam, writing in both Arabic and Persian, appealing to non-Arabs as well as Arabs in the highly stratified Seljukid society of eleventh-century Baghdad. Because he stood at a pivotal moment, a conjuncture, in Muslim history, Al-Ghazali is often credited with initiating two major developments in Sufism. They are changes that persisted through the Mongol period and into the emergent empires that came as successor states to the Khans. Both relate to the status of Muslims in society, that is, to class differences.

MARKING ALLAH AS UNKNOWABLE
YET NOT UNSPEAKABLE

One development from Al-Ghazali is the elaboration of theoretical Sufism in both prose and verse. It was dramatized by the literary legacy of the Andalusian Ibn ʿArabi (d. 1240 CE) and the Anatolian Jalal ad-din Rumi (d. 1273 CE), but they became mere nodes in a broad arc of literary production stamped by the Sufi quest. The other development was the emergence of the *turuq*, or brotherhoods, named after the central pursuit of the path, or *tariqa*, to truth. The brotherhoods provided institutional vehicles for channeling Sufi theory to all levels of society. Their masters or *shaykhs* are often credited with having introduced Islam into regions beyond the Nile-to-Indus heartland of Muslim rulers. They were the forward-moving face of Allah as the custodian of Muslims and the Islamic community but also the resource and goal of all humankind.

Both poetry and popular piety appealed to the lower classes, yet the distinctive social privilege of the upper class never disappeared, and within elite circles language remained an ambivalent, charged domain. While Tamerlane and Nasruddin Hoca met and joked in the public bath, they still refrained from God talk, or Allah discourse. That kind of discourse was the province of philosophers and mystics, for it revolved around the persistent need—at once annoying yet critical—to define what is named.

Among and beyond all names is the name Allah. The name Allah, as we indicated from the outset, shares with all references to the ultimate Other the problem of naming. Does not all speech turn itself back on its former statements, undoing them, when the referent is beyond human knowing? Many mystics have developed a language of self-suspicion, of essential doubt that language can even function in a one-to-one relationship with reality.

Michael Sells explores the tension between word and silence by distinguishing between *apophatic* and *kataphatic* modes of speech. Apophatic language enacts the process of "unsaying," a process that negates what has just been spoken. Its twin is kataphatic language, or the language of affirmation, declaration, and saying. The two must be paired because an apophatic statement presupposes a kataphatic one. In other words, something must be declared before it can be undeclared.[21]

In the *shahada*, the process is reversed: "there is no god," *la ilaha*, precedes the confirmation of Allah as God—*illa Allah*, "there is no god except the One, Only, Eternal God." And that same logic applies to successive efforts to understand Allah. Allah can be affirmed but never exhausted. Every saying produces an unsaying. Allah must be said before Allah can be unsaid; yet it is the unsaid, the unspoken, and the unspeakable "surplus" of the Thing, the Absolute, the One that is presumed to be the larger platform of reality.

There persists a further ambivalence about language that can only be expressed as a paradox. On the one hand, Islam, like every revealed religious tradition, rests on the authority of the Other, and to announce that Other in language is at once to claim knowledge of Its primal, basic source and to use special language to make that claim. In other words, all invocation of the Other must be suspect. All names for God, including God, are parochial to the extent that they reflect specific cultural traditions, linguistic conventions, and popular expectations.

At the same time, however, all names for God—from Elohim ("gods" in Hebrew) to Adonai, from Theos to Deus, from Allah to Khoda (Persian for "god")—are also nontrivial.[22] They evoke a power, a referent, and a resource beyond human sensory experience, and they are consequential insofar as their invocation, intercession, and application to this world shapes not just the hearts and souls but also the minds and deeds of those who address, beseech, and follow them.

For no group is the practice of remembrance more important than the followers of the Sufi path. It is their remembrance of Allah that occupies us in the next chapter, but let us first engage one other group of rationally engaged Muslims from the premodern period.

APPENDIX ON IKHWAN AS-SAFA

Consider the most illustrious tenth-century philosophical popularizers: the Ikhwan as-Safa, or Brethren of Purity. They made arguments for intelligent design of the universe, with Allah standing as the distant apex of all that we know. Some have even theorized that they were the precursors to an evolutionary view of creation, but of course with the premise of a divine origin.

Muslims were alert to the many ways of arguing for Allah as the Intelligent Designer. Islamic intellectual tradition was not only aware of the need for formulating the argument for intelligent design independent of the ontological premises that were at the heart of Islamic faith, but it also carried it out to its ultimate limits with increasing refinement. One can trace this thread from Muhasabi (d. 857 CE), with his teleological argument for the unity of the cause of the universe, to Qasim ibn Ibrahim (d. 860 CE), for whom the imprints of perfect wisdom and the signs of good governance manifest in the universe seem to prove that a wise and good deity must be responsible. But then the argument for design takes a new turn in the tenth century when Maturidi (d. 944 CE) extols the wondrous wisdom exhibited in the universe in his *Kitab al-Tawhid*. Maturidi becomes the precursor for the Ikhwan al-Safa, who offer a teleological argument for the existence of Allah in which the very structure of planets and stars supplies the evidence of design.

All of these traditional views maintain that in this manifest world, the flow is from the higher to the lower and not otherwise. Evolutionists envision the process in the inverse direction, from below upward, from earlier/primitive to later/refined, ascending from quantity toward quality, the higher evolving from the lower. All that Darwin did was to take the argument from design and reverse it, or so his opponents argue!

A NOVEL SENSE OF HIERARCHY

It is this difference in approach—assuming a Designer or looking only for the design—that separates all modern scholarship from the traditional scholarship on evolution, whether they are the classical *kalam* arguments used by scholars who adhered to the three Abrahamic religions or the viewpoints of Chinese sages or those who were rooted in some other premodern tradition. In this scheme of things, the universe is considered as one single unit, just as a city is one, or as an animal is one, or as man is one, as the Ikhwan noted in their *Rasa'il*.[23]

Ibn Hazm (d. 1064 CE) was an eleventh-century Andalusian scholar who added biological and botanical data to the astronomical data of the Ikhwan, along with evidence from aesthetics that would build on the functionality of the argument. He admires, for instance, the skill by which the limbs of the human body fit together and the texture of the palm tree fiber, so skillfully woven that it seems to be the work of a loom. But the important point to note is that Ibn Hazm's final appeal is to understand the Maker, Allah, via the intellect: it is in the human intellect that it must be undoubtedly known that the celestial and terrestrial regions must have come about by the deliberation of a Maker, one who exercises choice and invention. For Ibn Hazm, evidence from both the macrocosmic and microcosmic planes is sufficient to conclude not only

Fig. 6. Jabir and Ikhwan, according to M. F. Husain. Jabir ibn
Hayan Ikhwanusafa 2008.12.19. © Estate of M. F. Husain.

that the universe has a Maker, but also that the Absolute Thing is One:
there is a single Maker.

This appeal to intellect is as central to the Islamic rational tradition as
was direct laboratory experimentation. Some have argued that the Ikhwan, in relying on reason in order to deduce the nature of matter and the
five elements—earth, water, fire, air, and spirit—were disciples of the
eighth-century polymath Jabir Ibn Hayyan (d. 804 CE).[24] In the popular
imagination, as also in the history of Islamic thought, the Ikhwan and
Jabir are linked. The painting in figure 6 from M. F. Husain echoes this
long, intimate association.

And here is how the creation of the universe proceeds for the Ikhwan
as-Safa:

1. Creator (*khaliq*)—who is one, simple, eternal, permanent.
2. Intellect (*'aql*)—which is of two kinds: innate and acquired.
3. Soul (*nafs*)—which is of three kinds: vegetative, animal, and
   reasonable.

Allah Defined **79**

4. Matter (*hayula*)—which is of four kinds: matter of artifacts, physical matter, universal matter, and original matter.
5. Nature (*tabi'a*)—which is of five kinds: celestial nature (or spirit) and the four elemental natures.
6. Body (*jism*)—which has six directions: above, below, front, back, left, and right.
7. The sphere—which has its seven planets.
8. The elements—which are combined two by two: Earth—cold and dry; Water—cold and wet; Air—warm and wet; Fire—warm and dry.
9. Beings of this world—which are the mineral, plant, and animal kingdoms; each has three parts, with humans as a subset of the animal kingdom.

Underlying the elegance in this table of generation is a strong mathematical logic. The Ikhwan as-Safa divided the hierarchy of being into the fourfold division of God the Creator, Universal Intellect, Universal Soul, and *hayula* (primal matter). "The first four numbers are simple, universal beings," observed a leading scholar; "the numbers 1 to 4 already contain in themselves all numbers, since $1 + 2 + 3 + 4 = 10$—while other beings are compound."[25]

The Ikhwan as-Safa were able to produce a highly elaborate system that is universal in its intrinsic value; it has counterparts in Chinese, Indian, Greek, Christian, and Islamic cosmologies (figure 7). These conceptual dimensions of nature are integrally connected with the spiritual realization of the one who studies nature. According to the Ikhwan, the qualities and perfections belonging to the various levels of the hierarchy of being are not in any way subjective or anthropomorphic but visually observable and intellectually defensible. They are, or seem to be, genuine practitioners of *burhan*, or empirical demonstration as the path to truth, an emphasis that they share with their scientific predecessors, including Ja'far ibn Hayyan.

Figure 7 from the *Rasa'il* (or Letters) visually describes the interrelatedness of all things from the highest of the high to the lowest of the low. One might infer that the Ikhwan as-Safa support evolution in the Darwinian sense. "The chain of Being described by the Ikhwan," conclude two leading Muslim scholars, "possesses a temporal aspect which has led certain scholars to the view that the authors of the *Rasa'il* believed in the modern theory of evolution," yet skepticism about the source of

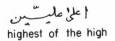

highest of the high

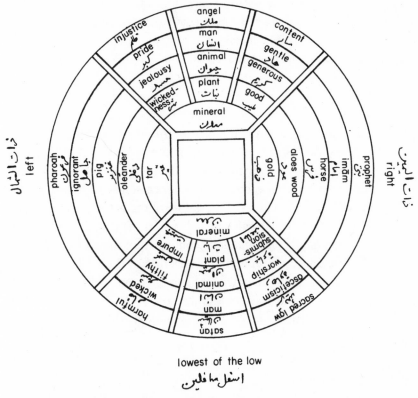

lowest of the low

اسفل ما فلين

Fig. 7. The Chain of Being, according to the Ikhwan as-Safa. From S. H. Nasr,
Cosmological Doctrines in Islam; courtesy of SUNY Press, Albany.

what evolves, namely, the divine origin of the universe in all its levels
and stages, is never voiced, either by the Ikhwan as-Safa or by their
opponents, the Ash'aris.[26]

A MAINSTREAM RETORT TO THE IKHWAN AS-SAFA

Less eloquent than the Ikhwan as-Safa but far more influential in ongoing debates among Muslims about Allah and creation are those claiming the mantle of Al-Ash'ari. The Ash'arites wrestled with the notion of
how Allah can be both Unseen and Unknowable, yet ever present and
vividly personified in Qur'anic references to the Supreme One, Author

Abu Hasan Al-Ashʿari

Abu Hasan Al-Ashʿari was a ninth-century rationalist in the first part of his career, but then he opted against the Muʿtazili view of Allah's Word (the Qurʾan) as created and instead attributed all power and knowledge to Allah without conceding that humans knew, or could ever know, the Thing, the Absolute, the One, the Divine Other.

of the Universe, Judge of All Humankind. Adding to the many spirited defenses of the Ashʿarite worldview over time are those of its modern claimants, many of which are now projected on the Internet. In describing a protracted battle between true believers and misguided others, one Ashʿarite cybernaut concludes: "The nature of the battle is the battle between *pure fresh wholesome milk* coming from the spring of the Book and the Sunnah and *blood, pus, and dung* coming from the spring and fountain of the language, *reason* and introspection of the Hellenized Jews, Christians and Sabeans—all of whom deviated from prior prophethood, and therefore used their own tools and resources to speak in matters of the unseen. Allah sent the Messenger to invalidate this falsehood and to revive the light of revelation."[27]

This same pro-Ashʿari website, however, claims that "the theological language of the Ashʿarites is founded on the conceptual tools and terminology of Aristotle bin Nichomas,"[28] so that even those who posit the language of the Book and the Prophet as supreme guides articulate their defense not from Arabia but from Athens. They use reason to defeat others' use of reason.

SUMMARY

Muslim society depended on an intellectual as well as a social hierarchy. The two were interrelated in premodern times. The social hierarchy was represented by the ruling classes, military and commercial but also juridical and educational. While two persons—Tamerlane and Nasruddin Hoca—represent the apex of fourteenth-century Central Asian Muslim society, their roles are mirrored and expanded by the philosophical and mystical elites of the Muslim Mediterranean world. All wrestled with the legacy of Aristotle—to use reason while embracing faith, to refine language but also acknowledge its limits, especially when talking about God or Allah. Even though it is possible to reduce all one's enemies to deviant falsifiers of the single, evident truth, the spectrum of choices and the sincerity of many seekers make that judgment suspect, even reversible. What is never disputed is the importance of remembering Allah, not just occasionally but on all occasions, and not just with the name Allah but with a panoply of access nodes that must be identified, pursued, and monitored. It is that intense, introspective labor of remembering Allah that will involve us in the next chapter.

There are two moments in life, and those moments are everything:
The present moment when we are free to choose
what we want to be;
and
The moment of death, which we cannot choose
but which depends on Allah's will.
If the present moment is good, then
the moment of death will be good too.
Mentioning Allah's name is the death in life,
and it will also be the life in death.
—Omar Khayyam

I see *a ladder of the Names* rising and falling,
Through it blowing a wind from south and north.
—Ibn 'Arabi, *Meccan Illuminations*

CHAPTER THREE

Allah Remembered

Practice of the Heart

OVERVIEW

Beyond invoking or defining Allah lies the task of remembering Allah, as both Omar Khayyam and Ibn 'Arabi understood intuitively.[1] At first glance, one might ask: what distinguishes invoking Allah from remembering Allah? The two seem very close. Both are practices dedicated to Allah, yet there is a discernible line separating them.

Invoking Allah is a performative activity; it becomes part of the inventory of activities expected of a devout Muslim. While it might be reflective, it can be, and often is, simply instinctual or habitual. Remembering Allah, however, requires an intense, dedicated practice of introspection. It begins with a specific intent to focus only on that name, that mood, that presence of Allah. Allah is not just Lofty and Exalted but also present, immediately and vividly present to the one remembering Allah, by whatever name He is remembered.

In the starkest language, all remembering of Allah presupposes invoking Allah. Allah cannot be remembered without being invoked. But Allah can be, and often is, invoked without being remembered. Alternatively, one might think of the invocation as utterance, and remembrance as self-conscious meditation on the utterance. The real goal, in either case, is not just invoking or uttering the name Allah; it is to project the Thing, the Absolute, the One as the *sole focus* of attention in the act of immersive remembering.[2]

THE MEDITATION OF A TURKISH MASTER

Sufis delight in the complex array of ways to approach the remembrance of Allah. To remember Allah through observation is the preliminary step. Twentieth-century Turkish master Sheikh Muzaffar Ozak Al-Jerrahi asserts that, far from being unscientific, remembrance is dependent on science, since it requires acute observation to understand how we humans are uniquely endowed with special skills among all Allah's created beings. Humans, and only humans, can and should note the *four perfections*—cosmic, terrestrial, bodily, and scriptural—which also evoke four reflexes:

- *Cosmic perfection* is reflected in the vast sky, with its daily and seasonal cycles. This is a cosmic sign, and it is confirmed again and again in the Qur'an (i.e., Q 10:5–6). It is based on a simple argument—what or who else but a superior mind/hand/heart could have constructed the universe as we know it? And so, do not all human beings share the reflex of cosmic wonder?
- *Terrestrial perfection* is detected in the planetary sphere, the earth, our common abode with its mountains, oceans, deserts, lakes, trees, flora, and fauna and its diverse peoples inhabiting and surviving in so many, often challenging, conditions. This is the terrestrial sign. It too is confirmed in the Qur'an (Q 36:71–73), and it can/should be invoked along with the cosmic order as another "natural," spontaneous reflex confirming the existence of Allah.
- *Bodily perfection* derives from the nature of the human body—as

found in the form of woman and man, with perfect parts: eyes to see, ears to hear, hands to hold, feet to walk, mind to grasp, and heart to feel. This is the self or psychological sign, an inner reflex also attested in the Qur'an, but with a twist that brings down the same creature who has been exalted: the noblest also can, and does, become the lowest:

We have made man in the finest order,
then We return him to the lowest of the low. (Q 95:4–5)

And this confronts us with human choice, the prospect of error. For the same Allah who created man of dust and clotted blood but in His image also taught the use of the pen and, with it, what man did not know. The Qur'an then goes on to warn that knowing is not sufficient:

Oh no! Man does indeed go to excess
In viewing himself as self-sufficient.
Yet all returns to your Lord. (Q 96:9–10)

That is, man will not recognize what he does not know; he will become arrogant and imagine that he is self-sufficient; yet he will be perfected when he returns, as all must, to the Lofty One, the Master of the Universe, his Lord.

• *Scriptural perfection* is channeled through the Divine Word. It provides for Muslims, as well as for Jews and Christians, a final index, a temporal reflex confirming Allah. This fourth proof of Allah's existence demonstrates His persistence over time. It is His constant reminder to humans through prophets and scriptures that there is a higher purpose, a single commanding presence, to all existence. This perfection, which is also the culmination, of all proofs, is known as the revelatory sign; for through it the One and Only inscribes a Preserved Tablet, a celestial scroll in which all commands and pleas, wishes and wanderings, are recorded. The Torah was its first installment, then the Psalms, followed by the Gospel, and finally the revelation in Arabic, the Noble Book, the Arabic Qur'an.

This capstone descent or disclosure of Allah, concludes the sheikh, looms as a work of genius, beyond human capacity to understand, exhaust, or reproduce it. It suffices as the sole "miracle" of the last prophet,

the Prophet Muhammad, but also the confirmation of all the prophets
who preceded him.[3]

Yet the Qur'an itself makes clear that human beings can never perceive or connect to Allah's essence; they only have access to His traits or
attributes, that is, the qualities that attach to His name, making of the
one name many names. Even though in this world it is impossible to see
Allah with ordinary human eyes, each person can and should try to perceive and comprehend the qualities of Allah. These are the Ninety-nine
Names, "the part of Him nearest to us," in Montaigne's haunting phrase.
The Ninety-nine Names are windows into the invisible. One might think
of them as portals of light onto a blinding flash, or handholds guiding us
through a fathomless depth, or, in terms of contemporary science, the
range of frequencies that transmit energy in the electromagnetic spectrum. In the words of a notable Sufi master, they can be "like patterns
on a great rug called 'the carpet of intimate conversation (*munajat*).'
Once it is spread wide for you, its patterns become endless. At times,
Allah seats you on the expanse of poverty and you call out to Allah, '*Ya
Ghani*! O self-sufficient One!' At times, Allah seats you on the expanse
of humility and you call out, '*Ya 'Aziz*! O mighty One!' At times, you are
seated on the expanse of weakness and you call out, '*Ya Qawi*! O powerful One!' There are other patterns on this widespread carpet, each corresponding to one among the Divine Names (*asma'*)."[4]

But why are there only ninety-nine names? Why do we have only
ninety-nine portals, lights, or patterns of the divine? And why are these
ninety-nine so vital to human well-being in this world and the next?
These questions will concern us below, but it is important to first note
the utter weakness of humans to grasp the enormous challenge of Allah.
In effect, we are all bounded by the limits of what is known or know-

able. Tibetan Buddhists tell the story of an old frog. He had lived all his life in a well. One day a frog from the sea got lost and came to his well. The sea frog told the well frog how much deeper and more expansive was the great ocean from which he came. The well frog followed the sea frog back to the ocean, but "when the frog from the well saw the ocean, it was such a shock that his head just exploded into pieces."[5]

And so, in the Muslim tradition of practicing restraint, many wise, well-traveled souls urge patience. Instead of venturing to the edge of an expanse that is mind shattering, Sufi masters commend the incremental approach:

> *O you who believe,*
> *remember Allah the Lofty*
> *with repeated remembrance.* (Q 33:41)

Recollection or remembrance becomes like an impregnable fortress, making it possible for Sufi adepts to surround their hearts with walls of light, each brick bearing the name Allah![6] The metaphor of the body as a house, and Allah as its (invisible) bricks and mortar, is extended to Allah as the very blood that flows through the veins of the devout Muslim in the act of remembrance. But remembrance requires persistence, along with patience, a keen appetite for discovering the true self that resides in each of us. This true self, the divine self within, is an echo of Allah.

THE NAME ALLAH AND THE TRUE SEEKER

A favorite Sufi story of this transformative process begins with Allah, intensifies in Allah, and finally becomes the echo of Allah. Sahl at-Tustari, an early Sufi master, said to one of his disciples:

> Strive to say continuously for an entire day: "O Allah! O Allah! O Allah!" and do the same the next day and the day after that. The disciple did until he became habituated to saying these words. Then the master bade him to repeat them at night also, until they became so familiar that he uttered them even during his sleep. Then the master said: "Do not repeat them any more, but let all your faculties be engrossed in remembering Allah!" The disciple did this, until he became absorbed in the thought of Allah. One day, when he was in his house, a piece of wood fell on his head and broke it. The drops of blood that trickled to the ground traced the name "Allah! Allah! Allah."[7]

And so the disciple who began wanting to connect with the name Allah ends by having his whole being, even his very lifeblood, suffused with the embodiment, which is also the projection, of that name.

TWO FACES OF THE ISLAMIC QUEST FOR ALLAH: IBN ʿARABI AND IBN RUSHD

The major difference between philosophers and mystics is etched in this strategy: to seek the Beyond by immersion in sincere remembrance rather than by feats of rigorous logic. The sincerity of both groups fuels the intensity of their divergent practices. The contrast between them has been etched in the encounter of Ibn ʿArabi, the Sufi, with Ibn Rushd, the philosopher. Ibn ʿArabi was a dazzled youth, Ibn Rushd a mature sage.

This is how Ibn ʿArabi describes his meeting with Ibn Rushd (d. 1198 CE), then the chief judge of Seville, but already in his lifetime a celebrated philosopher, not least due to his famous commentary on Aristotle in Arabic:

> I spent the day in Cordoba at the house of Abu al-Walid Ibn Rushd. He had expressed a desire to meet me in person, since he had heard of certain revelations I had received while in retreat and had shown considerable astonishment concerning them. In consequence my father, who was one of his closest friends, took me with him on the pretext of business, in order to give Ibn Rushd the opportunity of making my acquaintance.
>
> I was at the time a beardless youth. As I entered the house, the philosopher rose to greet me with all the signs of friendliness and affection, and embraced me. Then he said to me "Yes," and showed pleasure on seeing that I had understood him. I, on the other hand, being aware of the motive for his pleasure, replied "No." Upon this Ibn Rushd drew back from me, his color changed and he seemed to doubt what he had thought of me. He then put to me the following question, "What solution have you found as a result of mystical illumination and divine inspiration? Does it coincide with what is arrived at by speculative thought?" I replied "Yes and no. Between the Yea and the Nay the spirits take their flight beyond matter, and the necks detach themselves from their bodies."
>
> At this Ibn Rushd became pale. I saw him tremble as he muttered the formula "there is no power save from Allah." This was because he understood my allusion.[8]

Ibn 'Arabi is overly modest: the difference between him and Ibn Rushd is not that between the unworldly, unlettered mystic and the erudite philosopher. Ibn 'Arabi may have been a mere youth but he was neither unworldly nor unlettered in any orthodox sense.[9] Not only was he well versed in the philosophical thinking of his time but many of his books also deal specifically with philosophical problems. The real difference lies in the way in which knowledge is reached, whether by reflective thought or by mystical insight.

This unbridgeable chasm is graphically depicted in a second meeting, this time in a vision that Ibn 'Arabi had. There was "a thin veil that separated me and him (Ibn Rushd) in such a way that I was able to see him while he was unable to see me and was ignorant of my presence. He was so absorbed that he paid me no attention and I said to myself: 'He is not destined to follow the same path as me.'"[10]

Philosophical wisdom, it is implied, is based on rational analysis and so limited to the divided and personal realm of the "Yes" and the "No"; whereas mystical wisdom, which is founded on direct experience—often referred to as "taste"—is as incontrovertible as the acts of sense perception. The reality of the "thin veil" between the two is only seen from the side of mystical contemplation, though the possibility can be admitted philosophically.

Yet Ibn 'Arabi would be quick to assert that all beings have the selfsame capacity for mystical wisdom, just by the sheer fact of being human. It is not the privilege of a select few; it is open to all who choose it. What he strives for is the complete integration of the human being, with all his or her faculties, upon the task of fulfilling "that for which you were created," to be the vessel, the vehicle, the open channel of the divine soul (*ruh*) in the human self (*nafs*). In other words, the discovery of Allah is the ceaseless self-discovery of the individual's primordial being, at whatever stage in whatever place s/he finds herself/himself. According to Sufis, the world is not a staging ground but a launching pad for endless pursuit of the divine self within the human self. Not the outer material world but the inner spiritual world harbors the core of meaning, especially the meaning of the elusive One. The dynamic theatre of divine manifestation is the human heart; all else is a sideshow or a diversion from the central purpose of human existence. Every movement in life can, or should, be an inward movement toward love of Allah, not only the Great Beyond, but even more importantly, the Hidden Within. Allah is simultaneously "He" and "not He," just as the image of a person in a mirror is both that person and not that person.

THE PRACTICE OF *BASMALA*

For Sufis this task of discovering Allah by discovering the self comes through immersive remembrance—conscious, continuous, systematic, and disciplined remembrance—of the names given by the One Who Is Beyond Names. These ciphers of the Divine Other are derived from the Holy Qur'an, not just a book of law or worship but also the pathway to inner peace. The overall message of the 114 chapters of the Qur'an is summed up in the words of the *basmala* that opens the first chapter, and every other chapter but one: "*Bismi(A)llah ar-rahman ar-rahim*" ("O Allah Full of Compassion, Ever Compassionate"). Its opposite would be "*Bismi(A)llah al-mudhill al-mumit*" ("O Allah the Despiser, the Instrument of Death"). Many might be surprised to see these two sets of names side by side, yet both are clustered in the circle of names linked to Allah the Lofty, both in the Qur'an and in everyday usage. The play on pairs or doubles recurs, as in the wisdom of Seth, from Ibn ʿArabi's classic study, *Rings of Wisdom* (*Fusus al-Hikam*).

It is said that Seth, the third son of Adam and Eve (after Cain and Abel), was the conduit for two gifts, gifts from the Divine Names and gifts from the Divine Essence. And since it is the Divine Giver who tailors each gift to the recipient, they might be gifts given through specific requests (the names projected and perfected through remembrance) or gifts bestowed without request (an outpouring from the Thing, the Absolute, the One).[11] In other words, Allah can give out of His own lar-

> **Fusus al-Hikam: A Sufi Classic**
>
> The twenty-eight stories of the *Fusus al-Hikam*, each linked to a prophet, were revealed to Ibn 'Arabi in a single night. The most popular of his many, many books, it has often been heralded as the litmus test for esoteric wisdom about the Qur'an and Islam.

gesse, not solely and simply in response to human petitions, however sincere and persistent is the petitioner.

THE DIVINE NAMES IN A NUTSHELL

There are three basic questions about the Ninety-nine Beautiful Names.

Question 1: Why all the stress on names? The names are portals to the unseen, the essence of Allah the Lofty. They have to be opened to reveal the light behind, beneath, beyond them, but the portals are there within each human heart.

Question 2: Why ninety-nine? It is all about tradition, Prophetic tradition. As Imam Ghazali noted, there is a tradition, widely attested and ascribed to the Prophet Muhammad, that "Allah the Lofty has 99 names, and whoever recites them enters Paradise." Yet as Al-Ghazali also quickly notes, none of these genuine sources ever elaborates what are the exact ninety-nine names. It would be an infringement of the Thing, the Absolute, the One to be pinned down to a single name or to many names or to a roll call of specific names.[12]

Question 3: Why are most of the names active participles or adjectives? Participles are used because, in rhetoric, using an active participle or adjective in describing someone's quality is more forceful than using a verb to describe the same quality. Consider this depiction of Allah from the Qur'an: *"Allah it is who is the Best of Providers"* (Q 5:14, 22:58, 23:72, 34:39, 62:11). That is stronger than saying: it is Allah who provides, though just for emphasis in one Qur'anic passage both the active participle and the verb are used to stress Allah's all-encompassing character as the Provider. It is revealed in order to describe those who emigrated from Mecca to Medina to join the nascent Muslim community but then were killed or die on the way:

Surely, Allah will provide them
a fine provision,
for Allah is indeed
the Best of Providers. (Q 22:58b)

ARTISTIC RENDITIONS OF THE NINETY-NINE NAMES

Because of the prevalence of the Beautiful Names in practice and theory, and from medieval to modern times throughout the Muslim world, there have been many artistic attempts to depict the Ninety-nine Names of Allah. Most are marked by humility as well as beauty, since every artist, like every true seeker, recognizes the limits of human creativity. Few, however, are as extensive or as compelling as the Kaʿba Cube of the Egyptian artist Ahmed Moustafa (figure 8).[13] Somewhat resembling a Rubik's Cube, the exterior is black, to represent the black rock at Mecca, and the names are written on individual sub-cubes in geometric Kufic calligraphy. It cleverly unfolds (rather than rotates) to reveal each of the Ninety-nine Names in a space that allows them all to be seen fully.

It is difficult to reproduce the impression that this form makes on the observer, whether the person is Muslim or non-Muslim, Arabic speaker or innocent of that language. A newer version was released in 1998, and in the artist's words, what he has provided are "one hundred transparent methacrylate bars which—by means of illumination from the base—create a unique light effect suspended in space. The Hidden Dimension of the Cube is made of synthetic resin. The golden parts, representing the Attributes, are laminated with twenty-four carat gold. It can be a closed cube (as is the original Meccan structure) or an open sculpture, revealing the names, which the actual Kaʿba does not do."[14]

QURʾANIC PASSAGES ON THE BEAUTIFUL NAMES

The names themselves unfold in numerous Qurʾanic passages. The fullest citation comes at the end of Q 59, "The Mustering (on the Day of Judgment)":

He is Allah
Other than He there is no Allah
The knower of the Hidden and the Manifest

Fig. 8. Kaʿba Cube of Ahmed Moustafa. 1987. Calligraphy by Ahmed Moustafa.

He is Full of Compassion, ever Compassionate
He is Allah,
Other than He there is no Allah
The Sovereign
The Holy One
The Source of Peace
The Faithful
The Preserver of Safety
The Exalted in Might
The Irresistible
The Supreme
Glory be to Allah above the partners they ascribe to Him.
He is Allah
The Creator
The Evolver
The Bestower of forms
To Him belong the Most Beautiful Names;
All that is in the heavens and the earth praises Him,
And He is exalted in Might, the Wise. (Q 59:22–24)[15]

Most Sufis focus on the qualities of these Beautiful Names. According to a contemporary Sufi master, not all the names have the same value, just as the Ninety-nine Names are not always the same. There are seven key names or major attributes:

al-hayy (the Living)
al-qadir (the Powerful)
al-murid (the One Who Wills)
al-ʿalim (the All-Knowing)
al-samiʿ (the All-Hearing)
al-basir (the All-Seeing)
al-mutakallim (the One Who Speaks)[16]

Yet there is also another Sufi practice that foregrounds not seven but fourteen of the Beautiful Names of Allah. All evoke qualities or attributes that by their nature can and do refer only to Allah in Himself, Allah without parallel, that is, Allah as Allah beyond compare, even in metaphoric or rhetorical language, to traits of humankind, but they must be embraced in their intrinsic diversity: *Allah* is the first and foremost name, followed by two forms of the One, *al-wahid* (the Unique One) and *al-ahad* (the Absolute One).

Two other names come close to these two, approximating the nature of the ineffable, unknowable Other: *al-fard* (the Unique, similar to *al-wahid*) and *al-witr* (the Singular, similar to *al-ahad*). They are followed by *al-kabir* (the Great).

Among the remaining eight names, three mark transcendence (*tanzih*) with special force: *al-hayy*, *al-haqq*, and *an-nur*. They come up repeatedly as the links to Allah's unique qualities:

eternal (*al-hayy*, the Ever Living)
omniscient (*al-haqq*, the Absolute Truth)
luminous (*an-nur*, the Radiant, Unceasing Light)

The remaining five names stress His power both physical and metaphysical:

al-quddus (the Source of Sanctity)
al-ʿaziz (the Almighty)
al-ʿazim (the Magnificent)
al-jalil (the Majestic)
al-mutaʿali (the Most Exalted, Beyond Human Imagining, Knowing, or Comprehending)[17]

How then does one decide between seven, fourteen, or ninety-nine names? The seeker—even the most avid seeker—wants to find some order that reduces or redirects the names' multiplicity into a pattern, one that can be evoked, remembered, and also recited. Many admire, and seek to follow, the strategy of Shaykh al-Akbar, Muhyiddin Ibn ʿArabi, already noted and deemed by some to be the foremost Sufi exponent of the Path (*tariqa*). Let us call this strategy: *one plus three*.

Here is the *One*. In keeping with many others, Ibn ʿArabi gives the honor of first place to Allah. Why Allah apart from and above all others? Because we can only name Him by what He names Himself. While all the names connote His presence, the name Allah *is* the presence (*hadratu[A]llah*) that comprehends all presences. "Allah, Allah, Allah— His signs [*ayat*] have passed judgment that He is Allah. Glory be to Him! [*subhanahu*]—there is no Allah but He. He alone possesses a Name not shared by another."[18]

At the same time, there are clusters of *three*. Because they reflect Allah in different forms, Shaykh al-Akbar allocates all the other Beautiful Names, those beyond Allah but always linked to Him, into three distinct yet overlapping categories:

1. Affirmative attributes of the essence: knowing, powerful, willing, hearing, seeing, living, responder, thankful.
2. Relational or correlated descriptions: first and last, opener and closer, manifest and hidden, rich and enricher, guide and light.
3. Names that disclose acts: creator, provider, author, shaper, destroyer, abaser, death-giver.

In this way every possible quality or trait of Allah can be classified. All the Divine Names can be acknowledged as one of these kinds. Every one of them also denotes the essence, so that this Presence (Allah) contains all the presences, and He who knows Allah knows all things.[19]

Even those Sufi authors, adepts, and masters who find the metaphysical turns of Shaykh al-Akbar too intellectually tortuous still seek to pursue the pairing of the Beautiful Names that he has foreshadowed. Special focus is often directed to the Qur'anic passage that depicts Allah as "having two hands," that is, a constant, reinforcing polarity. The "two hands" embody benevolence and anger, fear and hope, intimacy and awe, but also knowability and unknowability, so that what might seem like apparent contradictions are not contraries but instead dyads—mysterious to humans yet part of *faydAllah*, the expansive surplus of the Lofty the Exalted. The metaphor is bodily, specific to the human form, but its significance is metaphysical, beyond what wo/man can know or imagine. There are many ways to grasp this notion of two proximate yet distinct qualities, but the best is *barzakh*, the space of connection/separation that permeates this life and the next, both the world beyond and every day in the present world.

Two examples of this approach reflect the medieval and the modern phases of Sufi practice. The noted fourteenth-century master Ibn 'Ata' Allah reckoned the two hands of Allah as His two decisive modes: the left hand symbolizes His majesty and power, the right hand His beauty and compassion.[20] In a similar vein, the contemporary South African master Shaykh Fadhlalla Haeri sees left-right as the gender complementarities of male (majesty: *jalal*) and female (beauty: *jamal*).[21]

Ibn 'Arabi was clear that not all contrasts were complementary. Two polar opposites in approaching the Other were to be avoided: 1) *tanzih*, transcendence, or thinking of Allah as so lofty that he could not be related to humankind and therefore reducing him to abstraction; and

Iblis and Adam

Iblis was an angel before he disobeyed a divine command and then became Allah's enemy, the Devil. In rebuking Iblis for his failure to bow down before Adam, Allah exclaims:

Iblis!
What has prevented you
From bowing to what I have created
With My own two hands?
Do you think you're too important?
Are you one of the exalted? (Q 38:75)

2) *tashbih*, immanence, or making Allah almost human, that is, anthropomorphizing his traits to the point of absurdity. Even though both poles were to be avoided, Shaykh al-Akbar favored the Sufis who embraced both, like the early master, Qushayri, or the common folk who only see Allah as *tashbih*. He disdained the scholars—both theologians (*mutakallimun*) and philosophers (*falasifa*)—who were prone to see only the Lofty and Exalted One, that is, the abstract Other, devoid of human connection except through the instruments of logic and metaphor.[22]

DIVINE NAMES BY THE BOOK: THEIR QUR'ANIC CITATIONS

It is possible merely to list many of the names with their Qur'anic occurrence(s). Less schematic in format, the scriptural notations allow one to cluster the most popular Ninety-nine Beautiful Names with minimum commentary on the taxonomic connections. Here is the briefest of direct citations for sixty-six, or two-thirds of all the names that recur again and again for the One beyond knowing or naming. He is Allah,

the Living (*al-hayy*, Q 2:255)
the Self-Subsisting (*al-qayyum*, Q 2:255)
the One (*al-ahad*, Q 112:1)
the Absolute (*al-samad*, Q 112:1)
the Truth (*al-haqq*, Q 22:6)
the Light (*an-nur*, Q 24:35)

the Self-Sufficient (*al-ghani*, Q 2:263)
the Comprehensive (*al-wasi*ʿ, Q 2:247)
the All-Wise (*al-hakim*, Q 2:129)
the Powerful (*al-qadir*, Q 2:20)
the Glorious (*al-majid*, Q 85:15)
the Strong (*al-qawi*, Q 11:66)
the Mighty (*al-ʿaziz*, Q 2:129)
the Great (*al-kabir*, Q 22:62)
the High (*al-ʿali*, Q 31:30)
the Exalted (*al-mutaʿali*, Q 13:9)

He is also known by epithets connoting intervention:

the Overpowering Restorer (*al jabbar*, Q 59:23)
the Subduing Dominator (*al qahhar*, Q 12:39)
the Constant Giver (*al-wahhab*, Q 3:8)
the Good Provider (*al-razzaq*, Q 51:58)
the Victorious Revealer (*al-fattah*, Q 34:26)

Allah is furthermore:

the Benevolent (*al-latif*, Q 67:14)
the Gentle (*al-halim*, Q 4:12)
the Generous (*al-karim*, Q 44:49)
the Sagacious (*al-khabir*, Q 6:18)
the Vigilant (*al-hafiz*, Q 34:21)
the Unshakable (*al-matin*, Q 51:58)
the Insuperable (*al-ʿazim*, Q 2:255)

Expressed by paired epithets, Allah is

the First (*al-awwal*) and the Last (*al-akhir*, Q 57:3)
the Manifest (*al-zahir*) and the Hidden (*al-batin*, Q 57:3)
the One Who Contracts (*al-qabid*) and Expands (*al-basit*, Q 2:245)
the Possessor of Awe and Kindness (*dhuʾl-jalal wal-ikram*, Q 55:27)
the Expeditor (*al-muqaddim*, Q 50:28) and the Postponer
    (*al-muʾakhkhir*, Q 11:8)

Elsewhere, He is also pervasive in His oversight:

the Reckoner (*al-hasib*, Q 4:86)
the Watcher (*al-raqib*, Q 4:1)
the Witness (*ash-shahid*, Q 3:98)

the Guardian (al-wakil, Q 3:173)
the Patron (al-wali, Q 42:9)
the Guide of Those Who Believe (al-hadi lilladhina amanu, Q 22:54)

And then in relation to his creatures and the universe, Allah is named

the Creator (al-khaliq, Q 59:24)
Who Is Constantly Creating (al-khallaq, Q 36:81)
the Creator of the Heavens and the Earth (badiʿ al-samawati wa
  l-ard, Q 6:101)
the Maker (al-bariʾ, Q 2:54)
the Shaper (al-musawwir, Q 59:24)

He also gives life and brings death (al-muhyi, al-mumit, Q 15:23), pre-vails over everything (al-muqtadir, Q 18:45), and assembles all on the Day of Judgment (al-jamiʿ, Q 3:9; 4:140).

Allah is especially known by names that denote mercy and forgive-ness. He is qualified not only as ar-rahman and ar-rahim (multiple cita-tions, including at the beginning of all but one of the Qurʾanic chapters) but also as:

the Kind (as-raʾuf, Q 2:143)
the Loving (al-wadud, Q 85:14)
the Resurrector (al-baʿith, Q 22:7)
the One Who Answers Prayers (al-mujib, Q 11:61)

Allah further abounds with forgiveness:

the Forgiving (al-ghafir, Q 7:155)
the Oft-Forgiver (al-ghafur, Q 2:173)
the All-Forgiving (al-ghaffar, Q 38:66; 20:82)
the Pardoner (al-ʿafuww, Q 4:43)
the One "Turned to" Humans with Favor (at-tawwab, Q 2:37)
Ever Ready to Acknowledge Their Gratitude (ash-shakur, Q 35:30)
While Also Exercising Patience (as-sabur, Q 8:46)[23]

ALLAH EMBODIED AS LIGHT

In the end, we are left with many nodes of connection, from the human to the divine, from the many to the One. While all function as part of the spectrum of immersive remembrance, a few traits or attributes stand out, not least because of their close association with the material world, and also with the human form. Might this practice be construed as anthropomorphizing Allah? Could one say that under the guise of the Many Names, seemingly devout Muslims are actually reverting to a form of idolatry, eschewing outer forms but still forming deep, inner attachments that divert them from the Thing, the Absolute, the One? The answer is: yes and no. Yes, for the literal minded, this practice could lead to heresy, but not for those pure in intent. Intense believers seek to connect themselves to Allah by any means possible. For them, the universe of letters, as also the parts of the human body, become the most immediate, the most palpable instruments for that vertical connection. The pervasive image, as also the dominant Divine Name, is *An-Nur*, the Radiant, Unending Light.

Consider how the famed fourteenth-century Persian poet Shabistari, (d. 1340 CE) conjures a secret vision of Allah for those privileged to be among the elect:

> The universe is Allah's book,
> And he to whom the vision of the Divine
> Is given
> Reads and understands:
> Substance is its consonants
> and accidents its vowels
> And different creatures
> its signs and pauses.
> The first verse is Universal Reason,
> The second Universal Soul, the verse of light,
> And this is a brightly shining lamp
> The third is the Highest heavens,
> the fourth the Throne.
> And after there are seven transcendent spheres,
> The chapter of the seven limbs,
> and forms of the four elements,
> Then nature's three kingdoms
> Whose verses none can count.
> And last of all came down the soul of man.[24]

While Ibn 'Arabi envisaged a ladder of the Divine Names, ascending and descending, Shabistari imagines a book with receding pages and unfolding insights.[25] "To him, whose soul attains the beatific vision," he observes, "the universe is the book of The Truth Most High. Accidents are its vowels, substance its consonants, while the grades of creatures reflect its verses and pauses. Therein every world is a special chapter, one may be the chapter *Fatiha* (Q 1), another *Ikhlas* (Q 112). The first verse of this book is Universal Reason, for that is like the B of *Bismi(A)llah* [the first word of the first *surah* and therefore of the entire Qur'an]. Yet its second verse is Universal Soul, the verse of light, for that is '*a lamp of exceeding light*' (Q 24:35). Following is the third verse: the Highest Heaven. That is, '*two bows' length from Him in heaven*' (Q 53:9)."[26]

It is the image of light that pervades, Allah as Light, the light of heavens but also the light among all the parts of the human body; our entire body is, as the *hadith* in the epigraph reminds us, "formed in the image of Allah."

ALLAH AS DIRECTIVE LIGHT

There are still other *hadith* or traditions of the Prophet that deflect the Divine Light but in another direction. From *Musnad Ahmad* comes the following: "Allah created his creation in darkness and then cast His light upon it. Those who were struck by that light were guided; those who missed it went astray. And this is why I say, it is only in the book of deeds (opened on Judgment Day) that we will learn the knowledge of Allah."[27]

According to Damascene theologian and Qur'an scholar Ibn Qayyim al-Jawziyya (d. 1350 CE), one of the foremost disciples of Ibn Taymiyya (d. 1312 CE), it is this *hadith* that "solves the mysteries of destiny and the wisdom hidden behind it." It demonstrates the limits of the pen while manifesting the dyadic splendor of Allah the Lofty the Exalted whose light before creation has directed believers to "another light, still greater and more brilliant and that is the light of Allah's sublime attributes, besides which every other light is dim." For

He is First before whom there is nothing. The Last after whom there is nothing. The Inward above whom there is nothing. The Outward beneath whom there is nothing. Glorified and Exalted is He, Most Worthy to be invoked. Worshipped and Praised. He is the First to be thanked. The One whose support is most desired. The Most Generous of those who possess. The Most Clement of those who have power. The Noblest of those who have a purpose, the Most Just of those who show anger. With His knowledge comes His forbearance. With His might His forgiveness. With His withholding His wisdom. With His excellence and mercy His guardianship.[28]

But how does a lowly creature connect to that Lofty Exalted One? "Remembrance," Ibn Qayim tells us, "is the main door to reach Allah. The door unto Allah opens to the one for whom remembrance has been opened. And it has four merits: it binds together what has been dispersed; it awakens the heart from its deep sleep, heedlessness to Allah; it is the tree which grows the fruits of insight sought by gnostics and ascetics alike; and Allah draws nearer, closer to the one who remembers Him."[29]

For still others the Divine Light becomes an outpouring or effulgence that at once captures and transforms the devotee. It is akin to different colorings, as Ibn 'Arabi explains:

> When the servant comes to know Allah in himself, he knows that he is not created according to the form of the world, but only according to the form of Allah (al-Haqq). Allah makes him journey through His names, in order *"to make him see His signs"* (Q 17:1) within him. Thus the servant comes to know that He is what is designated by every divine Name—whether or not that Name is one of those described as "beautiful." It is through these Names that Allah appears in His servants, and it is through Them that the servant takes on different "colorings" of his states; for they are Names in Allah but "colorings" in us. . . . For there is no Name that Allah has applied to Himself that He has not also applied to us: through His Names we undergo the transformations in our states, and with them we are transformed by Allah.[30]

Who could imagine that the One beyond knowing would make His deepest self known to mere mortals through colors? For Sufis, the different

facets of Allah as expressed by His many names are like a prismatic re-
fraction of white light into the multitude of colors; these colors reflect
aspects of what to us can only be thought of as beauty, subtle forms of
beauty, staggered and staged to match who we are before we recognize
them as part of our own deepest self.

AN EXUBERANT TAMIL PIR'S REIMAGINING
OF ALLAH AS NUR/LIGHT

This divine coloring excited and transformed the imagination of yet another Sufi master, the Sri Lankan twentieth-century exemplar Shaykh
Bawa Muhaiyaddeen. For Bawa, not only is the supreme name Nur/
Light but it is also the element beyond definition or restriction in the
divine panoply. It becomes the first quality of both Allah and Muhammad, so that Muhammad is known as Nur Muhammad. It is a cosmic
event, predating the formation of the world, which reflects the ninety-
nine qualities and actions of Allah in the ocean of *kalima* (that is, the
shahada or profession of faith). Indeed, "Allah will protect from destruction all those who have Allah's ninety-nine qualities, those who dwell
on the islands in that ocean, as well as those who dwell in the ocean of
His essence, His *dhat*."[31]

This variant of a Neoplatonic cosmology—an ascending spiral of
being that evolves from and dissolves into light—is not unique to Shaykh
Bawa Muhaiyaddeen, but he relates it to "true man," the "ordinary" believer, with a special fervor and series of homologies. In his book *Islam
and World Peace: Explanations of a Sufi*, he elaborates:

> Allah has said that man is the most exalted among His creations, be-
> cause he has divine analytic wisdom. If he becomes a true believer, he
> can know and see things that the heavenly beings cannot. Allah gave
> the jinn and fairies only thirty-six powers, but to man He has given
> ninety-six. Beyond those ninety-six powers are four more: true man,
> Muhammad, Nur and Allah.
>
> The state of a true man, the true form of Adam, comes into being
> once wisdom is resplendent. Then, when the heart becomes radiant
> and shines in the face as the beauty of that face, that is the state of
> Muhammad. And when the light of wisdom becomes complete and
> ever present, that is the beauty of the Nur, the effulgence of Muham-
> mad. Finally, when we block off everything else and stand in silence

as the *alif* (the first letter of the Arabic alphabet), and then raise our hands in praise of Allah (the *takbir*), that is Allah, resplendent as wisdom, the One who makes silent things speak and makes them become visible within. . . . Indeed, a man could not even move if Allah were not within him. And a true man is within Allah, hidden within Him, surrendered to Him. He keeps Allah within himself and Allah keeps that man within Him.[32]

Paralleling, complementing, and completing that macrocosmic picture is the microcosmic picture of Allah as Light. It is even more intensely related to Allah as internal to man: "Allah within himself, and that man within Allah." Allah pervades all the parts of the human body, from the crown of the head to the tip of the toes. This is an extended homology parallel to that accorded the sacrificial horse of Hindu ritual depicted in the well-known *Brihadaranyaka Upanishad*:

Om! That (Brahman) is infinite, and this (universe) is infinite. The infinite proceeds from the infinite.
(Then) taking the infinitude of the infinite (universe),
It remains as the infinite (Brahman) alone.
Om! Peace! Peace! Peace!
Om. The head of the sacrificial horse is the dawn, its eye the sun, its vital force the air, its open mouth the fire called Vaisvanara, and the body of the sacrificial horse is the year. Its back is heaven, its belly the sky, its hoof the earth, its sides the four quarters, its ribs the intermediate quarters, its members the seasons, its joints the months and fortnights, its feet the days and nights, its bones the stars and its flesh the clouds. Its half-digested food is the sand, its blood-vessels the rivers, its liver and spleen the mountains, its hairs the herbs and trees. Its forepart is the ascending sun, its hind part the descending sun, its yawning is lightning, its shaking the body is thundering, its making water is raining, and its neighing is voice.[33]

In a similar spirit of homologic invocation, the learned Sri Lankan Sufi master projects the anatomy of faith as the "perfect" form of Allah. It has no less than thirty-two parts—some of which are depicted below:

1. Allah the Lofty hovers above, and then,
2. the crown of the head is to have the certainty that M [Muhammad] is Allah's messenger,

3. the forehead is to be certain of the *basmala*, the Lord as creator, protector, and destroyer,
4. the eyebrows are the first utterance of the *kalima*,
5. the eye is to be the eye of NUN (in the divine name Nur),
6. the eye of attention,
7. the nose to discard all evil smells,
8. the moustache is to know the divine beauty resplendent in one of the three thousand attributes of Allah,
9. the lips are to close the mouth to bad words,
10. the tongue, to taste sweet sounds,
11. the teeth, all thirty two, are to refine different foods, while
12. the throat is to "swallow" truth, honesty, justice via the Qur'an,
13. the hands never still, with the right waging for purity, and the left upholding justice,
14. the chest exudes a triple radiance reflecting one hundred and twenty-four thousand prophets as also three hundred and thirteen chosen prophets (i.e., those with laws and books).

Like the Hindu text that precedes it, this list continues to enumerate qualities and duties, challenges and responsibilities, for all other parts of the body. But in a twist that goes beyond Hindu or other scriptural precedents, the *shaykh* focuses on two most in need of careful cultivation: *the heart and the stomach.*

THE HEART AND STOMACH OF FAITH, ACCORDING TO SHAYKH BAWA MUHAIYADDEEN

The heart is very treacherous terrain; it must be subjected to faith and truth. "Batter my heart," was the opening refrain of a John Donne sonnet,[34] and for Shaykh Bawa Muhaiyaddeen the heart must be battered repeatedly, then tamed with multiple sword strokes, daily administered 21,621 times each day, one for each breath (see figure 9). (For those curious about that number, one merely has to reckon, as does the *shaykh*, that each human takes about fifteen to sixteen breaths per minute, each requiring an inhalation and exhalation. That equals a total of 43,242 per day (15–16 breaths x 2 x 60 min./hour x 24 hrs./day).[35]

Yet the stomach is even more unruly than the heart. Instead of multiple sword strokes, it must be subjected to fifty commands. At first, what the *shaykh* commends seems like a meandering, excessive laundry list of dos and don'ts, but the commands actually sort out into disciplines that begin by being *moral* in nature and end up by being *didactic*. Sprinkled in their midst are commands that are either *dietary* or *devotional*. What is the point of such minute surveillance of the abdomen? It is to recognize its centrality for all remembrance of Allah. The central practice for Shaykh Bawa Muhaiyaddeen, as for all Sufi masters and adepts, is immersive remembrance. Did not Jesus command his disciples to pray: "Give us this day our daily bread"? We cannot connect to Allah, according to the *shaykh*, unless we first control the stomach and recognize its role in every activity of the heart, mind, body, and soul. The first eight guidelines are *moral* (M), followed by a *dietary* (D) injunction; the next eight are also moral, followed by another dietary injunction:

- to follow the truth in one's actions (M)
- to love other lives as one loves his own life (M)
- to abstain from speaking falsehood (M)
- to avoid stealing (M)
- to avoid treachery toward others (M)
- to avoid backbiting (M)
- to abstain from killing (M)
- to abstain from willful underpayment of wages (M)
- to control one's own hunger and appease the hunger of others (D)
- to perform charity in the right manner (M)
- to have compassion for other lives (M)
- to speak only the truth at all times (M)
- to live without swerving from justice and integrity (M)
- to live without slipping from one's duty and patience (M)
- to eliminate lust and wrath (M)
- to abstain from committing adultery (M)
- to abstain from desiring others' wives (M)
- to abstain from alcohol and other intoxicants (D)

At this point, the list veers into injunctions that combine a moral good (M) with a devotional intent (DEV), implying and requiring greater and greater self-awareness of *iman*/faith. These commands are eleven in all:

- to recognize the hunger in the face of a hungry person and to offer him food (M-DEV)
- to make the compassionate form of Allah appear within (DEV)
- to be born as man, to live as man, and to die as man (DEV)

- to cut away selfishness (M)
- to avoid quoting one law for oneself and another for others (M)
- to avoid cheating for treacherous self-gain (M)
- to avoid distorting justice for the sake of keeping up appearances and good relationships (M)
- to avoid suppressing the truth of Allah for the sake of one's own success (DEV)
- to abstain from ruining another so that one may prosper in one's own life (M)
- to abstain from disparaging elders and great ones (M)
- to avoid slandering, saying that one has seen something different from what one really feels within (M)

At this point, the "ordinary" believer may wonder how this list connects to the stomach, and just then the Sufi master delves even more deeply into devotional discipline (DEV), seemingly devoid of any connection to the bodily part under review:

- to worship *Allah ta'ala Nayan* day and night (DEV)
- to avoid breaking any of His commandments (DEV)
- to avoid trying to correct others when one has not attempted to correct oneself (M)
- to avoid scolding others without knowing oneself (M)

And then the emotive, devotional requirements become explicitly didactic, building in an intensity that encompasses each breath, each moment, each instant, each day of one's life (DID):

- to speak Allah's truths, and keep extolling those truths at every moment (DID)
- to preach the divine names of Allah to the good ones without failing for even a second (DID)

- to pray and worship in accordance with the wondrous truth of Allah, performing *sajdah* 70,000 times a day, *tasbih* 70,000 times a day, *dhikr* 70,000 times a day, and *fikr* 70,000 times a day (DEV-DID)
- to offer prayers of supplication (*du'a*) to *Allahu ta'ala Nayan* and to plead with Him and with His Messenger without ceasing for even an instant (DEV-DID)

And then three more intensely didactic directives:

- to expound to others the truths and beneficial laws given by the prophets, *awliya, qutbs,* great ones, elders, and those of wisdom (young or old) who abide by the laws of truth (those who have earned the praises of Allah, the king of justice) and also to teach them the truths that can be learned from the lives of chaste women and virtuous men of excellence, thereby making their faith steadfast
- to teach and to instill in others the faith of certitude, filled with faith, determination, patience, compassion, and perfect purity
- to expound *Allahu ta'ala Nayan*'s truth, the Prophet's truth, and the truth of the Noble Qur'an to others, and to gather all the good in these and preach it to them, *feeding them with it*

The metaphor of feeding circles the reader/listener/reciter back to the beginning, the faith of the stomach, and the last three directives relate the preceding forty-seven commands to the overall theme of this section of the bodily meditation deemed vital for the benefit and performance of the whole:

- to love others as one loves oneself, feeling the hunger of another's stomach as the hunger in one's own stomach (M-D-DEV)

And in this way, without moving a hair's length from Allah's truth,

Fig. 9. Bawa Muhaiyaddeen and his grave near Philadelphia.
Courtesy of Bawa Muhaiyaddeen Fellowship.

- to go on scooping up and imbibing those truths again and again until the hunger of one's soul is appeased—this will be the stomach of faith (M-D-DEV)
- thus, to sever and push away all the evil sins along with their roots and to scoop up and imbibe Allah, the Prophet, and the truth of the Qur'an, thus appeasing one's hunger—this will be the stomach of faith, called *Iman-Islam* (M-D-DEV)

The heart, the stomach, morality and abstinence—all merge in devotional dedication to the pursuit of truth/Truth at once outer and inner, part of each individual yet a link in the cosmos to the Thing, the Absolute, the One.

FROM DIETETIC TO CALLIGRAPHIC PIETY

Still, one must wonder: how is it possible to move from absorption with the body to focus on the meaning of letters? One must move vertically, through a descent of intense scrutiny, appearing as outward in name, but functioning as inward in force. After his forensic excursus into the stomach as the seat of reflection and activity to seed, develop, expand, and expound *iman*/faith, Shaykh Bawa Muhaiyaddeen makes several other stops before reaching the toenails. The toenails?! Yes, it is the toenails of faith that provide the bridge to a further meditation on Allah within each of us, and it is a bridge built on counting, first letters, then numbers, then levels of meaning. Though only ten in number, by the science of counting, the toenails of faith can be shown to include the twenty-four letters of the Arabic alphabet that form the *kalima*, aka, the *shahada*, or profession of faith in Allah. "That true state of Faith is: having come to know the twenty-four letters of the profession of Faith, to affirm the profession to the Prophet of Allah (that is, the second part of the *shahada*), and to have steadfast faith in him. This will be the feet of Faith. *Amin. Al-hamdul (A)illahi Rabbil-'alamin.*[36]

THE PROPHET AS PERFECT MAN, ISLAM AS A VAST OCEAN

And so the full impress of faith, from eyebrows to toenails, becomes the Prophet himself at thirty-two levels. The Prophet Muhammad reflects the perfect embodiment of faith, at each of these thirty-two levels or body stations, and his own "divine" face reflects the Qur'an in a culminating crescendo of homologies: "I have made your divine face into the

Noble Qur'an, the Noble Qur'an into perfect purity, perfect purity into faith, faith into certitude, certitude into the profession, the profession into Islam, and that Islam of perfect purity into a vast ocean, while I remain as the primal Lord, who rules that ocean. The water of that ocean is the profession, the shores of that ocean the Qur'an, the truth of the Qur'an the Prophet, and I the resplendence of the Prophet."[37] In other words, we are brought into the presence of the One beyond knowing, and privileged to listen to His own self-reflection on creation, almost as a form of spiritual eavesdropping.

FROM THE DIVINE OTHER TO THE DIVINE BELOVED

While the intricate prose of a Sri Lankan poet mystic arrays the body parts as points of access to Allah the Lofty the Exalted, other Sufis appeal to the sensorium, the full array of senses. Their intention also is immersive remembrance, or *dhikrAllah*, remembrance of Allah at every moment in every action in every thought. Their preferred medium is verse, abundant verse, most often imagined, spoken, and written as love poetry. In these lyrical volumes, known as *divans*, or collections of poems from a single author, the Divine Other becomes the Divine Beloved, while the human is cast as the seeker, at once the devout slave and the crazed lover of the Other.

The bard's task is to discover or recover Him. Recovery here is an especially potent process. It requires retrieval through remembrance, and it involves the entire sensorium.[38] The mirror is more than mere seeing; the body may be finite in existence but it becomes infinite in its response to divine stimuli. Verse, whether inspired or pain induced, or both, opens the whole range of human bodily connections to the material world—not just seeing or reading, hearing or speaking, but also smelling, touching, and tasting.

Comparison with Shaykh Bawa Muhaiyaddeen helps clarify the differences between his approach to Allah and that of his Persian language co-religionists. Their verses do not project the divine as the human, in the didactic style of Bawa Muhaiyaddeen, but instead allude to proximities, unions, secrets, dalliances, and sublimities that escape the register of most human experience. Those who are privileged to have a vision may see what escapes the rest of us. Such is the case with the Persian Sufi master Ruzbihan Baqli (d. 1209 CE). Known as the Shirazi falcon, Baqli left a diary of his theophany, in which he declares:

Divans of Persian Poetry

Though all verse epitomizes and condenses the range of human emotions, collections of Persian poetry, known as *divans*, provide a benchmark for recalibrating the spiritual quest as also a lyrical foray into the innermost recesses of the human imagination. Rumi, Saʿdi, and Hafiz (or Hafez) are the most salient of scores of poetic giants from the twelfth to the eighteenth century in the Muslim heartland. It is crucial to note, however, that the "drunken" character of poetry can be matched with the "sober" testimony in prose, often in the same person, as was the case with Rumi.

That Allah—glory be to Him who is transcendent—taught the messengers, the prophets, the angels, the saints about himself by signs. He displayed to them the lights of his presence, anointed their eyes with the balm of might, and showed them the sunbeams of his angelic realm. . . .

He also instructed them in the incantations of his names, and he taught them the subtleties of his qualities and characteristics. He made them inhale the perfumed breezes of the rose of near encounters and the herbs of proximities and unions.

He was expansive to them with his generous, intimate conversations [*munajat*], unveiled his secrets, was intimate with them with his beauty, and made them lovers of his majesty. . . . If they reach the position of standing firm after being ravished, Allah most high makes them the lamps of the age, the signs of mystical knowledge, the stages of reality, and the guideposts of the religious law—may Allah place us and you among the people of these states and stations.[39]

As intoxicated as this vision seems to be, it is still anchored in everyday society: the rhetoric does not conceal the reality of recognizing "the guideposts of the religious law," that is, the *shariʿa*, without which Islam ceases to have its fulcrum of norms and values, practices and institutions.

But there can be an even more dramatic shift in register, one that may seem imperceptible at first but is crucial. It marks the primacy of the person, the individual who experiences Allah the Beloved more than it does any connection to Allah or immersion in names of Allah, whether as invocation or remembrance. While Shaykh Bawa Muhaiyaddeen expanded *Allah ta'ala* to include *Nayan*, the Tamil term (the language of the people of South India and Northeast Sri Lanka) for the supreme Lord of life, and while Ruzbihan Baqli entreated Allah to unveil His secrets, other Persian poets defend the secret. They conceal Allah or *khoda* beneath a patina of terms for the beloved, whether *yar* (friend), *munes* (intimate companion), *deldar* (confidant), or *mahram* (protector). Love becomes the recurring theme of human existence, not knowledge of the beyond or engagement with Divine Names. One drifts up to the edge of silence; it becomes difficult to voice what can only be felt or experienced to be real. The supreme "drunken" Sufi, Mawlana Jalaluddin Rumi, even addresses Allah as his drinking companion:

> You are silent, you are silent, drink silently!
> Remain concealed! Remain concealed! You are a hidden treasure.[40]

Allah remains the Source, yet love reigns, as in this verse from the *Divan-i Shams* of Rumi:

> Everything is pretext, there is love and nothing besides love.
> Love is the house of Allah and you are living in that house.
> I will say no more for it is not possible to say;
> Allah knows how much more is in me crying out to be told.[41]

Whether as hopeless drunkard or dizzying dancer, the Sufi seeker is constantly in motion, always pulled toward the elusive, shattering Other, as in this further verse from Rumi:

> All the images in the world are running after His image;
> Like pieces of iron pulled toward a magnet.
> Rubies turn into stone, lions into wild asses;
> Swords turn into shields, and suns into dust particles in His
> presence.[42]

ALLAH: THE POISON OF SEPARATION

If constant movement and endless seeking underlie the paradox of those "standing firm after being ravished" [Baqli], the restless lovers also never cease to complain about the cruelty of the Divine Beloved. Even as they remember Allah with their entire being, they complain to Him about the intensity of their unrequited love. Among these mystically aroused complainants who preceded Rumi and anticipated him was the thirteenth-century Persian poet Muslih ad-din Sa'di (d. 1292 CE). Addressing Allah as the Beloved, he laments:

> Come! Out of the pain of love for You
> I am bewildered without You.
> Come! See in this pain how unhappy I am without you.
> O Beloved, not for one moment have You given me
> the drink of Your union;
> It is the bitter poison of separation that I taste forever.
> I have given the message, and I have said:
> "Come! Make me happy!" You have answered
> and said: "I am happy without you!"[43]

The physicality of Sa'di's poem privileges sight, followed by pain (reflecting touch), and then the taste of poison, "the bitter poison of separation." And in the same vein Sa'di occasionally invokes smell as an echo of separation:

> I live for your aroma, wherever you are.
> I long for the sight of you; where are you?[44]

But even more tangibly olfactory, evoking the very scent of the beloved's hair, is the verse of Jahan Malek Khatun (d. ca. 1382 CE). It is rare to find a woman's voice in this galaxy of supplicants for divine favor. Why? Because "women were considered to be private citizens who had no business in public affairs," notes a famed critic, here speaking about premodern Persian poetry, but also commenting about Muslim mores in general. Fortunately, Jahan Khatun, a fourteenth-century Shirazi bard and contemporary of the famed Hafez Shirazi, did write extensively, if in private, and when her complete poems were discovered and published twenty years ago, they included this verse:

> Sweet breeze return to me, you bear
> The scent of my beloved's hair.
> I suffered while you were away;
> You'll bring the balm for my despair.
> My doctors are so sick of all
> My sicknesses: but I know where
> The medicine lies—it's in the scent
> You'll bring to me from his sweet hair.[45]

ALLAH: THE TAVERN OF LOVE

For Rumi, however, the entire lyrical landscape becomes more than sightings or sickness, beyond cure or perfume. Love turns the heart upside down, inside out. It becomes a brawling tavern. Here is his most sensuous, if also paradoxical, verse. Through the raw physicality of wine and blood, he weaves a story that brings heaven to earth, rather than raising the dreamer into a divine embrace or the seeker into a connection with the Beautiful Name. Divine intoxication pervades the tavern of love:

> Who has ever seen such a mess?
> The tavern of love filled with drunkards.
> We drink the wine of our own blood, aged
> in the barrels of our own souls.
> We would give our lives for a sip of that nectar,
> our heads in exchange for one drop.
> Another morning! Pour the wine!
> A life without His love is nothing but slow death.
> It's up to you—accept the cry of the silent rubaab
> Or endure this burning heart filled with grief.
> O eyes, look only in His direction.
> O soul, hang your clothes on the wheel of life and death.
> O tongue, let the lover sing.
> O ears, become drunk with His song.[46]

"A life without His love is nothing but slow death." Hearing, drinking, singing, burning—all of these become a Sufi reflex, evocative of the twist toward sensory religion heralded in the twentieth century by William James, noted American philosopher, psychologist, and physician. Metaphysically Rumi anticipated William James, who over all other senses gave precedence to sight as inner feeling, or insight. Faith, for James, was "faith in the existence of an unseen order."[47] A radical empiricist, James was committed to a pluralistic view of things, but it was a plural view of sensory experience. What distinguished true religion was not outward observance but rather inner feeling illuminated by a deeply inner light.[48]

James, in his ascetic devotion to the mystical core of religion, might have been surprised to find himself in the company of Rumi and other Persian Sufis, but his awakening of the God within parallels the endless quest for Allah, as witnessed by the parade of Persian poets. All acclaim feeling as the deepest source of the divine, the pain of separation as the only path to true love, itself the path to true religion. Allah never ceases to move up and down the ladder of His names, but here He is marked as the transcendent/immanent Beloved of Persian verse. Thus He is ever sought but never caught. He remains the object of endless sighing, the throb of ecstatic singing, beguiling yet eluding the poisoned, besotted, burning lover.

SUMMARY

If the ordinary believer asks for guidance through prayer and invoking Allah's name, the devout Sufi seeks to access the One beyond and before all that is, or ever will be, through remembrance. Remembrance is an intense, unending pursuit of the deepest interior connection with Allah. Sufi masters have traveled the perilous path (*tariqa*)—through poetry and prose, music and dance, with dieting and fasting—to find the Divine Beloved. The pain of separation is palpable as well as visible in what we have as records of this quest, and the vast sensorium of appeals includes taste, so much so that one Sufi master has given a lengthy list of rules to pursue in conquering the stomach's appetite and redirecting its longing as a spiritual channel to Allah. The psychological reflex of remembrance is so varied, so intense, and so persistent that it anticipates the insight of the father of modern psychology, William James, for whom belief in God was less important than how one *felt* about belief in God. Sufis would agree, but substitute Allah for God, as the gut feeling of their own lifelong quest to connect with the Beloved.

Yet even James could not have anticipated how all reflections on Allah—as also reactions to Him, His Messenger, His Book, and His many names—would be confounded in the Information Age. All that Sufis admire, seek, embrace, and feel is too often refracted through the lens of disbelief, compounded by anger and fear, turning the Hidden Treasure into the Guardian and Goal of terrorists. The debate about Allah, always simmering, has intensified during the decades since the end of the Cold War, abetted by American involvement in two overseas wars in majority-Muslim countries. It is that debate that occupies us in the next chapter.

And do you think that unto such as you
A maggot-minded, starved, fanatic crew
God gave a secret, and denied it me?
Well, well—what matters it? Believe that, too!
—Omar Khayyam

CHAPTER FOUR

Allah Debated

Practice of the Ear

OVERVIEW

Debunking Allah is the pastime of cynics, critics, and mimics. Sometimes the most intelligent people engage in these activities, and because
of their mass appeal, now expanded by the Internet and the World Wide
Web, they must be acknowledged. Are they largely polemical? Yes. Is
there a small residue of truth in their disparagements? Yes, and for that
reason, and only for that reason, must they be acknowledged, their perspectives explored, their grievances aired.

The Omar Khayyam cited here mimics the secret prized by Sufis. Can
it be read as a rejection of Allah (here translated as God)? Yes, especially
if the reader is Christopher Hitchens. We start with a short discussion
of Hitchens's atheistic views on religion—almost exclusively targeting
Islam—and then follow with thoughts on his harsh criticism of Islamic
claims about the sanctity of the Qur'an when read or understood only

Christopher Hitchens died on the same day that the Iraq war
(allegedly) ended: December 15, 2011. His life as a public polemicist
and prolific journalist was intertwined with defense of the U.S.-Allied
invasion, and any effort to justify its curtailment or cessation for
him was an act of treason. The Taliban and the neoliberal antiwar
establishment were equally hectored by his lapidary style and acerbic
tongue.

in the Arabic language. This inexorably leads us to a broad-ranging discussion of the role of violence (and nonviolence) in Islam. Violence is
rooted in pre-Islamic mores, and redefined in the Qur'an. Though im-
plemented by Muhammad, it is also curtailed by him. Not so by later
actors, who respond to contexts beyond those confronted or imagined in
seventh-century Arabia. Especially notable is the evolution of views that
inform modern-day jihad and jihadists. More than Qur'anic wisdom, the
skillful manipulations of Osama bin Laden illustrate the power of the
new Information Age, the subject of our final chapter.

CHRISTOPHER HITCHENS ON ALLAH

Christopher Hitchens, a noted British-American author and journalist
best known among the theological intelligentsia as a confirmed atheist,
begins where others have begun—not with Allah, but with Allahu Akbar.
The choke point for such folk is the utterance—Allahu Akbar!—God is
Great, or Greater (than anything or anyone else imaginable). This shibboleth is often viewed as the triumphal moment of Muslim conquest or victory, not the entry point for Muslim ritual prayer and submission to Allah.

So common is the phrase Allahu Akbar—God is Great—that when
Hitchens opted to write his manifesto against *all* religion, he did not
title it Allahu Akbar but instead paraphrased the negative of that phrase,
"God is *not* great," in English. In fact, Hitchens, ever the nimble satirist,
went one better: he reversed the capitalization as well, so that the title
of his best-selling book from 2007 reads: *god is not Great.*

Neither the word Allah nor the phrase Allahu Akbar appears anywhere in his text, yet in a screed that lampoons all revealed religion, Hitchens gives pride of place to Islam as the religion that not only imposes circumcision, as does Judaism, but also relies on the value of one language—Arabic—for access to "the unknowable and ineffable creator."[1] It is the linguistic barrier of Arabic that grates Hitchens: Islam remains coded in Arabic through the Arabic Qur'an, accessible only to believers who know the original language. Sardonically he asks: "Even if god is or was an Arab (an unsafe assumption), how could he expect to 'reveal' himself by way of an illiterate person [alluding to Muhammad] who in turn could not possibly hope to pass on the unaltered (let alone unalterable) words?"[2]

SATIRE AND WAR FATIGUE

Many have dismissed Hitchens's authority to speak about religion in general or Islam in particular, and some will no doubt be offended that I give him any space in this book. Yet Hitchens offers a critique of the "Arabicity," or Arabic language priority, of the Qur'an that also applies to Allah. Is Allah only the god of the Arabs, the lampooned moon god of Jack Chick comic strips, or is He God the Lofty One, who spoke to Arabs but also to others through the archangel Gabriel when the Qur'an was first revealed about 1,400 years ago? This claim needs to be reviewed in 2015 as the United States winds down from two wars in Muslim-majority countries—Afghanistan and Iraq—but remains perplexed about the role it plays, or should try to play, in the future of not just the Middle East but also the more than fifty other countries of Africa and Asia with sizable or majority Muslim populations. The central question is not whether or not Islam needs to have a reformation (*pace* Hitchens), but whether Islam is understood as the message of peace announced in the greeting: Peace be on you! Is the central message of Islam peace, or is it instead warfare: Kill the unbelievers, wherever you find them. Both passages are Qur'anic but which should prevail as the will of Allah?

Like the Hebrew Bible and the New Testament, images of the Thing, the Absolute, the One, vary within the fold of Holy Writ. If one wishes to engage Allah today, one must first understand Allah's role in the formative phase of Islam as the Qur'an was being revealed. As Michael Lambek tersely but correctly observed, "Texts by themselves are silent. They become socially relevant through enunciation and acts of interpretation."[3] The Qur'an, like the Bible, has a deep, long, and complex history; it has been subject to myriad, often conflicting interpretations; it cannot, and does not, have a single, monolithic perspective on truth.

VIOLENCE AND ISLAM IN CONTEXT

Is Islam violent? Of course it is, but of course it also is not. Is Allah a deity of wrath and vengeance? In some instances it would seem so, but in most instances not, and how does one resolve the tension, as also the seeming contradiction, between two sides of the same One, Absolute, Other?

Context is crucial to answering any question about Islam or Allah.[4] War and jihad were not always linked, and to understand Allah in the time of the Prophet Muhammad you have to delink them. Early seventh-century Arabia was not only home to Muhammad but also to numerous forms of societal violence. These included, for instance, female infanticide, along with the abuse of orphans, the poor, and the marginal. Against such forms of societal violence, the revelations from Allah/God mediated through the Archangel Gabriel to Muhammad were clear, incontrovertible challenges to the social order of tribal Mecca. They prohibited the pre-Islamic Arabian practice of female infanticide as well as other bodily and social abuses through directives set down, encoded, and transmitted in the Qur'an. Reflect on the following:

> And when the infant girl who was buried alive is asked
> For what offense she was killed [the person who killed her will have to
>   answer for his sin on Judgment Day]. (Q 81:8–9)

> Do not kill your children out of fear of poverty;
> We will provide for them, and for you.
> Indeed, killing them is a great sin. (Q 17:31)

What these two passages reflect is that in pre-Islamic Arabia killing of
female infants was very common; often the moment a female was born
she was buried alive. Islam not only prohibits female infanticide, but it
forbids all types of infanticide, irrespective of whether the infant is a
male or female. Consider the following:

You should not kill your children on account of poverty—
We provide for you and for them.
And do not approach the property of the orphan,
except with what is better till he comes of age.
Take not life which God has made sacred. (Q 6:151–52)

CHILDREN AS WELL AS WOMEN MERIT LIFE AND JUSTICE

And linked to the concern for children was a parallel concern for
mothers. In the Qur'anic chapter dedicated to women (Q 4), Allah directs the Prophet:

Give orphans their property,
Without exchanging bad for good;
And if you fear you cannot do justice by the orphans,
Then marry women who please you,
Two, three, or four;
But if you fear you won't be equitable,
Then one, or a legitimate bondmaid of yours,
That way it is easier for you
Not to go wrong. (Q 4:2–3)

The irony of this passage is its misapplication during subsequent Muslim history. In the course of centuries, Islamic law overlooked both the

context for this revelation—to care equitably for the orphan—and its qualification—if you cannot be equitable to two, three, or four women (who have been previously married and have children now orphaned without a father), then marry but one woman or cohabit with a legitimate bondmaid, as Abraham did with Hagar, producing Ishmael. Caring for orphans is the critical rationale for plural marriage during the earliest period of Islamic history. It could even be argued that it is the sole rationale for plural marriage, and so the first signpost of violence in Islam is not the violence inherent in Allah's dicta to Muhammad but rather the greater violence of the preceding, non-Islamic period known as *jahliyya*, or period of ignorance. And so one can deduce that the initial revelation of the Qur'an, along with the early formation of a Muslim community (*umma*), was intended to curtail rather than to expand or export violence.

THE FIRST EXODUS, FROM ARABIA TO AFRICA

If it was difficult to sustain the purity of thought and the dedication of purpose indicated in those early revelations, it is nonetheless crucial to see how they shaped Muhammad and emboldened him to persist when others could, and did, fail. The so-called Meccan chapters were revealed to the Prophet over twelve years, from 610 to 622, and during that time Muslims were the nonviolent members of Arabian society in general, and in urban Mecca in particular. At one moment, it seemed that Muhammad's nonviolent responses to the provocations of his hostile countrymen would jeopardize the entire Muslim experiment. In 617 the Prophet sent some of his closest followers and relatives next door, across the Red Sea, to Abyssinia (Ethiopia). Their enemies followed them and demanded that the traitorous Muslims be handed over to them and returned to face justice, that is, certain death in Mecca. When the Christian king asked the fearful Muslims to explain their faith, one of them recited to him a revelation that had just come to the Prophet. It included the first forty verses of Q 19, Sura Maryam. So closely did these words from Allah parallel Christian scripture, belief, and hope that the king granted them asylum.[5]

That first *hijra*, or exodus, was yet another instance when violence was prevented, rather than abetted, by the earliest Muslims, and the medium of their pursuit for justice, peace, and equality were those revelations from Allah that later became the Holy Qur'an, also known as the Noble Book.

THE SECOND EXODUS, FROM MECCA TO MEDINA

Later the bar of restraint for Muhammad and his followers was raised yet higher. By 622, life had become intolerable for the hardy cohort of Muslims, and Muhammad, with his band of followers, moved to Yathrib/Medina in the second *hijra*, which became also the first year in the subsequent Muslim calendar. Once Muhammad established a community of followers in Medina, he had no choice but to fight his Meccan enemies who continued to pursue him. But he could not fight without license from the Thing, the Absolute, the One, and as the Qur'an records, Allah did acquiesce to limited war: *"Permission to fight is given to those on whom war is made"* (Q 22:39).

In other words, war was always and everywhere to be defensive. The war Muhammad waged against Mecca was not a struggle for prestige or wealth; it was, in his view, a war for survival, of both the community and the faith. In December 623, more than a year after the beleaguered Muslims had fled to Medina, Muhammad ordered a small detachment to spy on a caravan to the south. It was proceeding along the route to Yemen, at the oasis of Nakhlah that links Mecca to Taif. Since it was a holy month, he had ordered his followers not to attack, but they disobeyed. Killing some, they took others captive and brought the caravan back to Medina. Muhammad was appalled. Not only had his followers disobeyed him; they had disobeyed the command of Allah to fight only in defense of one's own life and property. Their actions mirrored his leadership. He was responsible. The prophet who had pledged to be a divine mediator had betrayed his own prophecy. Riven with distress, he prayed to Allah. He needed guidance from above. And when it came, it was at once clear and compelling:

They ask you about war in the holy month.
Tell them: "To fight in that month is a great sin.
But a greater sin in the eyes of Allah is to hinder
people from the way of Allah, and not to believe
in Him, and to bar access to the Holy Mosque
and to turn people out of its precincts.
And oppression is worse than killing."

They will always seek war against you till
They turn you away from your faith, if they can.
But those of you who turn back on their faith
and die disbelieving will have wasted their deeds
in this world and the next.
They are inmates of Hell,
and abide there forever. (Q 2:217)

MUSLIM WARFARE SANCTIFIED

This revelation from Allah via the Archangel Gabriel had replaced a rule of principle with one of practical moral value. Yes, killing is forbidden in the sacred month (Q 2:191), but worse than killing is oppression, hindering people from the way of Allah. Empowered by this divine dictum, Muhammad waged war, and then divided the spoils of war among his followers at Nakhlah.

More war lay ahead. Muhammad and his followers entered into an unending conflict with their Meccan kinsmen and opponents. From 623 to 632, Muhammad planned thirty-eight battles that were fought by his fellow believers. He led twenty-seven military campaigns. The nonviolent protestor had become a general, waging war again and again. The first full-scale military campaign came at the wells of Badr, in 624, less than four months after the skirmish at Nakhlah. Muslims chose to attack a caravan coming south from Palestine to Mecca. The Meccans learned of their attack, opposing them with a force that far outnumbered the Muslim band. Muhammad and his followers should have lost; and they would have lost, except for the intervention of angels (Q 3:122–27), not just angels but angels as emissaries of Allah, the One beyond knowing but also beyond doubting.

While the Battle of Badr projected the small Muslim community onto a cosmic stage, with divine intervention as the basis for military victory, its outcome provoked fear in the Meccans. If Allah was made known to Muhammad in the still voice of Gabriel in the cave of Hira outside Mecca, He continued to speak, in both words and deeds, through the trials of Medina. The Battle of Badr was the first clear signal that the upstart Muslim community seemed to be protected by forces beyond their reckoning. It also made their Meccan enemies even more resolved to defeat the "lucky" Muslims.

By 625 the mighty Meccan general Abu Sufyan had assembled a huge army of foot soldiers and cavalry. He marched toward Medina. The Muslims countered by moving out of the city proper and engaged their adversaries on the slopes of a nearby mountain, Uhud. Despite the Meccan's superior numbers, the battle went well for the Muslims, until some of Muhammad's archers broke ranks too early to pillage the Meccan camp, in anticipation of another victory such as Badr. The Meccans counterattacked, and Khalid ibn al-Walid, one of the brilliant Meccan nobles, led his cavalry to the unprotected rear of the Muslim formation and, catching them unawares, slaughtered them. The Muslims were soundly defeated, and Muhammad himself wounded in the mayhem that day.

Yet the Prophet did not believe that Allah had forsaken him on the battlefield. He resolved to learn the deeper lesson behind this bitter defeat. He regarded the defeat of Uhud to be as important for Islam as the victory of Badr, for in defeat as in victory the Muslims had to acknowledge that their fate was not theirs but Allah's to decide. Allah's superseding knowledge is echoed throughout the Qur'an but nowhere more directly than in Ayat al-Kursi, the Throne Verse, earlier cited and here cited again:

Allah knows what is before them,
and what is after them;
but they do not encompass anything
of His knowledge,
except as He wills. (Q 2:255)

In 627 there followed the major Battle of the Trench. Abu Sufyan, the architect of Uhud, again led a mighty Meccan army against the Muslims. But when he tried to invade Medina to defeat and destroy Muslims once and for all, he failed. Far from rejoicing in this revenge after the humiliating defeat at Uhud, the Muslims credited Allah—and Allah alone— with their victory. In the aftermath, fierce foes such as Abu Sufyan and the fiery Khalid ibn al-Walid ceased to oppose the Muslims and instead joined their ranks.

MUHAMMAD THE COMPROMISER AND PEACE MAKER

Beyond the battlefield, Muhammad never ceased trying to convert his Meccan opponents to the religion of Islam. Though he had forsaken non-violence, he had *not* embraced violence as a way of life, only as an expedient to a higher end. He contacted the Meccans to propose a peaceful pilgrimage. Though he assured their leaders of his intention, they doubted him, perhaps not surprisingly. It took until 629, seven years after he had left Mecca, before he and his followers were allowed to re-enter their native city. At last all Muslims—those Meccans who initially had emigrated to Medina, those Medinans who had joined them, and other tribes who had become their allies—submitted to Allah, and all were able to return to Mecca in a peaceful pilgrimage.

When they returned in January 630, Muhammad made a singular, perhaps well-calculated, decision. Instead of vengeance, he again forgave all but his bitterest enemies. Yet another military encounter quickly followed on the heels of the peaceful pilgrimage. One month later, in February 630, was a battle larger than any Muslims had seen since Uhud. It came not from Mecca but from beyond. Led by the Hawazin, many Bedouin tribes who were opposed to Islam saw the reentry to Mecca as an opportunity for their own ferocious, full-scale assault on the Muslims. The Battle of Hunain (one of only two battles mentioned by name in the Qur'an) was a fierce battle, but also a curious one, one that reflected the value of intelligence, harassing attacks, and the role of decisive leadership. The Muslim army, having spied out the Bedouin movements, moved into the valley, but the Bedouins had expertly deployed spies to track the Muslim movements, and after they had set up camp the Bedouins harassed them with stones and showers of arrows. This so demoralized the Muslim army that it was near collapse. But Muhammad invoked Allah and shamed his army, restoring their confidence, ultimately leading to a major victory. Once again, from the Muslim point of view, it was the Thing, the Absolute, the One, working through the angelic host, that brought them victory. It was not Muslim numbers or military prowess that decided the outcome. The Qur'an once again marked the event:

> Indeed Allah has helped you on many occasions,
> even during the battle of Hunain,
> when you were elated with joy at your numbers
> which did not prove of the least avail,
> so that the earth and its expanse became too narrow
> for you,
> and you turned back and retreated.
> then God sent down a sense of tranquility
> on His Apostle and the faithful;

and sent down troops invisible
to punish the infidels.
This is the recompense of those who do not believe. (Q 9:25–26)

THE DEATH OF MUHAMMAD

After the death of Muhammad in 632, his movement, based so squarely on his personal authority, almost came unhinged. It was a delicate moment when a new leader, one of his trusted followers, Abu Bakr, was elected his successor, or *khalifa*. Several tribes tried to withdraw from the treaty that bound them to Muhammad, yet Abu Bakr fought them in what became known as the Ridda wars, the wars of apostasy or repudiation of Islam. For many scholars, this period initiates the practice of open warfare in the name of Islam. It is said to be the time when jihad, or war in defense of the faith, came to be associated with Islamic expansion. Muslims were a single, indivisible community united by faith, worshipers of the one and universal God, but at the same time they must, and did, accept the notion of a central human authority transferable from Muhammad to his successors. And there was also the notion not just of revelation and acceptance of its divine truth but also of obedience required to its divine dictates. Consider how the *lex talionis* (that is, the protocol of equivalent retaliation, e.g., "eye for an eye") was modified through the Qur'an:

Believers, requital is prescribed
for you in cases of murder;
the free for the free, the slave for the slave,
and the female for the female.
But if anyone is forgiven
anything by his brother,
let fairness be observed,
and goodly compensation. (Q 2:178)

And do not take a life
that Allah has made sacred,
except for just cause.
And if anyone is killed unjustly,
We have given his next of kin
a certain authority;

but he should not be excessive in killing;
for he has been given divine support [to be restrained]. (Q 17:33)

Especially crucial is the protocol for requital among believers, announced in Sura an-Nisa, which is pivotal for Muslim attitudes toward interpersonal violence. It details the instructions of Allah as both All-Knowing (*'alim*) and Most Judicious (*hakim*), two of the Ninety-nine Beautiful Names:

It is never right
for a believer to kill a believer,
except by mistake;
and one who kills a believer by mistake
is to free a believing slave,
and compensation is to be handed over
to the family of the deceased,
unless they forego it to charity.
If the deceased was from a people
warring against yours,
yet was a believer,
then free a believing slave.
But if the deceased was from a people
with whom you have a treaty,
then compensation is to be paid
to the family of the deceased,
and a believing slave is to be freed.
and if one has not the means,
then one is to fast
for two consecutive months,
as an act of contrition granted
as a concession from Allah.
And Allah is All-Knowing, Most Judicious. (Q 4:92)

THE ORIGIN OF JIHAD

All of these conditions—Allah as authority, the community as resource, the successor as leader—are critical for defining both the Islamic state and its impetus for expansion through war. Jihad, when it does occur, appears only as an ancillary, incidental concept. Of course, early Mus-

Jihad

Jihad, after *shari'a*, is the single most controversial notion in Islam, but its historical context demonstrates how variable, and secondary, it was as a pretext for war in the initial period of Islamic expansion (prior to the Crusades).

lim warriors were motivated by the prospect of either booty (if they survived) or paradise (if they were slain), but jihad entered as "a product of the rise of Islam, not a cause of it—a product, to be exact, of the impact of the new concept of the *umma* on the old (tribal) idea that one fought, even to the death, for one's own community."[6] While there is a lot of fighting depicted in Islamic histories, such military encounters are known mostly as *maghazi* (raids) or *futuh* (conquests). Whenever jihad is invoked, it is a sidebar, not a central feature of the narrative of early Muslim warfare.

Over time what had been an incidental, qualified part of the Qur'anic message and the earliest Islamic worldview became an independent force on its own, so much so that some have declared jihad to be a sixth pillar (beyond the standard five) that defines Islamic belief and practice. The seminal text cited by all proponents of jihad as a collective duty incumbent on all Muslims is Sura at-Tawba (Q 9). Here, Muslims are told that idolaters must be fought and polytheists leveled, and that the reward for those who struggle will be paradise:

But the messenger
and those who believe with him
struggle with their possessions and their persons.
So the good things are for them,
and they are the successful ones.
Allah has prepared gardens
under which rivers flow,
where they will abide.
That is the great attainment. (Q 9:88–89)

Yet neither this verse nor other Qur'anic verses motivated Muslims to engage in perpetual warfare against Byzantines, Sassanians, or other *ahl al-kitab* (People of the Book), after the death of Muhammad. It was not until the eleventh century, with Saladin and the Crusader conquest of Jerusalem, that jihad was revitalized. The key events were the fall of Jerusalem to the Crusaders in 1099, the recapture of Edessa from the crusaders by Saladin's father, Zengi, in 1144, and then, in 1187, Saladin's recapture of Jerusalem.

It was during the fateful twelfth century that the doctrine of jihad was revived and heralded as a paramount duty to preserve Muslim territorial, political, and symbolic integrity. Indeed, it seems that "the Crusades triggered the jihad mentality as we know it now." It was in response to the Crusades that Zengi and Saladin produced, for the first time in Islamic history, "a broad scale propaganda effort to praise jihad and jihad-warriors. Jerusalem became the center of jihad propaganda, and Saladin extended its sanctity to Syria, reminding everyone that Syria too is the Holy Land and that Muslims are responsible for defending and protecting it against foreign assaults."[7]

Later, the doctrine of jihad was amplified and applied anew in the thirteenth and fourteenth centuries after the Mongols plundered Baghdad, ravaged the Muslim world, and then themselves became Muslims. It was Ibn Taymiyya (the influential thirteenth-century Islamic scholar, theologian, and jurist) who inveighed against the Mongols, and his favorite tool for anathematizing them was jihad. It was not just external but internal enemies of Allah who incurred the wrath of Ibn Taymiyya. Ibn Taymiyya saw the Muslim world assailed by external and internal enemies of all kinds, and in his strong desire to purify Islam and Islamic territory from all intrusion and corruption, he declared, "the only solution [is] to wage jihad so that 'the whole of religion may belong to Allah.'"[8]

From medieval to modern to contemporary history, the trope of Islam as religiously motivated and divinely sanctioned violence has continued to focus on jihad. So it is important to note how those who came to be labeled fundamentalists invoked the early experience of the Prophet Muhammad and the revelations of Allah in Medina to proclaim jihad. None did so more stridently or effectively than Sayyid Qutb, a member of the Muslim Brotherhood who opposed Nasser, the Egyptian president from 1954 to 1970. Before being executed on charges of sedition in 1966, Sayyid Qutb produced a series of writings, many from prison, which exposed modern-day nationalism as a form of *jahliyya* (i.e., the reliance on manmade laws rather than the Qur'an and *shari'a*). In effect, he equated nationalism with the kind of tribal order that Muhammad had opposed and overcome, together with his early followers, in order to establish the *umma*, or single supra-tribal Muslim community. In one of his most memorable string of homologies, Qutb reappropriated nationalism for "true" Islam: "Nationalism is belief, homeland is *Dar al-Islam*, the ruler is Allah, and the constitution is the Qur'an."[9]

AFTER QUTB, BIN LADEN

Qutb's message and his resort to jihad as the just cause for Muslims under threat resonated through Egypt and the Arab world, but also with the Taliban and the attackers of 9/11. It is impossible to make this temporal transition from the seventh to the twenty-first century without noting how eschatological religion becomes at once more vivid and more accessible through modern means, not least of all martyr operations. The master of that shift from premodern to modern instruments of ending time, and doing so in the name of Allah, was Osama bin Laden (aka OBL). But it was not Bin Laden as a religious warrior like other, earlier Muslim warriors; it was instead OBL, the Islamic apocalypticist mediated through modern visual and satellite technologies. Since his 2011 death at the hands of a U.S. Navy seal team in Abbotabad, Pakistan, it has become possible to reflect on his impact on Islamic notions of Allah as a violent, wrathful, vengeful God. In the several messages that highlight Bin Laden's public utterances, his relationship to Al-Jazeera proves to be almost as important as his decision to wage jihad. Prior to December 1998, when the United States and Britain launched an attack on Iraq called Operation Desert Fox, Al-Jazeera had been a local satellite news service. Founded in February 1996 by the emir of Qatar, its goal was to promote freedom of information among Arabic-speaking citizens of the Gulf and its neighbors. In 1998, the Baghdad office got their big break when they filmed the missiles being launched against Iraq from British and American airplanes. Bin Laden gave an interview that was broadcast on Al-Jazeera in December, and he became an instant international attraction. So significant was the impact of this interview that, nine days after September 11, 2001, it was rerun by Al-Jazeera. Accompanying the ninety-minute video were pictures of Bin Laden firing a gun. The message, in images as well as words, was that Allah has ordained war, that war is between aggressive crusaders and defensive believers, and that Muslims have a stark choice, either to side with the infidel oppressors or to support the beleaguered but pure and resolute Muslim defenders.

In essence, it is an updated version of the message attributed to Ibn Taymiyya. The latter used much the same argument to justify jihad against the invading Mongols. But here it is recrafted for a modern audience through twenty-first century media. And it is the same message that was articulated in all of Bin Laden's subsequent epistles that were broadcast via Al-Jazeera before his death in May 2011. Each was tailored to the audience he addressed. As pious public lecturer, militant jihadist, and disenfranchised scribe, Bin Laden excoriates ruling Saudi leaders for corruption, fiscal mismanagement, human rights abuses, and especially for their alliance with "American Crusader forces" since the Gulf War of 1991. These accusations take on religious significance for Bin Laden, who sees them as apostasy (*shirk*) insofar as Saudi leaders are represented as relying on manmade state law instead of on true Islamic law (*shari'a*). What is *shari'a*? For Bin Laden, it remains confidently underspecified. Overall, the pious tenor of his epistles is consistently maintained as an act of remembrance (*dhikr*), not in the traditional Sufi sense, but as a central dimension of Islam's message: humankind is by nature, and also by practice, forgetful; all persons are in need of constant reminding.[10]

These epistles functioned as sermons. They were delivered from on high and projected globally in ways that enhanced Bin Laden's charismatic stature. Those to the Iraqis were elaborated with scriptural and historical citations and also with poetic verses, some from his own pen. His epistle to the Afghans flowed with cascades of Qur'anic citations as he reminded them of his struggle on their behalf against the Soviets. His letter to the Americans and Europeans, by contrast, contained an unadorned accusation: they were blindly following leaders who were dooming them to an endless war of attrition. In every instance, he was an anti-imperial polemicist on behalf of global jihad, shaping the message to reach and motivate the audience.

One of his most stellar performances was a sermon delivered in 2003 on the holiest day in the Islamic calendar, 'Id al-Adha, wherein he combines elements from all his letters and declarations to address Muslims around the world. He talks to individuals directly, commending each one's worthiness to participate in global jihad and accusing their leaders of criminal corruption. Like the first encounters that the seventh-century Arabs had with unbelieving Persians, the current jihad pits absolute good against absolute evil. Psychologically speaking, it is as though Bin Laden is charged with a paranoid certainty about the end-time, the apocalyptic moment in which all are living but only he and the guided warriors from Al-Qaida understand fully how close the end is. Numerous Qur'anic citations and prophetic traditions are woven into his fervent appeal to believers to take up arms against the United States, Britain, Israel, and their collaborators in the Arab world. Like the Prophet Muhammad's followers, Bin Laden's Muslim armies will prevail. They have a recent history of victories over the superpowers. Who was it that defeated the Soviet Union in Afghanistan and the Russians in Chechnya? Many may try to take credit, he observes, but it was in fact a divine glory, parallel to Allah's earlier victories of the first Muslims against unbelievers. In the late twentieth century the beneficiaries of that glory were the Afghan-Arab mujahidin. Was it not they who conquered the Americans in Lebanon, Somalia, Aden, Riyadh, Khobar, East Africa, at home, and, most recently, in Afghanistan? The myth of American democracy and freedom has been shattered, al-hamduli(A)llah! And then, remarkably, he concludes with his own poem in which he vows to fight until he becomes

a martyr,
dwelling in a high mountain pass
among a band of knights who,
united in devotion to Allah,
descend to face armies.[11]

Unfortunately, due to the dizzying shifts of technology in the Information Age, it is easy to underestimate how dramatic Bin Laden's moves as a risk taker were. A modern linguistic anthropologist especially attuned to Arabic speech practices explains:

> Bin Laden's bald comparisons between hallowed personages of early Islamic history and contemporary actors and events subject him to decided risks. Not only does he hazard alienating Muslim listeners by compromising the unique role that the Prophet played in Islam; he also risks becoming a poor historian, one whose antiquarian zeal fails to re-connect narrated events with present concerns. It is precisely here that *Bin Laden adopts an entirely new tactic, one that moves him from his role as pious public lecturer to the roles of tribesman, poet, and ultimately cosmic warrior.* In the midst of this set of transformations, the temporal distinctions of "then" and "now" become entirely blurred. Listeners are mesmerized, then invited, through the most sonorous and impassioned portions of the cassette, to mobilize as eternal holy combatants.[12]

The oracle speaks then as a cosmic warrior; it is he who can augur both the end-time and its "certain" outcome. The role that had been reserved for Allah the Thing, the Absolute, the One is now channeled through His "servant," Osama.

While Bin Laden undoubtedly mastered and benefited from modern media, no one should assume that such benefits, particularly in the case of Al-Jazeera, were without some cost to his project. The channels of influence and of risk taking cut in two directions across the religio-political landscape. Bin Laden advocated the maximal response to imperialism — constantly demanding sacrifice, especially of youths through martyrdom for a greater cause. Yet he gave no hint of a future frame beyond the shibboleth "Islamic state" or "rule of Allah on earth." The emptiness of his political vision was made clear in the Taysir Alluni interview in October 2001 when he declared that jihad will continue until "we meet Allah and get His blessing!" While the reference to meeting Allah echoes Bin

Laden's confidence in the Day of Judgment, it is in the here and now, not the hereafter, that he seeks, and needs, the divine blessing. Bin Laden had no cogent strategic endgame in mind. Earlier, in an August 1996 epistle, he seemed to call for a deferral of apocalyptic rewards, insisting on the value of oil revenues for a near-term Islamic state: "I would like here to alert my brothers, the Mujahidin, the sons of the nation, to protect this (oil) wealth and not to include it in the battle as it is a great Islamic wealth and a large economical power essential for the soon to be established Islamic state, by the grace and permission of Allah."[13]

Still later, in his second letter to the Iraqi people, he called again for establishing the rule of Allah on earth but only through incessant warfare against multiple enemies, with no agenda for a structure or network to succeed the current world system.[14] While there are many ways to connect Bin Laden to the early generation of Islam, perhaps it is more penetrating to see how he contrasted the perfection of early Islam with the desecration of the twenty-first century. In the same way that former president George W. Bush saw freedom and democracy as standards of global virtue, projecting both holistic soundness and indivisible oneness for "the axis of good," so Bin Laden saw sacrifice and war as the dual emblems of early Islam, emblems that persist until today as "the axis of hope" for all committed Muslims who recognize the seriousness of the moment, as also the unfailing guidance of Allah.

Yet his was a hope with no terrestrial future. It could never be realized under the current world order since all its denizens were living in an end-time of total crisis. There was no rush to restore the caliphate or to remake the Ottoman Empire in the pre–World War I image of a pan-Islamic Muslim polity. Instead, the ultimate criterion was "meeting Allah and getting His blessing." That was a deferred hope, one that could not be achieved in this world during the lifetime of Muslim martyrs but instead was deferred for all humankind to experience in the terrible reckoning that the Thing, the One, the Unique and Eternal has prepared.

ALIF THE UNSEEN

From Al-Qaida to fiction, from actual devilry to Internet myth and magic may seem like an unlikely journey, but it is one that we daily make in negotiating the parallel universes of the twenty-first century. While the headlines mark mass media attention to threat, horror, and fear, the by-lines make us look at what is fantastic yet real, touching the inner space

Jinn or Genie

Jinn (also spelt *Djinn*) are mentioned in the Qur'an and in *hadith*, or traditions linked to the Prophet Muhammad. Unlike angels, they eat, drink, marry, have children, and die. So they seem like human beings, except that they live longer and have unusual abilities, both to work good and to do ill, in the lives of actual humans.

of our insistent search for truth, justice, hope, and love. Consider the best-selling novelist Willow Wilson, author of *Alif the Unseen*. Like Bin Laden, Wilson is a devout Muslim and a committed activist, but with one major difference. Bin Laden, before his death, related his militantly destructive quest to Allah, and saw but two realms: belief and unbelief, this world and the next. Willow Wilson, however, relates her lyrically instructive novel to multiple realms, the visible, the invisible, and in-between spaces. The *barzakh* realm—both/and, neither/nor—is her domain. She projects a cosmology that includes in-between creatures, not just humans and angels but also mixed creatures, *jinn* or genies.

In her 2012 novel, Wilson charts the adventures of Alif, an Arab-Indian computer whiz who lives in the Gulf. Alif takes his name from the first letter of the Arabic alphabet. It is also the first letter for the name Allah. Like the One whose name he echoes in shorthand, Alif engages the Unseen. The title conveys the mystery behind the seeming sameness of all the wealthy Arabs who inhabit the newly rich Gulf Emirates. The nameless island state in which Alif lives is repressive; its controlling force rests on the computer codes that are manipulated by henchmen of the state. To break repression, Alif "the Unseen" must break the code, and as a young hacktivist he finds an unsuspected parallel to the bureaucratic terror of the state apparatchiks. There is within and behind the city another city, one inhabited not by humans but by *jinn*. The *jinn* are like humans, except they have different bodies, different talents, and also different means of communication. All these parallels play out not only in the characters of the novel but in its central trope: a book, an ancient book, a mysterious book, one that contains a code parallel to the code of the computer but more powerful because its secrets disguise even the identity of the one who uses it. The secrets cannot be seen, but they can be heard—if one reads out loud and listens patiently to the messages of the text. That text is *Alf Yeom*, the Thousand and One Days, itself a parallel universe to the *Alf Layla*, the ancient text known in English as the *Thousand and One Nights*.

The mood of this novel is frolicking but serious. The first story that the hero, Alif, reads comes from the sole "real" copy of the book that he received from his girlfriend. Intisar turns out to be unfaithful to Alif but unwittingly shares with him a book that transcends her infidelity. She is writing a dissertation on this book. Titled *Variations of Religious Discourse in Early Islamic Fiction*, her dissertation begins:[15]

> The suggestion that the *Alf Yeom* is the work of jinn is surely a curious one. The Qur'an speaks of the hidden people in the most candid way, yet more and more the educated faithful will not admit to believing in them, however readily they might accept even the harshest and most obscure points of Islamic law. That God has ordained that a thief must pay for his crime with his hand, that a woman must inherit half of what a man inherits—these things are treated not only as facts but as obvious facts, whereas the existence of conscious being we cannot see—and all the fantastic and wondrous things that their existence suggests and makes possible—produces profound discomfort among precisely that cohort of Muslims most lauded for their role in that religious "renaissance" presently expected by western observers: young degree-holding traditionalists. Yet how hollow rings a tradition in which the law, which is subject to interpretation, is held as sacrosanct, yet the word of God is not to be trusted when it comes to His description of what He has created.
>
> I do not know what I believe.

And then Alif finds that his feckless girlfriend, Intisar, is using Douglas Hofstadter to decode *Alf Yeom*. Without ever mentioning the title of Hofstadter's book (*Gödel, Escher, Bach: An Eternal Golden Braid*), she (Intisar, but also the author, Willow Wilson) is echoing the thesis of his 1979 Pulitzer Prize–winning, best-selling meditative book, to wit, that there is a relationship between the visible and the invisible world. In scientific terms, there are hidden links between formal systems, to such an extent, argues Hofstader, that the formal system underlying all mental activity transcends the system that supports it. So, if one can imagine how life evolves from the chemical substrate of a cell, or consciousness from a system of interactive neurons, then does it not follow that computers might attain human intelligence? And might they not attain a level of intelligence that surpasses each individual and cumulatively approaches omniscience, and omnipotence, qualities linked traditionally with the Thing, the Absolute, the One? That is the eureka of modern science, the holy grail of the human search for a formal system of such intricacy and accessibility, at once material and conscious, that it models God/Allah. *Gödel, Escher, Bach* conjures "an eternal golden braid" as the metaphor for such a God-like machine, and in Willow's novel, the chief protagonist, Alif, pursues pseudo-mathematical logic exercises with the same intent: to shadow and so evoke the divine through a numerical model. In one of these exercises, which happens to be written in English, Alif recognizes: "GOD = God Over Djinn [playing on the initial letters, and recognizing djinn as the equivalent way of writing jinn in English]. GOD = God over Djinn over Djinn. GOD = God Over Djinn Over Djinn over Djinn."[16]

In short, Alif recognizes, as he is reading Intisar's thesis about *Alf Yeom*, that she has hit upon the importance of recursive algorithms, a pivotal element in cognitive science. "'Douglas Hofstadter,' he repeated, 'Intisar has one of his recursive algorithms in her thesis. God equals God over jinn—they spell it with a *d* in English. It is a mathematical model in which God sits on an infinite pillar of jinn who hand our questions up and down, and the answers down and down. The joke—or maybe it's serious—is that GOD can never be fully expanded.'"[17] Not fully expanded except within the '*d*,' which provides an infinite regression through the world of the *djinn*! A scientific tall tale? Yes, but also a journey through the *barzakh* realm of the *djinn* into another glimpse of the Thing, the Absolute, the One.

SUMMARY

Allah is no more violent than Yahweh of the Hebrew Bible or less loving than the Triune God—the Father, Son, and Holy Spirit—of the New Testament. What is most necessary is also the most difficult: to restore context, and so introduce nuance, into each statement that begins *"Islam is . . . ," "The Qur'an says . . . ," "Muslims believe . . ."* All three points of access to a global civilization—the religion, Islam; the book, the Qur'an; the community at large, Muslims—have enormous internal variety. If one only looks at the earliest period, Muslims are more peaceful and nonviolent than Mahatma Gandhi or George Fox (founder of the Quakers), but if one looks at the most recent period, from Sayyid Qutb of the Muslim Brothers and Osama bin Laden of Al-Qaida, one could argue that the most radical religious activists link themselves to the Qur'an, see themselves as Muhammad's loyal followers, and justify their destructive acts with the clarion cry: *Allahu Akbar.*

But one must be careful at the same time not to draw the wrong conclusions from these observations. It is a miniscule minority of fundamentalist activists, led by a charismatic leader and bolstered by the tools of the Information Age, who have created a wholly different and largely negative view in the public's mind regarding Islamic war or jihad—and by extension about Islam in general, to wit, that Islam has espoused violence since its origin. However, the vast majority of the 1.6 billion Muslims in the world have more immediate concerns for survival as citizens within viable nation-states. And though their voices are seldom heard in the drone of crisis reporting, one can scarcely doubt that most Muslims, like most non-Muslims, are appalled by what is being done to them also in the name of Islam. To the extent that Muslims struggle under the banner of jihad, they subscribe to the original interpretation of jihad in the Qur'an; they view it in its more limited context, that is, as primarily a defensive action against persons and property. Since the Iranian Revolution of 1978 and even more since the horror of 9/11, it has been all too easy, and too frequent, to condemn Islam and all Muslims for violence done in the name of Allah. That reflex needs to be kept in check and balanced by the long view of history. Most Muslims are no more bound by the acts of terrorists than are Christians or the Catholic Church for murderous events during the days of the Crusades or the Inquisitions that persisted from the twelfth to the mid-nineteenth century.

And among those who have a more sanguine view of the cosmic drama played out in the world beyond, but also in this world, is the novelist Willow Wilson. The counterpoint that she provides in *Alif the Unseen* to Bin Laden's stark vision is also echoed in the creative work of other representatives of Islam who, like her, are devoted to the truth of the Qur'an and the message of Allah as announced by Gabriel, revealed by Muhammad, and recorded in the Qur'an. It is a vista of hope not doom, confidence in Allah's mercy rather than complicity in his wrath, and some of its most ardent advocates are also cybernauts, those Muslim trollers on the World Wide Web whose numbers and influence have increased dramatically in the past twenty years. We will explore their approach to Allah in the next chapter.

The part mirrors the whole.
All information is stored in every volume of space.
—Ahmed Hulusi

When it comes to God's Word, I would say that only the latest edition of God's
Word is in Arabic. God's Word has been revealed in other languages; for example
God did not speak Arabic to Moses or Adam. Arabic is merely the language of the
latest God's Word edition and thus a useful tool to understand it, but it is
not intrinsically any more sacred than other languages.
—Jalees Rehman

CHAPTER FIVE

Allah Online

Practices in Cyberspace

OVERVIEW

It has often been remarked that Arabic is the sacred language of Islam,
so much so that one cannot imagine Islamic discourse or ritual or community or piety without Arabic. To put that pronouncement in perspective, one needs only to consider that over 80 percent of the world's
1.6 billion Muslims are not Arabs. They neither speak Arabic nor have
Arab ancestry. They are non-Arabs. Most come from two parts of Asia:
the Indian subcontinent, or South Asia; and the Pacific archipelago, or
Southeast Asia. Yet the last prophet, in an Islamic calculus, was the Arab
merchant turned messenger Muhammad, and the language he spoke,
as the language of the Book in which God's Word was revealed to him,
was Arabic.

One might ask: *If* Allah had revealed His Final Dispensation to an
Englishman, would it not have been possible for Allah to have provided
the right English words to convey the same rich nuances and mean-

ing in English to Prophet William (hypothetical) that the Arabic Qur'an evokes through the Prophet Muhammad (actual)? The answer would be YES, but only if we can also imagine English to have evolved as a different instrument of human communication than it now is. The nature of Semitic languages in general and Arabic in particular diverges from Indo-European languages, and the challenge of translation persists to the present day.[1] Parallel to that challenge is the challenge of making sense of Arabic in our time: What are we to make of the role of Arabic in the twenty-first century, in real space but also in cyberspace?[2]

TWO OPPOSING VIEWS OF ARABIC AND ALLAH

If the distance between Islam's origins and its current demography has produced divergent reactions, the two quotations at the head of this chapter mirror the opposite perspectives on Arabic. Ahmed Hulusi tells us that all information is contained in the smallest dot, with the dot under the first Arabic letter *b*, which begins the Qur'an, being the index of all space. But Jalees Rehman informs us that there is no singular or intrinsic sanctity to Arabic; it just happens to be the language of the last installment of God's Word, the divine revelation, given to an Arab prophet.[3]

What is more remarkable than either of these assertions is the authority of their authors. One is a self-described Sufi master from Turkey now living in North Carolina. The other is a medical researcher from Pakistan now living and working in Illinois. Neither is an Arab by birth, neither speaks Arabic as his native tongue, and neither has any serious credentials as a religious scholar. Nor do they represent the knowledge class of traditional Islam (the *'ulama*). Instead they project their views through the Internet, and so what they say is equally as accessible as views that can, and do, claim to represent the mainstream, orthodox view of Islam, the Arabic language, and Allah.

VIRTUAL ACCESS TO ALLAH: A TWENTY-YEAR ODYSSEY

The upsurge of virtual authority has come without checks or balances, so much so that it might be called pseudo-authority. The dominance of the World Wide Web has been as swift as it was unexpected. It has exploded in less than two decades, with dizzying changes. Since the mid-1990s the Information Revolution has transformed all facets of global communication, with a marked impact on Muslim references to sacred texts and sacred names, including Allah. Until the mid-1990s three forms of media defined the Information Age: print (newspapers, books), audio (radio, telephone, tape cassettes, and cell phones), and audiovisual (television and movies). But since then the Internet, global cellular service, and satellite television have dramatically reshaped the landscape of communication and knowledge management. Consider satellite television, which, after overcoming local censorship barriers, has played a huge role in Muslim countries. Al-Jazeera was established in the late 1990s, created by BBC-trained reporters and sponsored by the Emir of Qatar. During the post-9/11 period this satellite television station broadcasting from the Arabian Gulf became as familiar to American viewers as CNN. It provided the world with otherwise unavailable coverage, and in a virtual theater brought together viewers from all over the Arab, Muslim, and even non-Muslim worlds. But even Al-Jazeera has been less revolutionary in the marketplace of ideas than has the Internet.

In Saudi Arabia, AwalNet was the first Internet service provider in the kingdom. On 7 November 1999, it published an article online in which it promised to "marry the Internet and Islam for the millennium."[4] Linking people, places, ideas, and commodities with an immediacy that seems to conquer space, the Internet has engendered a new way of being in the world that the French philosopher Paul Virilio's calls "tele-presence," or the technologically enhanced capacity to "be" in several places at the same time. Muslims may also form contingent virtual communities at the collective and individual levels to provide safety, companionship, social support, and a sense of belonging, as in the case of WLUML.

Tele-presence enables a new form of association that compels a reconsideration of the meaning of community. What is community when participants do not share place but can communicate as if they do? There have long been disparate communities, but they have never been as rapidly connected or as broadly inclusive as those facilitated by the World Wide Web. If shared physical place is not a necessary condition for aggregation and collaboration, is the notion of community as embodied contact merely the romantic projection of an idealized past? The answer of the Internet, Facebook, Twitter, and Blogspot has been a resounding: YES! Newly formed virtual communities require only shared ideals, along with the commitment to advocate for common interests by any means possible.

The Internet has compelled a rethinking not only of communities

WLUML in Virtual Space

WLUML is the acronym for Women Living under Muslim Law, a women's advocacy group begun in France in 1984 but then accelerated first on the Internet and now on Facebook, expanding its influence through a global solidarity network in French, English, and Arabic. Its self-declared goal is to "provide information, support and a collective space for women whose lives are shaped, conditioned or governed by laws & customs said to derive from Islam."

and communications but also of places. One must revisit and reimagine cities, states, and boundaries. This extraordinary acceleration in global connectivity produced a tsunami of Muslim networks that are equally committed to Allah, His Messenger, and His Book, yet also compete with each other. It is hardly a battle of equals. Afro-Asian Muslim students who came to the United States to be trained as engineers in the 1970s were the first to create Islamic websites (notably, through Muslim student associations) and to become catalysts for digitizing Islam. They put scripture online, making available many renditions of Qurʾan and *hadith* that facilitated the production of new *ijtihads*, or interpretations of foundational texts.

WHOSE ALLAH ONLINE?

The central question raised by these student groups and other Muslim cybernauts was: "Can humanity's relationship with Allah be projected through a digital interface?"[5] In its initial phase, individual Muslim engineers online answered affirmatively, but their enthusiasm led others to adopt what have been called officializing strategies. Instead of allowing a bottom-up, grassroots approach to flourish, mainstream intelligentsia and national orthodoxies attempted to control digital resources in order to project—and protect—their view of Islam in cyberspace. What mattered was not just who could read the Internet but who controlled the webmasters and the websites that claimed to speak on behalf of all Muslims. Among the fiercest battles has been the contest to define or redefine Allah.

These efforts from national groups, or groups that support national

Whose Islam Online?

The mainstream Sunni site islamicity.com ranks thirteenth among all Islamic websites, while the smaller Shiʿi community has its portal al-Islam.org ranked fifteenth. The dissident Ahmadiyya, with the fewest numbers, still reach many cyber searchers through alislam.org and rank twenty-third, according to an authoritative website.

interests, are not always transparent. Consider one of the most frequented Muslim websites, IslamiCity. Ranked thirteenth in one popular Web-monitoring site, it is an offshoot of HADI, or the Human Assistance and Development International, a Saudi overseas holding company based in California.[6] In Arabic *hadi* means guide or leader, and this site guides Muslim cybernauts toward Saudi norms and values. It reflects the effort of the Saudi government to project itself as the bastion of Islamic orthodoxy.

The HADI-sponsored websites are very different from those created by a socially active but numerically small Shiʿi subcommunity, the Ismaʿilis. In turn, their sites are internally highly diverse. Even within this demographically tiny subset of the Muslim community there is a huge diversity of ethnicity, faith, and practice. The Agha Khanis (a subsect in the Shiʿi community) contrast with Bohras (another Shiʿi subsect, predominately in India), who themselves are divided between progressives and conservatives.[7] One of the most dramatic, if little reported, contests is for the portal name "Islam." The Twelver Shiʿis, representing the major group of those self-identified as Shiʿi Muslim, obtained the portal al-Islam.org, while the major Sunni site became islam.org, islamic.org, and islamicity.org before settling on islamicity.com. At the same time, a group representing a Sunni offshoot, the Ahmadiyya, obtained the portal name alislam.org.

As confusing as are all these website names, online sites have proliferated at such a dizzying rate that one of the experts in Muslim cyberspace has contrasted the predigital with the digital era as follows: "The Internet opens up opportunities for further access to insider perspectives and analyses from specific worldviews. Unfortunately in some cases this material comes shrouded in either anti-Islamic rhetoric or in content that seeks to present a homogenized interpretation of Islam focused on one

The Case of Islam Online

A popular website linked to Sheikh Yusuf al-Qaradawi, a leading religious scholar from Egypt now living in Qatar, was shut down in 2010 when the government decided not to support the "moderate" views of the sheikh. Though now funded from alternative sources, it is still a much-visited website, ranking nineteenth among Islamic websites by one estimate, but it no longer has the broad appeal that it enjoyed before being censored. Its scope and pronouncements are restricted to conservative or Salafi interpretations of Sunni Islam.

school of thought. Often, grassroots material produced on blogs and in social-networking contexts may have a greater resonance than staid official sites."[8]

The message in cyberspace is clear: there is no single Islamic orthodoxy that can claim the mantle of virtual authority. In the name of Allah, rival orthodoxies have proliferated; each proclaiming to show what devout Muslims must do to conform to their sacred trust. The analogy posed by the intellectual historian Gertrude Himmelfarb applies to Islam as to all other online advocates. "Like post-modernism, the Internet does not distinguish between the true and the false, the important and the trivial, the enduring and the ephemeral."[9] Without virtual authorities or consensus ethical standards, the trillions of sound bites, images, and recordings provided on the World Wide Web produce not clarity but cacophony, and this chaos poses severe problems for those who seek Allah as Truth (*al-haqq*), another of the Beautiful Names. It reflects a larger dilemma facing all surfers of the Internet, or cybernauts, but nowhere more so than when what poses as sacred narratives conceal less than sacred sources.

TWO PROFESSORS TRACKING ALLAH ONLINE

Perhaps the most astute observer of Islam on the Internet today is the British Islamic studies scholar Gary Bunt. Not only does Bunt track what he calls cyber-Islamic environments (CIES) but he also demonstrates how Islamic source codes, as well as blogospheres, work. As one would expect, a major focus of attention is the online presentation of daily ritual elements, the crucial centerpiece being the *adhan*. This is the five-time call to prayer that begins with the *takbir*, or pronouncement of *Allahu Akbar*. As Bunt explains, the range of options is itself dizzying: "there are many versions available for download for use on a computer, an MP3 player, or a cell phone or to be burned into a CD/DVD. They may come with commentaries and translations or be available to view on YouTube or MySpace."[10]

Despite the blizzard of information and ways to secure that information, it is possible to sort out hyperlinks on Islam, that is, online resources that examine every facet of Islamic history, scripture, ritual, and practice. If one had to choose but one comprehensive site, it might be the webpage of Georgia University professor Alan Godlas. This Sufi scholar turned cybernaut offers a feast of options, often identifying whether or not a specific link is Sunni or Shi'i, Salafi or Sufi, convert or immigrant, Middle Eastern, North African, or South Asian in its outlook.[11] Almost a decade ago I was trying to imagine how the Internet would impact the servants of Allah, that is, the global Muslim community, or at least those members of the *umma* who use the Internet as a major resource for faith as well as commerce. What I said then remains true today: "The Qur'an stands as the linchpin of Muslim belief and practice. It affirms Allah as the One, the God of creation and judgment, both in this world and the next. Yet we must ask, and Muslims also must and do ask: who interprets the Qur'an, and what makes one interpretation more valid than another?"[12]

VIRTUAL ISLAM BEYOND MUSLIM RELIGIOUS SPECIALISTS

A contemporary Muslim scholar has provided one pathway in the twenty-first century. "The greatest challenge for both Muslims and non-Muslims," writes Ziauddin Sardar, "is to read the Qur'an on its own terms, to engage with its text unencumbered by prejudices and preconceived ideas, to free our minds as far as humanly possible from what we have been told to understand, and encounter its words anew."[13] Aware of this awesome challenge, he adds: "I write as Every Muslim; as an individual trying to understand what the Qur'an means to me in the twenty-first century. . . . To accept the Qur'an as eternal means acknowledging that there is always more to the text than our partial intellect will comprehend, and to begin one's reading from that premise with humility."[14]

Yet there are those others who also add to this debate: "Muslims who advocate, or allow themselves to be convinced by, a literal reading of the Qur'an; worse, they insist that this literalism contains all the answers necessary to live in the twenty-first century." Even religious specialists have to be distrusted, for most of them "exist in hermetically sealed religious and cultural capsules, and can spout little more than slogans that are dangerously obsolete. . . . Muslim scholars and experts should not be gatekeepers, permanently excluding the rest from using their own knowledge and insight to make sense of the Qur'an for themselves."[15]

THE SECRET MADE PUBLIC

Nowhere is the need for pragmatic guidance, both to the Holy Qur'an and to Allah online, more evident than in the field of Sufi studies. Among the most impressive websites are those that emanate from Turkey, whether it is the Gulen movement; its precursor, the Nursi movement; the less circumspect Harun Yahya;[16] or the vibrant Allah watcher Ahmed Hulusi. All these individuals can be found through generic or their own branded websites. For instance, http://www.en.fgulen.com includes a prayer to Allah to limit damage from Hurricane Sandy, which wrought havoc on the U.S. East Coast in the fall of 2012. No less virtually omnipresent than Gulen is his predecessor and inspiration Bediuzzaman Said Nursi. Both have extensive websites in English as well as Turkish, and http://www.bediuzzamansaidnursi.org/en provides the iconic glaring stare of Nursi, along with the entire 6,000-page *Risale-i Nur*, a kind of patchwork Qur'an commentary, with numerous references to Allah. At http://www.harunyahya.com one finds Allah repeatedly extolled, but always with attention to the brand name of His most vocal advocate, Harun Yahya. And then there is yet another Turkish exile in

Gulen in America

One of the most powerful expatriate voices on Islam in modern-day Turkey, Fetullah Gulen has been a U.S. resident since 1999. He and his movement are the subjects of heated debate in the public media, not least due to his advocacy of a strong role for charter schools to jumpstart science education in America. The intent of the Gulen charter schools is commendable: to provide the next generation of American youth with sorely needed arithmetic skills. But their advocacy of Turkish cultural nationalism still worries many.

America, Ahmed Hulusi, less famous or controversial than Gulen, but he too offers a feast of novel and traditional insights into Allah at http://www.ahmedhulusi.org/en.

While it is impossible to do justice to all these sources, one can, and must, note that what they share is a common interest and a persistent dedication to connecting Islam in general and Allah in particular to the claims of modern science. How can that be done? By trying to trace numerical patterns, often with a blinkered focus on the number nineteen as a hidden Qur'anic code confirming Allah's creation of the universe. The hero, or some might say villain, in this ongoing saga is Rashad Khalifa. The son of an Egyptian Sufi master, he was a biochemist who emigrated to the United States in the late 1950s and became a naturalized citizen, living and working in Arizona. Though he had no credentials as a Qur'anic scholar, he had a passion for discovering mathematical secrets that "proved" the divine authorship of the Qur'an. He produced several books between the early 1970s and the late 1980s. All were self-published, and all focused on the mysterious properties of the number nineteen. He was murdered in 1990, and in a strange twist of fate it was not till nineteen years later that his assailant was arrested, arraigned, and convicted of first-degree murder.[17]

ALLAH AND MODERN SCIENCE: THE EDUCATION OPTION

More serious and sustained on the Internet is the effort to marry God with science by matching some dimension of the Beautiful Names with a scientific insight or discovery. Bediuzzaman Said Nursi, the predecessor to Fethullah Gulen, personifies this quest in twentieth-century Turkey. Born in 1873 in the village of Nurs (southeastern Turkey), Said Nursi was deeply influenced by the curriculum of scriptural studies as well as the conservative atmosphere of his region. At first, he hoped to revive religious learning in Ottoman institutions while opposing the secular spirit of Kemalism that dominated Turkey after World War I. Until the mid-1920s he charted a course separate from the fierce politics of Republican Turkey and opposed it publicly when a separatist Kurdish revolt broke out in the southeast in 1925. Yet the Kemalists distrusted him and succeeded in having him deported from his hometown and the region where he had lived. From his deportation to approximately the beginning of 1950s, Said Nursi remained remote from politics, dedicating his time to writing and sharing his ideas with newly converted disciples and followers. But he did not live in quiet seclusion. Even after his deportation, he was considered enough of a threat to the stability of the state that he was arrested and imprisoned for eleven years (1935–46). Most of what is now known as *Risale-i Nur* was in fact written in prison. It was here where he converted his first followers and where his thought evolved from the goal of Islamizing the state to the more encompassing objective of Islamizing the spirit of Muslims through education.

Education became the enduring legacy of the movement named after him, the Nurcu Movement. Said Nursi turned his ban from public life into a virtue. Not only did he remain aloof from politics but he denounced the politicization of religion. He called on his followers to refrain from any involvement with a party or political movement; they were to concentrate on the teachings of Islam and the role of Allah in their everyday life. Islam meant redirecting oneself to Allah through the private practice of ritual duties, while at the same time pursuing the public advocacy of education, especially scientific education. In his view Islam must be modern to survive, and for him the development of Islam in the context of modernity had to come through mass public education. Allah was not just the Lord of Creation and the Revealer of the Qur'an but also the Guardian of Today's World and the Force behind Modern Science.

Modern science, in Nursi's view, had two different but complementary aspects. First, he saw technology, and especially telecommunications and the media, as a tool for disseminating his ideas and attracting the younger generation. In this respect, he was far more advanced than most secular Turkish modernists as well as his religiously minded compatriots. Second, Nursi focused on the principles of science, and the defining spirit and required syllabus. Very early, he advocated updating the classical approach of the *madrasa*, or Islamic school, by introducing mathematics, physics, and logic into the educational curriculum. He had a single, overriding objective: to demonstrate that Islam belonged to the present and the future just as much as science and modernity did. Though not everyone followed the logic of this spiritual entrepreneur, he remains arguably the most influential force in contemporary Turkish culture; many share, and promote, his vision of combining secular with religious elements in Turkish society.[18]

THE CASE OF AHMED HULUSI

To see how Islam is married to science through the Internet, consider the eccentric role of the last of the four Turkish public figures cited above, all with major audiences beyond Turkey, many in North America and the United States. All are committed to cyber jihad of Allah ta'ala through the World Wide Web, and all have a lively presence on the Internet. Here is how the fourth of them, Ahmed Hulusi, presents Allah in his latest online book, also self-published in paperback. The critical argument comes in the subtitle: *A Sufi Perspective in Light of the Letter B*. Later it is summarized with a gloss on two key Qur'anic verses as follows:

> *O you who have believed*; Aminu B'illahi, That is, O you who have
>   believed, believe in Allah in accord with the meaning signified by
>   the letter B. (Q 4:136)
> And of the people are some who say, *"We believe in Allah* (in accord
>   with the meaning of the letter B—that His Names comprise
>   our being) *and the life after* (that we will forever live the
>   consequences of our deeds)," *but they are not believers* (in accord
>   with the meaning of the letter B). (Q 2:8)

While the approach of the author is fascinating, even within a Sufi worldview, it is not novel. Others have tried to fathom what is the meaning of the *b* in the *basmala*, which is itself the first mention of Allah in the name of the Noble Book, the Holy Qur'an.[19] What is novel here is the author's unabashed commitment to linking his interpretive strategy to modern science. In the prologue to *Decoding the Qur'an*, Hulusi offers a quote attributed to Muhammad: "The part mirrors the whole." Paired with it and given equivalent space is a dictum from modern physics: "All

Quantum Mechanics and Holographic Principle

The *Holographic Principle* is a property of quantum gravity and string theories that suggests a description of, or information about, how a volume of space can be encoded on the boundary of the region. *Quantum theory* in physics describes the interactions of atoms, protons, neutrons, electrons, and other subatomic particles. *String theory* (in one of five different versions) proposes that all subatomic particles and forms of energy could be explained by one-dimensional "strings," and that the universe is made up of multiple dimensions, indeed multiple universes. *M-theory* is a modern attempt to mathematically reconcile the disparate "string theories"—resulting in a *Theory of Everything* that would rationalize the theory of relativity, space-time, gravity, and quantum theory.

information [that can be accessed] is stored in every volume of space" (quantum mechanics and the holographic principle).

"He who wants to observe the reality," we are then told, "can do so even on a single verse. . . . Whether manifest in worldly form or a literal verse encrypted in the Qur'an. . . . For just as the part contains the whole, so a single verse can be a gateway into endless realizations, both inward and outward."[20]

What we have here is an argument that connects the infinitely small to the unimaginably large—from the underlying fundamental particles and energy to the cosmic universe(s). We follow a chain of logic that begins with the Qur'an but weaves its message through modern science, in this case, quantum mechanics and the holographic principle. The beauty of the argument is that all of creation seems to be derived from, and confirmed by, the Qur'an. At the same time, however, the core of the Qur'an—its rich rhetorical storehouse of Divine Names—is here linked to the first name Allah, but more precisely to the preposition *ba*, and even more precisely to the dot that is beneath that preposition in Arabic.

In effect, we are presented with a regressive argument. It recedes back to smaller and smaller elements to test its validity. The serial reduction of focus goes from Creation to Qur'an to First Chapter to First Verse to First Word to First Letter to First Mark under the First Letter. It is the Arabic *'ism*, "name," which introduces Allah in the phrase *ba-*

ism-Allah, and from this elision and compression we have the *basmala*: *bismi(A)llah.* The author explains the *basmala* as a trigger system.[21] He uses it to decode the Qur'an and, by inference, all of Creation, the Universe, Human Destiny, and Final Purpose. Once properly and sincerely invoked, the *basmala* unlocks all the mysteries of the Qur'an through the invocation of the 'B,' with special attention to the dot under the B!

While seemingly seductive in its integration of Sufism and science, this is a dangerous, double game, for once the revealed word of Allah is taken to be authoritative, not on its own merit but because its content is confirmed by the discoveries, the practices and the claims of modern science, the vector of authority is reversed: science confirms Allah, not Allah science. By the logic employed by Ahmed Hulusi, and not only him but also numerous others who have sought to reconcile modern science with *Allah ta'ala,*[22] it is science that confirms Allah's Word, the Qur'an, not the Qur'an that confirms science. Traditionally, the trust of Allah to humankind has been expressed in, and measured by, the final revelation to Muhammad, the Noble Book, the Holy Qur'an. But now the Qur'an ceases to be a book apart from other books; it becomes instead a book that stands tested, and confirmed, on the anvil of modern science, with its scientific method, hypotheses, empirical evidence, guidelines, and protocols. The question raised by modern science is the same question raised in every age: which authority is it that makes and shapes and confounds the world? Is it Allah or science? If they are elided, which is prioritized? The Thing, the Absolute, the One? Or the contingent, the finite, the many? While Allah is invoked, it is scientific authority that pervades, at once verified and expanded, online. The mystical and the metaphysical become the litmus test of truth as measured by quantum physics and cosmology. Forgotten is the nature of knowing. All science is subject to change. A pursuit of human knowledge, it is always limited by its agency, and even at its apogee it cannot be the same category of either knowing or being (epistemology or ontology) linked to the One beyond knowing.

NAWAL SAADAWI AND ALLAH AS ALLAT

Along with Sufi exponents of scientism, feminist advocates have joined the virtual quest for Allah during the past two decades. Not only the mystical and metaphysical but also the feminist pro-goddess approach to Allah has been enhanced online since the beginning of the Information Age. Often what is virtual is also linked to what is literary. Not all books have been discarded, not all writers have ceased to write or to publish novels. And one Muslim woman who embodies the two vectors—virtual and literary—also sits astride the real-time battle between male triumphalists and female advocates for the heart of the Muslim world.

It was back in the mid-1990s that my friend, the Egyptian author and activist Nawal Saadawi, asked me to consider the relationship between Allah and Allat. "Might there not be two creator gods in pre-Islamic Arabia?" she asked, "and if so, what did that mean about orthodox notions of Allah?" She broached this precise question in her novel, *The Innocence of the Devil* (*Jannat wa Iblis*) (1994). It is only when the heroine of the novel dies and is lying in a coffin that her true name appears:

Ganat Abd Allah Abdil Illah!

Her eyes opened wide and the pupils grew bigger and bigger. It was as though she were seeing her triple name for the first time. Abdallah? Who was Abdallah? Was it her father's name? Abdil Illah? Was it her grandfather's name? Her memory awakened little by little. Her grandmother's voice echoed in her ears like a whistle. She was calling her grandfather Abdillat, changing the h into t. Her grandfather almost jumped out of his high-backed chair.

Abdil Illah not Abdillat

Her grandmother opened her mouth wide, took a long deep breath and expelled it slowly. She stuck out her tongue between two parted lips to pronounce the letter properly, but it seemed to twist from her and change the h into t.

> ### The Significance of A'udhu bi(A)llahi
> The last two chapters of the Qur'an (Q 113, 114) are called
> *Mu'awidhatayn* because they begin with this phrase. They are said
> to have special apotropaic powers, and the phrase *A'udhu bi(A)llahi*
> *min ash-shaitan ar-rajim* ("I take refuge in Allah from the accursed
> Satan") is so important that it is often recited before the *basmala* of
> the Qur'an. The reciter protects himself from the Devil before uttering
> the Word of Allah.

And then the debate goes on about which pronunciation or name is correct, and to help the reader a footnote explains: "Illat in the Arabian peninsula was a female goddess before Islam. Her name was written in the same way as Illah/Allah, the monotheistic God of Islam, but two dots are added to the last letter."

And later in the dialogue, the grandmother, speaking to Ganat in her grave, observes: "Making a history out of two dots. Turning the world upside down just because of two dots. May God take you from this world."

In another flashback, the deceased Ganat remembers that as a student in school the Devil, the other protagonist in the novel, had constantly called on her to recite *"A'udhu billahi"* ("I take refuge in God") but to modify it and to substitute *"A'udhu billati"* ("I take refuge in the Goddess"). As an antidote to that mistake, the teacher has all the girls, not just Ganat, recite the verses from the Qur'an (Q 53:19–22) that refer to the three goddesses (Al-Lat, Al-Uzza, and Manat).[23]

For those cybernauts who want to contest Nawal's heroine, or perhaps to support her case for expanding the reference field of Allah to include Allat, there are multiple online references to Allat and her crucial role in pre-Islamic Arabia. One hyperlink depicts Allat as a primal mother goddess, and also the mother of all the Arab tribes. She is said to be among the earliest deities and to be a consort of Allah.[24] Allat is lauded, above all, as a goddess of fertility and wisdom.[25]

Despite the repeated efforts to marshal evidence of a Muslim conspiracy to disconnect Allah from Allat, the actual history of these two names is well recorded in Islamic sources. Some of the best-attested versions of Allat's pre-Islamic history come from feminist blogs. There we are informed that Allat was worshiped by all of the tribes and in all of the kingdoms of ancient Arabia, a claim that cannot be verified even though inscriptions and god lists from various cities do show her to be among the most powerful and revered goddesses of Arabia. The Thaqif tribe from Ta'if held her in especially high regard, and it is perhaps more than coincidental to note that Mecca and Ta'if were competitive trade centers in early seventh-century Hijaz. In effect, the supremacy of Allah also registered the supremacy of the Meccan God over the Taif Goddess, though that link remains conjectural.[26]

It could be deduced that in pre-Islamic Arabia Allah and Allat were allied, not so much as deities of specific natural forces but as pan-tribal deities. At the same time, Allat was also often seen as the protective deity over a specific tribe, the Thaqif in Ta'if. Those who search for the divine feminine will continue to see her as the shadow, or partner, of Allah, especially in the many virtual communities that now dot the World Wide Web.[27]

ALLAH AS HU: OFFLINE

No less haunting than the connection of Allah to Allat is the repeated accent on Allah as *huwa* or *hu*, reflecting the importance of the pronoun *hu*, or "he" in many of the Qur'anic passages extolling Allah. On the World Wide Web one can quickly scan Allah as *hu* and find over 13 million sites. One of them is a song by the world-famous Sufi vocalist, or *qawwal*, Nusrat Fateh Ali Khan. It is titled *Allah Hoo Allah Hoo*.[28]

I do not have to go online to be reminded of the power of the pronoun *hu* to represent Allah. Daily I experience the force of that name from the unseen, unknowable world projected to the everyday visible world of my life. Each day I am reminded of this connection when I return home, whether from work or from travel, and look at my living room wall. There hangs a picture from the Moroccan artist Mohamed Melehi (figure 10). This image compels me to ask, and to ask repeatedly, the now-familiar question: Is there a supreme name for God? Is it Allah or one of the other ninety-nine names? Or is it instead just the pronoun *huwa* or *hu* that is represented in the Moroccan artist's notion of primal forms and colors, each unfolding but also recoding their source—*hu* or *huwa*—staring out like an eye at all that surrounds, reflects, yet also eludes the One, the Source of Light/Dark, Life/Death, Male/Female.

Once when I was in the company of Ibrahim Abu Nab, a noted Pal-

Fig. 10. *Hu* in bright acrylic colors by Mohamed Melehi. Ha 2, 1984.
Courtesy of Mohamed Melehi.

they are "*Qul huwa (A)llahu Ahad Allahu Samad.*" Ibrahim indicated that repetition produces results not otherwise imagined. Try it, he said, and we did. After myriad repetitions *Samad* and *Ahad*, two of the most prominent Beautiful Names, seem to merge with Allah. One ceases to say the whole phrase, and instead just focuses on "*Qul huwa Allah, Qul huwa Allah.*" These three words become the next series of vocal foci, but again after a long period of repetitions, Allah folds into *huwa*, yet without Allah *huwa* becomes simply *hu*, and so the final phase of repetitions is an increasingly intense recitation of *hu, hu, hu.*[29]

THE SUPREME NAME FROM A CHISHTI MASTER

Whether looking at a painting, speaking with a spiritual giant, listening to music, or surfing online, one cannot escape the fascination with seeking the supreme name of Allah. Among Sufi cybernauts is a Chishti *shaykh*, a Sufi master in the lineage of Mu'in ad-din, Qutb ad-din, Farid ad-din, Nizam ad-din, and Nasir ad-din Chiragh-i Delhi. So absorbed was he in the quest for the supreme name that he posted an anecdote to illustrate both its importance and its elusiveness.

> Someone asked him if Fakhr ad-din Razi was right when he said that the Supreme Name is a specific name and that people are able to know it. Some of the names suggested are:
>
> *Hu* or *Huwa* (He)
> *Allah*
> *Al-Hayy, al-Qayyum* (The Living, The Everlasting)
> *Dhu'l-jalal-wa'l-ikram* (The Lord of Majesty and Bounty, the name from *Surat ar-Rahman*)
> The supreme name may also be found in the "isolated letters" at the beginning of several Qur'anic chapters [different suggestions are offered]

> Baba Farid, who is one of the most important Chishti masters, prefers the third option (*al-Hayy al-Qayyum*), but here is what ar-Razi writes about it:

> > It has been reported that Abu ibn Ka'b asked the messenger of Allah (Allah's blessings and peace be upon him) to teach him the

supreme name. He answered: "It can be found in these words: '*Allah! There is no god but He, the Living, the Everlasting*' (Q 2:255) and in these words: '*A, L, M. Allah! There is no god but He, the Living, the Everlasting*'" (Q 3:1–2).

The companions, hearing this, said: "It cannot be anything else than saying Allah! There is no god but He, as it can be found in a great number of verses. But because of the fact that the messenger of Allah has indicated that the supreme name can be found in these two verses, he has taught us that it cannot be anything else than the Living, the Everlasting."

Without further comment Fakhruddin Razi told this story: Someone once asked Ja'far as-Sadiq a question about the supreme name. To the man who asked him about the supreme name Ja'far answered:

"First, take a bath and purify yourself and then I'll teach you the supreme name." The man went into the bath in order to make a complete ablution. At that time, as it was Winter, the water was extremely cold, but every time that the man wanted to leave the water Ja'far ordered his companions to make it impossible for the man to leave the water. They pushed him back several times and his pleading was of no avail. Eventually he started to believe that they wanted to do something bad; perhaps they even wanted to kill him. He began to implore Allah to help him escape from their hands. When they heard him say this prayer, they allowed him to leave the water.

Immediately the man went to Ja'far as-Sadiq and begged him:

Fakhruddin Razi and Ja'far as-Sadiq

Fakhruddin Razi and Ja'far as-Sadiq are intellectual giants with contrasting pedigrees. While the thirteenth-century Razi is the most famous rationalist commentator on the Qur'an, the eighth-century Ja'far is a direct descendant of the Prophet Muhammad honored both by Sufis and Shi'is alike. Not only did Ja'far author his own commentary on the Qur'an, but his eldest son, Isma'il, also became the eponymous founder of the Isma'ili subset within Shi'i Islam, precursors of the Agha Khan and his followers.

"Now, please teach me the supreme name of Allah!" Ja'far replied: "My dear friend! You already have learned the supreme name by which you have implored Allah, and He has answered you by granting what you asked." "How is that?" said the man. "No name of Allah," replied Ja'far, "No name of Allah, no matter how great it might be, can be useful, if you are invoking Him while your heart remains attached to another than Him. But if you invoke Him after you have lost all your desires and turn only to Him, then whatever name you use, becomes the supreme name. When you thought that we wanted to kill you, you lost hope and in your heart trusted only in the compassion of Allah. In such a state whatever name you might invoke, that is the supreme name."[30]

SUMMARY

No roadmap exists in virtual space. There is a surfeit of information with a lack of guidelines or guideposts. What we have reviewed here are some of the opportunities, but also some of the dangers, of searching for deeper insight into Allah on the World Wide Web.

The last story quoted, however, does underscore the insistent emphasis in Islamic spirituality on intention. It matters what you intend to do. It also matters how you feel about what you decide or intend to do. Had the American psychologist William James heard this last story, he might have quipped: "It's not what you believe; it's how you *feel* about what you believe." Whether online or offline, there is no end to the quest to understand Allah. What must, and does, create a lingering pause on any quest in real space or cyberspace is the *basmala*, that is, the pronunciation of Allah as both the source of compassion and the endless resource for all who seek compassion: In the name of Allah, Full of Compassion, Ever Compassionate.

Invoked and redefined, remembered and cyber tested is a god who is neither male nor female, but who expresses the female attribute of motherly concern for all her offspring. To move deeper into that mystery is to seek the unseen and the unknowable, to find poems—or music or dance—to express the ineffable. Finally one must end where all circumspect Muslims end: *Allahu a'lam bis-sawab.* God alone knows what is right!

Yet doubters, tongue twisters, literalists, and even terrorists are not satisfied to end at the edge of the ocean. Like the frog from the well, they must leap in—and so yet one final chapter is required to conclude our review of those who seek meaning. They are a motley crew. They seek levels of meaning within the Thing, the Lofty and Exalted One, yet some despise the One sought, while others disregard those (other than themselves) who seek the same One.

It is obvious from our own personal experiences and this short foray into exploring Allah in cyberspace that the Information Age has fundamentally changed the way we live, do business, communicate, travel, and share knowledge. It has also changed our views of what constitutes a "community," as it expands beyond local limits to global horizons. It has provided opportunities for those not engaged in scholarly or literary activities to express more easily their own voice and proffer opinions to vast audiences beyond previous means of distribution (e.g., books or movies). But the fact that there are no "peer reviews" or adjudication of the truth or fiction of what is published makes this new freedom problematic, perhaps even dangerous. An actor in a recent U.S. insurance company commercial is asked, "Where did you hear that?" He responds: "On the Internet, and you know they can't put it there unless it's true." Too often those who troll the Internet for information about Allah, the Qur'an, and other topics of religious interest intuitively assume that what they find is "true." Thus the Internet has opened up the possibility of religious "cyber war," with groups attempting to steer readers and the faithful into whatever they advocate, whether fundamentalism, orthodoxy, or splinter terrorist groups. As we have seen here the Internet has the power to expand ideas, but the question remains: Whose ideas and to what goal or outcome? That requires attention to artists, photographers, and writers, all of whom seek the same connection to Allah as mystics, philosophers, cybernauts, and everyday believers. Their participation in the search for Allah will occupy us in the conclusion.

Conclusion

OVERVIEW

How to think the unthought or imagine the unimaginable?[1] It is at once a project and a challenge—to the mind, to the heart, and even to the notion of self for all those attached to the Name, the Thing, the Absolute, the One: Allah. It has occupied wordsmiths, intellectuals, scholars, mystics, and mainstream practitioners—from the seventh century to the twenty-first century. It has also occupied artists whose language is channeled through the hand and directed to the eyes, the ears, and also the heart. Artists ask: How can art redefine, and reconfigure, what is meant by Allah? Convention and orthodoxy resist both innovation and stimuli for creativity. Though artists often find space at the margin of social acceptability, sometimes in their attempt to bring others into a higher state of awareness, they go beyond what others accept and expect as normal. It is notable how often women have been the pioneers for renewed artistic attention to Allah in recent decades.

There is no single group of either men or women who can be labeled

Muslim artists, and so the conclusion would miss the point of exploring Allah if it only looked at Muslim performers or painters, as though they represented "true" Islam, or took an alternate perspective and looked at Muslim videogames and their entrepreneurs as though *they* were the custodians of Allah and His Word. Both these groups do project a view of Islamic creativity in the public domain. While we will examine representatives from several regions of the Muslim world, we will end with an embodied approach to Allah that circles back to those spiritual warriors known as Sufi masters, featured earlier in chapter 3.

IN THE NAME OF ALLAH: FIGURAL DEATH

To highlight the importance of performance art we begin the conclusion with a picture: in this case an Indonesian woman artist holding aloft a plate with Allah written on it in Arabic (figure 11).

More than just another creative project, the Allah plate is intended to raise a crucial, oft-ignored perspective: there is no normative ethics for works of Muslim art with respect to their disclosures or affective aims. Arahmaiani is a contemporary Javanese performance artist, committed to Islam (her father's religion) but also engaged by Hindu Buddhist beliefs (her mother's persuasion). Whether or not she recognizes Om to have a similar power to Allah in evoking the Eternal Absolute,[2] she aims to shock the sensibilities of Muslim viewers and participants re Allah. In her performance of *Breaking Words*, she wrote *Allah* in Arabic on white ceramic plates. She invited audience members to write on them as well, and then smashed them against the wall.

This iconoclastic gesture took advantage of the bundled material properties of ceramics and inks, but it also suggested the symbolic power of Arabic orthography. Its intent was to shake participants loose from attachments that, in Arahmaiani's view, border on the obsessive and compulsive, not just to know and obey Allah but to presume to act as Allah's sole custodian. For at least several viewers, the smashing of the plates was a hurtful, even hateful blow to Allah and to their affective attachments to Allah through material form. Complaints were lodged with the police at the opening performance and also in subsequent forums at which the artist appeared.

What can we say about the moral status of this artist and her work? "If some artists aim at ethical pleasure through their work," noted a prominent scholar of Indonesian culture, "perhaps we may say that

Fig. 11. Performance artist Arahmaiani with Allah plate.
Courtesy of Arahmaiani and photographer Shu Yang.

Arahmaiani's strives for ethical hurt (not harm) or, better, ethical un-
ease. Arahmaiani is an artist of conscience, yet different people are
made happy by different things [and so] object choices are not equivalent." Arahmaiani seeks to raise the serious but tangled question: in
what context, and with what memories, does one appeal to the sacred as
an unequivocal source of happiness? In shattering the Allah plates, she
hopes to trigger others' awareness of the history of injustice occluded
in the aura of happiness. Her ultimate aim, one might say, is to expose
unhappy effects, to reimagine what else may count as the good life; but
in order to find alternative models of the good, one must first "touch"
the ultimate source of good and bad, hope and despair: Allah. Arahmaiani is even prepared to kill some forms of joy that her viewers take
for granted when they see the name Allah. She also recognizes her own
risk at having to live with the consequences of her provocation.[3]

Part of the outcry against Arahmaiani, of course, was not just her "harm" or "offense" to Allah, but also her resort to visual art, and to performance, as a means of communicating her message. Using Arabic as a pictorial rather than verbal sign is itself an Indonesian reflex that has other parallels, notably in the work of Abdul Djalil Pirous, not least of which is his acrylic representations of the Chapter of Sincerity (Sura Ikhlas: Q 112) and the Chapter of the Forenoon (Sura ad-Duha: Q 93).[4]

But it also resonates with Iranian women artists; among them the University of California, Berkeley, educated Shirin Neshat. Neshat has mounted several exhibits of her photography, including the series *Women of Allah*, shown during the 1990s at major museums across the United States. Its centerpiece is a self-portrait of the artist holding a gun in front of her veiled countenance, with Persian writing scrolling across her face. In explaining the layered elements of this photograph, Neshat notes its three components: the body, the veil, and the text, with an accent on the last. And it is this text that counters the visual veil, as though "through literature, one can show how Islamic women have historically 'unveiled' their feminist views, in order to transform their societies."[5] It dramatizes a little-known aspect of life under the Islamic Republic of Iran between 1980 and 1989, when women as well as men served in the horrific war with Iraq, and many of them were injured, maimed, or killed. But before Neshat's art most of these women were not recognized as warriors or soldiers. To recuperate "lost" Iranian women fighters may be a utopian project, on the edge of Muslim self-expression but still within the scope of a quest to engage, and so be faithful to, Allah.

IN THE NAME OF ALLAH: CENSORSHIP, PRISON, AND PHYSICAL DEATH

Among those prepared to kill when offended by what they perceive to be an abuse of the name Allah are those who monitor public space in Egypt today. In 2011 Egyptian writer Karam Saber published a set of his short stories with the provocative title *Where Is Allah?* In these stories the writer, also a social activist, questions how an omniscient, omnipresent Other could be divinely monitoring what is happening in the world of the twenty-first century. Writing in the aftermath of the Tahrir Revolution (January 2011), Karam Saber was monitored by foreign media tracking Egypt. When he was brought to trial for insulting religion, the court found him guilty and he was sentenced to five years in prison. While his case is under appeal, it has continued to attract the attention of international media, including NPR, which broadcast his story in early summer 2013.[6]

Yet Karam Saber was luckier than other Egyptian writer-activists who have sought to shine light on injustice and to rally others to a higher commitment to justice through invoking the name Allah. In the 1990s, the Egyptian novelist Nawal El Saadawi had to leave Cairo after the assassination of a fellow writer-activist, Farag Foda. On 8 June 1992 Foda was murdered while leaving his home, his murder justified by a *fatwa* declaring him an apostate. While in exile, Nawal El Saadawi wrote and published a new book in the form of a play, entitled *Allah Resigns at the Summit Meeting.* In it she too boldly suggested a divine absence instead of omniscient presence, a rejection of hope, not an acclamation of belief, when facing the spectrum of (in)justice that defines our contemporary world, not least in the Middle East. In satirical terms, she suggested that if Allah looked at all that is happening in today's world, much of it in His name, He would resign. He would be offended by the hypocrisy of those who invoke His name but do not follow His command, above all, the command for balance, equity, and justice. Saadawi's play was intended to draw attention to the deficit in the contemporary world, not to offend any belief or practice linked to religion, but the play was banned in 2006. Religious authorities took her to court in 2007 accusing her of apostasy and heresy. She was not acquitted till 2008. In the meantime, her publisher received so many warnings that she withdrew the book from print publication, though it persists in cyberspace and remains available online in a Kindle edition.[7]

PROVOKING WITHOUT OFFENDING:
THE CASE OF M. F. HUSAIN

Women have pioneered new—some would say, audacious—ways of reimagining Allah. There are also some bold male artists intent on pursuing the same project. One of the greatest challenges is to create powerful images that evoke the Thing, the Absolute, the One with dignity but also with provocation. Earlier, we introduced then explored the Ka'ba Cube as reimagined by the Egyptian painter Dr. Ahmed Moustafa (see chapter 3). Now we turn to an extraordinary evocation of *Allahu Akbar* in its foundational seventh-century context that is also linked to the twenty-first century. It comes from the Indian/Qatari artist M. F. Husain (figure 12). The artist created this painting when he was in his nineties and

Fig. 12. Bilal, according to M. F. Husain. Bilal. 2010.1.7. © Estate of M. F. Husain.

living in exile in Doha. The image is simultaneously political and cultural, connecting as it does, though obliquely, Bilal al-Habshi, the first African Muslim and first Muslim prayer caller (*muezzin*) with President Barack Obama. Integral to Husain's imagination was bringing together past and present. He conjoined incongruous moments and actors in ways that seem far-fetched yet real, at once implausible and celebratory. The Bilal-Obama connection was inspired by the 2008 U.S. presidential election. Husain had stayed up late to listen to the results in Doha. He was so elated by the outcome that he could not sleep, and so he instead devoted himself to a painting of Bilal, one of the first converts to Islam and the first *muezzin*—who also happened to be Ethiopian.

The phrase *Allahu Akbar* is forever identified with Bilal because he was the first muezzin in the new Islamic faith, and so the words mark his identity. The phrase *Allahu Akbar* looms large at the bottom, with the name BILAL written across the middle of the figure with upraised arms. One has to know the painter's story of its inspiration to conclude that Barack Obama is projected as the modern-day equivalent of Bilal al-Habshi. "It took America two-hundred years to do what Islam did in less than ten years," Husain quipped to me when I asked him about this painting: "make a black man its major icon to the outside world." Bilal was, of course, not Muhammad; he was only the leader of ritual prayer in Medina, not of the entire Muslim community. Yet the comparison reflects the long reach of *Allahu Akbar* beyond its everyday evocation in Muslim public space or its signature use by terrorists or suicide bombers in their final moments. It projects the artist's—in this case, M. F. Husain's—ability to cross religion and politics, enriching one by contact with the other, while also denying either ultimate authority over the individual. Arguably, the painting has not offended or caused public outrage because it is part of a series on the Arab world commissioned by Sheikha Moza, the wife of the former Emir of Qatar, and it is also not yet on full display in any public venue.[8]

VIDEOGAMES WITH ALLAH THE AVENGER

Alas, neither Arahmaiani nor Shirin Neshat nor M. F. Husain represents the only artistic response to the search for Allah in today's conflicted, asymmetric world. One of the most pernicious effects of the Internet Age is the preference for images of warfare that involve a Wahhabi-like image of Allah the Vicious and Vengeful, rather than Allah the Lofty and

Exalted, to pervade and prevail on the Internet. Games on CD-ROM had long predated the Information Age, but with the expansion of the World Wide Web they have found another audience of consumers, many addicted to images of violence. Consider the game Maze of Destiny, introduced in 2002 by a company called Islam Games as the first in a trilogy of titles pitched to a young audience; the later sequels were Ummah Defense I and Ummah Defense II. Since there is lots of poisonous nonsense on the World Wide Web, one could question why in a book on Allah one might even visit the website of a violent-videogame maker. Since I first stumbled onto the site over two years ago, it has relocated. Intriguingly, if one tries to access it in 2014, the Google search engine takes you to the CIA.

And with no sign or even hint of irony, here is how the lodestone of American intelligence and data collection on Muslim terrorists characterizes the game Maze of Destiny. Classified under: "The Terrorists' Network: An Analysis of 'Pro-Arab' Video Games" the explanatory text reads:

> Ummah Defense's objective is to unite the world under Islam. It introduces young children to Islam. Maze of Destiny has players rescue chapters of the Quran from thieves. It will not be long before a game is created to reflect the latest war between Hizbullah and Israel, but also the latest rows "between East and West," with Danes drawing enflaming cartoons and Pakistanis burning down embassies. Pundits will myopically focus on which side will create that videogame first and what its ideological underpinnings will be. They will forget the intricacies inside and beyond the screens. Is it a real life story or a political propaganda? You have the right to decide.[9]

But actually you do not have the right to decide, at least since 2007, for if you visit another website, Digital Islam, you will discover a portal that features videogames. The Maze of Destiny is listed but is no longer available. In 2007 it was removed from cyberspace, but still circulates in CD-ROM and can be obtained through mail order. The actual game is also cleverer than the above sleuth warning suggests. The plot revolves around the secrets of Allah as they are conveyed in the Qur'an. It features an evil wizard, Darlak the Deceiver, who wants to destroy the Book of Allah, and to that end has imprisoned the teachers of the Qur'an. Your task is to find their location, set them free, and reform a world made dark by the near destruction, and total isolation, of the Book of Allah.

That is the hook, but it also poses a formidable obstacle. Darlak has hidden these Qur'an teachers in his dungeon, and he has set his evil minions there to guard them. The path to the dungeon is fraught with those videogame staples—"deadly traps and creepy crawlers." Armed only with your wits, and your faith in Allah, you must dare the depths of Darlak's dungeon.

And here is the ultimate challenge: "Can you recover the missing letters of Surah Fatiha (which have been forgotten while the Qur'an teachers are imprisoned)? Just figuring out how to get the letters and free the prisoners (in one piece) becomes a puzzle in itself." And so you need to trust: "May Allah guide you and help you on your quest. Remember to stay on the right path!"[10]

That last injunction comes directly from the "lost" *sura*: "*Guide us on the right path*" (Q 1:6), and the game is no worse, and no better, than many other videogames that invoke religious themes and high-stakes warfare in order to attract viewers/players. But the Maze of Destiny, like other Islam-themed games, becomes problematic in the context of early twenty-first-century Allah image making. What is now portrayed as religious struggle or outright warfare echoes too closely the combat that has involved Euro-American others, mostly non-Muslim, fighting Muslims in different parts of the Middle East, Africa, and Asia. The reasons for the warfare are never cited as religious by the invading warriors, but the protracted nature of the conflict—the United States has been in Afghanistan since October 2001—makes the religious appeal of evil intent, desecration of the Holy Book, and loss of true devotion to Allah seem real to many Muslims, not just videogaming youth.

Yet not all seekers of Allah have experienced the extreme alienation from the West as those of the Wahhabi/Salafi proponents. For many it is trying to survive in circumstances of duress that marks the engagement with Allah, not least under the punishing gaze of one of those religious specialists or *madrasa* (seminary) teachers so well known from the Asian subcontinent, especially Afghanistan.[11]

FROM AFGHANISTAN: A CHALLENGE TO "SEE" ALLAH

Consider the plight of an Afghani school child named Fazil. He is one of the several Afghanis featured in *The Bookseller of Kabul*, Asne Seierstad's international best-selling view of life inside Kabul during the thirteen years following the American-led NATO assault on the Taliban in

October 2001. In a chapter titled "Can God Die?" Fazil is detained after school for some as yet unnamed infraction and ordered to do punitive homework:

> He must write ten times what God is: God is the creator, God is eternal, God is almighty, God is good, God is truth, God is life, God sees all, God hears all, God is omniscient, God is omnipotent, God rules all, God. . . .
>
> The reason for the detention was his inability to answer correctly during the lesson on Islam. "I never answer properly," he moaned to his mother, "Because when I see the teacher, I get so nervous I forget. He's always angry, and even if you only make a tiny mistake, he hates you."
>
> He had answered a battery of questions about God: Does He die? No, because He is eternal. Does He speak? Yes, through the Koran, but then he was asked: Can God see?
>
> "Yes," said Fazil.
>
> "How does He see? Does He have eyes?"
>
> Fazil hesitated before saying: "I've never seen God. How do I know?"
>
> The blows [from the teacher's ruler] rained down over Fazil until the tears flowed. He must surely be the stupidest boy in the class. The pain was nothing compared to the shame of standing there. Then he was given detention homework.
>
> "If you cannot learn this, you cannot continue in the class," the teacher concluded.

Eventually Fazil memorizes the "correct" answers and is allowed to continue in the class, but the larger lesson that reverberates from this story is the huge, and detrimental, influence of the instructor: Allah is communicated not just by the Qur'an but also by those who teach the Qur'an, and in the hands of an autocratic, blinkered literalist, its lessons can be subverted, even nullified.[12]

THE ALLAH BRAND NAME: YUSUF ALI USURPED

And so we must continuously ask: Who is Allah in the twenty-first century of the common era? For Muslims Allah is still divine, but for many non-Muslims Allah is now the divide—between East and West, between the United States and the Middle East. Among many Muslims as well there is a divide between the "true" literalist believers in God's Word (the Qur'an) and others who seek to see God manifest in His creation and also in His creatures. Allah is no longer a monitor for humankind but instead a moniker for one brand of sectarian rage, replacing a community united by faith with a maelstrom of competing ideologies. The current public outcry in Malaysia over Christian use of Allah is yet another instance of Islam politicized, with Allah center stage in a media war to claim ownership of the One beyond naming, or owning, or outlawing.[13] Where is the balance, the middle point, the broad way or *sirat al-mustaqim* that is announced as the Muslim path in the first chapter (Al-Fatiha) of the Noble Book?

To move beyond the dyadic choices and the perpetual warfare heralded by the Maze of Destiny, we must return to where we began in the introduction: can or should Allah be translated as God? William Chittick, a seasoned observer of Islam with a strong Sufi bent, says yes. But the answer is emphatically no from the leading propagators of Islamic orthodoxy, located in western Saudi Arabia in the two holiest cities of Islam: Mecca, the hometown of the Prophet and pilgrimage site for Muslims, and Medina, the city to which Muhammad migrated and where he died and was buried. The Saudi religious authorities have resolved the question of choice between Allah and God: they always substitute Allah for God, even when the text that they use as an English translation of the Qur'an comes from a translator who elected to use God instead of Allah.[14]

Abdullah Yusuf Ali was perhaps the most successful, and certainly the most famous, translator of the Holy Qur'an into English. An Indo-Pakistani civil servant from colonial India, he first published his Qur'an translation in Lahore in the mid-1930s. Its odyssey has been bizarre. It would be the stuff of fiction were it not the staggering byline of actual history, amply marked at several stages. Yusuf Ali began his translation in the 1920s, after he had retired from the civil service and settled in the United Kingdom. First published in 1934, his original translation was already in its third printing at the time of his death in 1952.

But then in 1980, the Saudi religious establishment felt the need for a reliable English translation and exegesis of the Qur'an; they wanted to make an official Saudi-approved translation available for the increasing English language readership across the globe. After surveying the various translations in print at the time, four high-level committees under the General Presidency of the Department of Islamic Research chose

Abdullah Yusuf Ali's translation and commentary as the best available for publication. No reason was ever given why the work of Marmaduke Pickthall (an English convert, whose translation is also well known) or some other translator was not selected, but significant revisions were made in the Yusuf Ali translation in 1985 before it was endorsed and then printed by the King Fahd Holy Qur'an Printing Complex.

In 1989, Amana Publications, which in 1977 had first introduced the Yusuf Ali translation to a wildly enthusiastic American audience, published a "new" fourth edition. It featured revision of the translation and commentary undertaken with the help of the Saudi-funded International Institute of Islamic Thought. The new revised Amana print reached its eleventh edition on May 2004. Among the several departures from the original of Yusuf Ali is the shift from God to Allah. Allah to God to Allah? Why? The awkward shift has been described by one Muslim writer as "the decision to 'detranslate' the word 'God' back into the Arabic Allah in the 1989 New Revised Edition (of Yusuf Ali) by Amana."[15]

Though there is no commentary on the reasons for the change, it is implied that Allah has so thoroughly replaced God (for Muslims) that Allah, and only Allah, has become closely identified with the Abdullah Yusuf Ali Qur'an translation. One can surf the Internet in search of the original translation, but literally nothing will be found. It is a sad irony that some websites blandish the altered translation, substituting Allah for God while retaining Yusuf Ali's preface in which he makes clear that it is Allah as God who for him shines through the pages of the Holy Qur'an.[16]

Despite the flaws in the original rendition, as also the manipulations of the successive versions printed from Amana (including the detranslation of God to Allah), the appeal of the Yusuf Ali original translation endures. Yet its checkered history cannot be traced on the Internet. Despite the dizzying plurality of sites on Islam, Allah, and the Qur'an, there is none that details the saga just depicted.

As it happened, the modified Yusuf Ali Qur'an translation served as the officially sanctioned English translation of the Saudi religious establishment for slightly more than a decade before it in turn was deemed unsuitable and replaced by the still more distorted Al-Hilali and Khan translation in 1998. In the words of a leading Muslim scholar, this translation "turns the Qur'an into a blueprint for replicating the xenophobic and misogynist Saudi society in every detail."[17] Others have also criticized the severe biases that make this not only an awkward, stilted, dry, and literalist rendition of the Noble Book but also one that is aggressively puritanical, authoritarian, misogynous, anti-Jewish, anti-Christian, and antipluralist.

Perhaps none of this would matter, except that the Al-Hilali and Khan English translation has been distributed largely free through mosques, seminaries, religious organizations, and Muslim bookshops throughout Africa, Asia, Europe, and the United States. Often, on my own trips to the Kingdom of Saudi Arabia, it is the Al-Hilali and Khan version that I find in my hotel room, tucked away in a drawer of the bedside table. In this version, there is no doubt that Allah literally does all the things that stumped poor Fazil, the student derided in a Kabul classroom a decade ago. All the words from Allah, and all the descriptions of Allah, in the Qur'an must be literally true; all the prescriptions attributed to the Thing, the Absolute, the One must be slavishly, unquestionably followed. And, above all, Islam must be sealed off, kept free of contamination from other Abrahamic religions. Whether it is Osama bin Laden and Al-Qaida, or Muhammad and the Muslim Brotherhood, or Sheikh Nasrollah and Hizbullah, all these individuals, and the groups they represent, seek to distance Islam from its Semitic neighbors, reinforcing negative stereotypes that much of the world already has of Islam.

SUFI SEQUEL TO WAHHABI PROHIBITIONS: BAWA MUHAIYADDEEN ON ASMA AL-HUSNA

One might, and some do, succumb to despair and doomsday predictions. The punitive Allah of videogames, the harsh Allah "seen" in the Taliban texts of Afghanistan, and the tribal Allah of Saudi orthodoxy—all project images of Allah that will persist, but will they dominate the imagination of this generation and future generations? Will Muslims and non-Muslims alike accept these images, and ignore others that also claim to project the Thing, the Absolute, the One, the Lord of Both Worlds, the Endpoint, as also the First Point, of All Life?

The strongest, most persistent retort to literalist notions of Allah comes from the rapt attention and insights of Sufi masters. They, along with their devotees, take comfort from *Asma al-Husna*, the Beautiful Names. There is a strong moral dimension to that meditative practice. Recall the advice from the Tamil master, Shaykh Bawa Muhaiyaddeen. We saw earlier (in chapter 3) how the *shaykh* projected Allah as Light through the body of Faith. Elsewhere he also links each name to the notion of duty, and divides the human heart into two sections. In its innermost part is the kingdom of Allah, and there His essence can be found as also the names, the Beautiful Names:

The *Asma al-husna* (ninety-nine beautiful names) of Allah are the plentitude of the ninety-nine duties of Allah; the *sifat* of His *dhat*; the manifestation of His essence. The states of His qualities are His manifestations that emerge from Him. He performs His duty when these manifestations are brought into action, then they become His *wilayat*, the actions which stem from the manifestations of His essence.

The *Asma al-husna* (beautiful names) are the 99 names of His duties. They were revealed to Prophet Muhammad in the Qur'an, and he explained them to his followers. This is a vast *bahr al-dawla*, a very deep ocean of His grace and His limitless, infinite, and undiminishing wealth.

If we go on cutting [the heart, as if cutting tissue from its perimeter], we will cut one of these 99 *wilayat* over and over again, taking one piece at a time. We will see 99 particles revolving one around the other without touching. This applies to each one of the 99 *wilayat*; this is the *Asma al-husna*. As we go on cutting, we lose ourselves in that. We die within that.

How can we ever hope to reach an end of the 99? If we receive only one drop of that, it will be more than sufficient for us. The person who has touched the smallest, tiniest drop becomes a good one. These are merely His powers. If you go on cutting just one of His powers, it is so powerful that it will draw you in. That power will swallow you up, and you will become the power (*wilaya*). Then you come to the stage at which you can lose yourself within Allah; you can disappear within Allah.[18]

A FINAL QUEST TO INVOKE AND EMBODY ALLAH

Still another Sufi effort to expand the core of Islamic devotion to an inclusiveness that at once embraces Indian spirituality and yet rejects Salafi repudiation of all nonliteral approaches to Allah/God comes from Scott Siraj al-Haqq Kugle. An American, a Muslim, and a Sufi, Kugle is also a scholar, and in a recent book he evokes many of the themes explored above: devotion to the Word and to the world, acknowledging Allah as transcendent, beyond human knowing, yet so close as to be part of the body. Kugle focuses on five spiritual exemplars who exceeded the boundaries of their temporal context. One was particularly prescient. Hajji Imdadullah not only performed the *hajj* or pilgrimage to Mecca, as his name implies, but also embodied, as his name further suggests, *imdad Allah*, the support of Allah, his own agency as Allah's instrument for his age.

Hajji Imdadullah was a Chishti master living in what Kugle calls a *barzakh* era. It was late nineteenth-century North India. Though the British dominated South Asia, seeds of change had been planted even before the Mutiny of 1857. The Mughal Empire, after more than three hundred years of rule, was in sharp decline. Though commerce ruled, it was commerce that originated from Europe not Asia. As the East India Company expanded from a trade network into a military force, it reduced the Mughal emperor to a vassal; it also reduced Muslims to a disempowered minority in a non-Islamic and rapidly modernizing state.

Because he lived at a time of political transition and social uncertainty, Hajji Imdadullah focused on inner, spiritual revolution. He crafted his own strategy for focusing on the heart as the seat of all emotions and also all outcomes, "allowing the heart to reveal its deeper nature as the wellspring for God's presence in the world."[19] His instrument was a training manual: *The Brilliance of Hearts*. The hierarchy of leader and disciple permeates its pages, yet its focus on immersive remembrance of Allah reflects an intense mixture of psychological insight and anatomical training peculiar to the Chishti tradition. It draws on its own lineage of past masters, including its initial Indian emissary, Mu'in ad-din, and the Mughal paragon Abdul-Quddus. But it is Hajji Imdadullah who recasts their teaching in a modern idiom.

The goal for Imdadullah remains the same as that announced by Mu'in ad-din, his thirteenth-century precursor: "To bring the body into harmony with the cosmos, allowing the ego to dissolve into union with God."[20] For Imdadullah, however, the goal of self-purification and harmony with the cosmos was not an end goal, as it had been for his predecessors; it was instead instrumental to the higher goal of performing the *sunna*, the Muhammad model, while obeying the outer law, or *shari'a*, since its requirements encompassed both the individual believer and the collective good of the Muslim community.

Indeed, the outcome of all these spiritual techniques for Imdadullah is "to accelerate the spiritual disintegration of the self to erase the will and achieve union with God, allowing the performance of *sunna*."[21]

By prioritizing *sunna* over solitude, Imdadullah reinterprets the spiritual mandate of his Chishti predecessors, yet he maintains their reliance on sainthood as the key to both sanctity and *sunna* observance. On this critical point he departs from the practices that are advocated by his fellow Muslim, Wahhabi contemporaries. For the latter, all Sufis are deemed to be unbelievers, and all saintly devotion condemned as tomb worship, itself a form of idolatry.

The critical locus of difference between Sufis and Wahhabis, however, is their view of the body. The central figure of Wahhabi belief is their eponymous founder, Ibn 'Abd al-Wahhab. While Ibn 'Abd al-Wahhab did not condemn the Sufi vision of God's nature, human nature, and ascetical practice, he was obsessively fixated on the human body as the source of all temptation, evil, and idolatry. Looking at acts, not intention (*niyya*), he attributes the most crass motives to all dependence on bodily practices or human exemplars. The Prophet Muhammad is stripped of any link to the Light of Allah. Instead of the Perfect Man of Sufi reflection, he is reduced to being the storehouse, conduit, and announcer of God's Word. The Prophet Muhammad becomes, in Kugle's words, "nothing more for the Wahhabis than a mere megaphone for God's speech; they cannot see the human body as an assembly of the signs of God."[22]

In effect, Wahhabis are Arab Cartesians. "For while Descartes attempted to gain distance from the body in order to achieve intellectual certainty, the Wahhabis sought religious certainty and, along the way, abdicated intellectual clarity (by decrying the body). Both are united in the drive for certainty and commit ideological violence against the body in order to banish it as a source of moral doubt and ontological ambiguity."[23]

These are not mere differences in outlook among pious Muslims. The ideological brinkmanship of the Wahhabis, according to Kugle, also fuels more extreme expressions, and often acts of violence, that privilege jihad as a monolithic reflex of Islamic loyalty. So much so that in the aftermath of the Cold War, "al-Qaeda, the Taliban, and other splinter groups of Wahhabi-inspired militants express this ideology's most violent inner drive. These radicals who cannot or will not engage in military jihad engage in cultural jihad by prohibiting body images in other ways: suppressing women, denouncing Sufis, or reviling as idolatry technologies of visual communication (like photography, cinema, and television)."[24] Jihad is no longer a metaphor of self-perfection but an instrument for endless warfare.

THE SUMMARY OF SUMMARIES

We cannot avoid warfare, both physical and metaphysical, in the name of Allah. The inventory of battles over the Thing, the Absolute, the One is lengthy. The skirmishes are far from over. The greatest danger of these ongoing skirmishes is that both Muslims and non-Muslims will be debarred from the power of Allah. It will not matter whether Allah is presented in the unadorned Arabic of the original revelation, or mediated and then transformed through intense reflection on that name, or one of its ninety-nine facets, as it has been in the history of Islamic spirituality. That will be a loss, not just for Muslims but also for humankind.

And so what are the guideposts, and the takeaway message, from our review, our engagement, and our struggle with multiple practices that focus on Allah? No matter how intense or persistent our quest, it hinges on a single question: what are we to make of Allah? Who *is* Allah? The question remains as haunting, its answer as elusive, at the end of this quest as at the outset. What we have reviewed, examined, analyzed, and projected are but the fragments of a millennial odyssey. It encompasses the history of Islam and beyond. It echoes the shifts and challenges of human society across time and place, from the seventh century to the twenty-first century, from Arabia to Asia, Africa, and now America. It also reflects varied groups within Islam, many mainstream and respected, but also others marginal, questioned, or even rejected by the majority of Muslims.

And so instead of one overarching conclusion we have three possible conclusions. Let us call them sociological, existential, and skeptical, each with their distinctive perspective and separate audience.

The *sociological* approach focuses on persons: WHO seeks to connect with Allah, and WHY? In the resources scanned and the sources cited above, we find mostly urban men of culture, education, and wealth enjoying public acclaim during, and also after, their lifetime. The champions of Allah are also the heroes of Islam: Al-Ghazali, Ibn ʿArabi, Rumi, Nursi. The voices of women, especially radical revisionist women such as Nawal El Saadawi and Shirin Neshat, are few and recent. One could argue that their impact today, like that of the Brethren of Purity from the eleventh century, affects only a few, but will not they too linger as part of the larger legacy of Islamic creativity across centuries? Dissident artists such as Arahmaiani and M. F. Husain still invoke Allah. They see themselves in the image of the Thing, the One, even if it is not the image imagined or embraced or acceptable to their coreligionists. It is Allah on the edges or at the margin. Each end heralds a new beginning. The quest has amplified without exhausting the Thing. It remains the One, beyond knowing yet ever inviting us to know.

> To Allah we belong,
> and to Allah we are ever returning." (Q 2:156)

The second conclusion veers to the process, the search itself. It is an *existential* process. It focuses on WHAT is linked to Allah, and HOW? Its advocates dwell in the mystery of the Name. Allah exceeds the Name, even as the Name itself becomes a focus of attention on Allah as immeasurable force, the source of life and death, good and evil, hope and despair. Smell the bouquet, hear the echo, see the rainbow, join the feast, and feel the fire—of Allah, Khoda (a Persian word for God), and Tanri (a Turkish word for God). All the senses, not just the mind or intellect, attune to the beyond which is also within, yet one cannot speak of Allah without first feeling the spark within, either as the second person "you" in English, or the third person *hu* ("He/Him") in Arabic. Mirror, mind, moment are not goals but goads: how to see Him/*hu* in the mirror, how to imagine Him/*hu* in the mind, and how to feel Him/*hu* in each moment, the present moment, neither past nor future, beyond birth and rebirth, the Eternal Now? That is the mainstream Muslim quest for Allah, the Sufi search for the Beloved. It parallels the quest for a cosmic *qibla* (at once daily focus and final vista) in every religious tradition or spiritual path.

Yet neither the sociological assessment nor the existential response will satisfy the *skeptic*. The skeptic may be a believer or unbeliever but she never ceases to ask: WHERE is Allah, and WHEN does the quest end? We began with Montaigne, a devout skeptic from the seventeenth century, and his counterpart today would be the computer geek who sees all the evidence and arguments about Allah as human toying with the metaphysical lines of regressive theory. At the least, she asserts, there is no supreme name for God. Allah, like Adonai or God, Khoda or Tanri, Om or Om Shanti Shanti Shanti, may not exist or may exist but only as Being—infinite, timeless, and unknowable. To the extent that He is a being, His ipseity (that is, who He is at His core self), goes beyond description, beyond naming. The Thing is ever more, and always other, than what is named the Thing, the Absolute, the One. It appears as an ethereal image traced by *jinn* but not by "real" people. It resides in the *barzakh,* not in heaven or hell or on earth or in the sky but at the margins of each and within each simultaneously. Unthinkable, untraceable, it has no true Name since any name, whether God or Adonai or Allah or Allat, confines Him/Her/It. At best there are a surfeit of names for Allah, at least ninety-nine, though likely many more. All pale beside the infinite reality—Allah simply "is"; all the names that we devise or use mere artifacts. Fickle humans are not only mortal and finite, they are also feeble; they cannot truly conceptualize the eternal, the immortal, the infinite. The Unseen persists as the Unknown and the Unknowable. The Thing and the Name elide but never equate. The search is endless, the goal unattainable. Neither patience nor piety satisfies. Only loyalty and love endure. Only they can—and *inshallah* they will—prevail.

Glossary

'abd: Servant, one who serves, as in the name *'Abdallah*.

'Abdallah: Name meaning Servant of God, acknowledging God as creator, guide, and judge.

Ahl al-bayt: The household of the Prophet; those Muslims loyal to the Prophet's immediate family, specifically 'Ali, his wife, Fatimah, and their two sons, Hasan and Husayn; Shi'ites, defining themselves apart from, and over against, dominant Sunni Muslims.

ahl al-kitab: The People of the Book; those who acknowledge God as creator, guide, and judge of humankind; Jews, Christians, and others who have a divine scripture that was revealed by God before the final Book, the Qur'an.

Allahu Akbar: God is Greater (there is none greater than He).

Allah: God; the first and foremost of the Ninety-nine Divine Names.

As-salamu 'alaykum: The Peace (*salam*) of God be upon you; the most frequent and important of Muslim greetings.

Asma'allah al-husna: The beautiful names of God, totaling 99 in the canonical list but including up to 300 in other lists; the Divine Names.

ayah (pl. *ayat*): Verse(s) from the Qur'an; a sign pointing to God.

baraka: Blessing or benefit or grace, conferred by God on the believer.

basmala: Technical name for the phrase, *bismillah ar-rahman ar-rahim* ("In the Name of God, Full of Compassion, Ever Compassionate").

Din: The last and perfect religion given to the last Prophet of God for humankind, namely, Islam; any religion that addresses the divine.

Du'a: An invocation or prayer addressed to God that is not part of the five daily prayers (*salat*).

Dunya: The material world, or (excessive) concern with material, worldly goods.

Fiqh: Knowledge acquired by studying the book of revelation and the book of nature; the science of Islamic law(s).

hadith (pl. *ahadith*): Reports containing the statements made by the Prophet Muhammad, eyewitness accounts of his actions as well as his endorsement and approval of other people's actions; transmitted by his companions, *ahadith* collectively define the Prophet Muhammad's *sunnah*, or exemplary conduct.

hajj: The canonical pilgrimage incumbent on Muslims once in a lifetime, to visit Mecca and its surrounding places for five days during the last month of the *hijri* calendar and to perform specific acts of worship there.

Halal: What is permitted by divine decree.

Haram: What is forbidden by divine decree.

hijra: The date of Muhammad's separation from his city of birth, Mecca, and his relocation in Yathrib (later Medina); the benchmark for the Muslim lunar calendar (July 622 CE).

Ihsan: A desired perfection to comply fully with divine commands; the state of mind of one who strives to be in full compliance with these commands.

'Ilm: Knowledge, but specifically knowledge of God that is collected and systematized.

imam: Leader at canonical prayer; the one designated to lead the Muslim community for his generation (Shi'ites).

iman: Belief in God as creator, guide, and judge of humankind; belief in God and in Muhammad as His last prophet.

Islam: Surrender to God; the last religion of God delivered to the last prophet through the revelation of the Qur'an.

jihad: Struggle for the collective good or public welfare of the *umma*; as armed warfare or political struggle, it is sometimes defined as "Holy War."

jinn: Ambivalent spirits that inhabit an intermediate world between the known or material world and the unknown or spiritual world; the English counterpart is genie, as in "don't let the genie out of the bottle."

kalima: Witness, affirmation, profession of faith in two stages; first, in Allah as the Absolute One and second, in Muhammad as the final prophet, the perfect messenger, and the devoted servant of Allah. See also *shahada*.

khalifa: Successor, but especially one of the four successors to the Prophet Muhammad in the Sunni tradition: Abu Bakr (632–34), 'Umar (634–44), 'Uthman (644–56), and 'Ali (656–61). Collectively, they are known as *al-khulafa al-rashidun*, or just the *rashidun* ("the right-guided ones").

Kitab: The Book; the metabook of all divine revelation (*umm al-kitab*), but also the Qur'an as the final form of that book and therefore the most authoritative.

Muhammad: The Last Prophet of God, directed to deliver the Final Book (itself a portion of the *umm al-kitab*) in Arabic to Arabs, but with a message encompassing all humankind and all eras of history.

Mu'min: The believer; one who professes belief in God, the Prophets, and Judgment Day; a member of the *ahl al-kitab*.

Muslim: The one who surrenders to God; member of the *umma*, or worldwide community of Muslims.

Qibla: The orientation of Muslims for *salat*, or ritual prayer, at first to Jerusalem, and then to Mecca.

Qur'an: The final revelation of God to humankind, given to the last prophet, Muhammad ibn 'Abdallah, as the complete message encompassing and perfecting the books given to earlier prophets, including Moses and Jesus; the 114 chapters that comprise the book known as the Noble Qur'an.

Rasul: A messenger, whose message comes from God Almighty in the form of a scripture to be heard then recorded for future repetition as a perpetual guide to correct conduct in this world and preparation for judgment in the next.

salam: Peace, specifically, the peace conferred by God on those who accept Him, worship Him, and obey Him as creator, guide, and judge, both of humankind and of all sentient as well as nonsentient beings.

salat: The daily act of worship, consisting of five prayers, addressed to God at specific times from sunrise to early evening.

shahada: The witness, or affirmation, that there is no god but God, and that Muhammad is his (last) prophet, his (greatest) servant, his (complete) messenger; the first, necessary step to become Muslim and a member of the *umma*.

Shahid (pl. *shuhada*): Witness(es), specifically, those who witness to the truth of Islam by becoming martyrs, dying while fighting for the common good (*maslaha*) of the Muslim community (*umma*).

shari'a: The collective name for Islamic normativity; often equated with the requirement to comply with Islamic law; a Muslim guide to correct and good living that encompasses religious and liturgical but also ethical, juridical, and daily activities.

shaykh (or *sheikh*): An illustrious scholar or spiritual leader, often the foremost person of his generation, at least in the eyes of his followers and contemporary elites.

Shi'ites: Those Muslims who believe that succession to Muhammad was designated by divine revelation and prophetic authority; linking themselves to the Prophet Muhammad's immediate family, they prefer 'Ali over any other Muslim leader; they oppose the Righteous Caliphs and instead obey the *imams*, beginning with 'Ali and his two sons, Hasan and Husayn.

sunna: The pattern of God in ordering the creation and function of the material world; the exemplary conduct of the Prophet Muhammad, conveyed in reports of his deeds, dicta, and endorsements (*hadith*); the necessary companion and complement to the Qur'an for many Muslims.

Sunnis: Those Muslims who believe that succession after Muhammad was to be decided by the community of believers and not by divine authority or prophetic appointment; they accept the history of the first *hijri* century and the authority it conferred on the Righteous Caliphs; they acknowledge 'Ali as the Fourth Caliph but not as the First Imam. Their successors are the Umayyad, then the 'Abbasid Caliphs.

sura: A chapter, specifically one of the 114 chapters that together comprise the Noble Qur'an.

Tafsir: Commentary on the meaning of the Qur'an, mostly confined to verses with an evident and commonsense message.

ta'widh: The invocation of God's mercy and protection from the forces of evil, specifically the wiles or insinuations of the Devil.

'ulama: The custodians of *'ilm*, or knowledge, who transmit it from generation to generation as teachers and jurists within the *umma*.

umma: The worldwide community of Muslims.

Umm al-kitab: The metabook of all divine revelation, preceding the Qur'an and finalized in the Qur'an; it includes the Torah for Jews and the Injil, or Gospel, for Christians as well as other scriptures, notably the Zabur, or Psalms, sacred to both Jews and Christians.

Notes

INTRODUCTION

1. Quoted from the *wird* (devotion) ascribed to the famed collector of traditions about the Prophet Muhammad, an-Nawawi. See http://www.naseemalsham.com/en /Pages.php?page=readDynamicCom&id=38938&comid=94&name=About%20a%20 Book&sub=Al%20Imam%20An%20Nawawi (accessed on 11 June 2014). This is but the first of many citations from the Internet that will appear in the pages that follow. The use of Internet references, and resources, will be explored in chapter 5. Further, note that the expression "no power except through Allah" is an oft-repeated refrain.

2. "St. Patrick's Breastplate" is attributed to the fifth-century Irish saint, but it was a late nineteenth-century English woman, Cecil Alexander, who rendered it into English meter. See http://www.cyberhymnal.org/htm/s/t/stpatric.htm (accessed on 11 June 2014).

3. Montaigne, *Essays*, 106. The emphases are mine. "Montaigne, much like Augustine, was known due to his association with religion. However, his actual religious beliefs are unknown, to such an extent that the way he writes makes it impossible to tell whether his remarks and comments toward the Christian faith are sarcastic or genuine." An anonymous source accessed on google.docs on 15 August 2013. See https:// docs.google.com/document/d/1SOBPJ1cA7hODFeRMLMp-7WtKAZd6h_EmTlKYPD MyEK4/edit.

4. While it may sound strange to use "Thing" as an apposite name for Allah, it is a usage well marked in the Qur'an: "Say, what thing is the greatest (in witness)? Say, Allah is a witness between you and me" (Q 6:19a). "Thing" is also traced in Islamic speculative theology (*kalam*). Muhammad ibn ʿAbd al-Karim ash-Shahrastani (d. 1153), renowned for his broad-gauged study of diverse religious communities and sects, also authored a Qur'anic commentary, *Mafatih al-asrar wa masabih al-abrar* (*Keys to Secrets and Lamps for the Pious*), in which he discusses the meaning of each of the letters of Allah. "The *alif* is for grammatical definition (*tarʿif*), the *lam* is to affirm possession (*tamlik*), while the *ha* is for reification (*shayʾiyya*)." And then, as the endnote explains, the word *shayʾiyya* literally means thingness or "acknowledging that God is a 'thing.'" Shahrastani, *Keys to the Arcana*, 144, 230n674. Given the importance of Allah, God is not a thing, however, but the Thing, as also the Absolute (*samad*) and the One (*ahad*), to gloss Q 112 *Surat al-Ikhlas*, as does Shahrastani himself a page later (145).

5. There is, of course, the deeper issue of linguistic potential. In Arabic there is no neutral pronoun, just "he" or "she," and so if one wants to translate Allah as both-neither, in order to convey the transgendered nature of the One, either pronouns must be omitted altogether or "One" substituted for every use of "he" (*huwa*) in the Arabic original of the Qur'an. That makes for awkward translation choices, as Scott Kugle

demonstrates in translating Q 112 *Surat al-Ikhlas* as, "In the name of God the Compassionate One, the Caring One. Say, God is a singular One, the eternal One, never begetting and never begotten, to whom no other bears comparison." Ibn ʿAtaʾ Allah al-Iskandari, *Book of Illuminations*, 373. Kugle also goes on to note the ultimate irony: "all translations are betrayals of the original. The real question for each translator is which style of betrayal effectively communicates the essential meaning to the perceived audience" (377). Similarly, the problem of how to render the gender ambiguity about the divine, and to avoid a simplistic equation of gendered God talk as always "masculine," occupies Saʿdiyya Shaikh. See Shaikh, *Sufi Narratives*, 29–31.

6. http://www.huffingtonpost.com/2011/01/27/new-pew-forum-report-proj_n_814 818.html (accessed on 11 June 2014).

7. On the disparate uses of *Allahu Akbar* attributed to Neil Armstrong and for its polemical citation, see the following obituary on Neil Armstrong: http://www.jihad watch.org/2012/08/neil-armstrong-first-man-on-the-moon-dies-at-age-82.htm (accessed on 11 June 2014).

8. http://www.islamic-dictionary.com/index.php?word=Allah (accessed on 11 June 2014).

9. Hawting, in *Idea of Idolatry*, dedicates an entire chapter (20–42) exploring what he calls the distinction "between a straightforward evolutionary approach and one associated with the notion of primaeval monotheism" (25). In other words, how do you choose between an idea of making the One God appear from the many or seeing the One God appear, disappear, and then reappear (in this case, with Muhammad). The outcome of that debate is important for academics but not for most practicing Muslims.

10. Cragg, *Call of the Minaret*, 37.

11. There is a Chishti website that provides details gleaned from diverse etymological cum theological explanations for the origin of the name Allah. Too long to include in the body of the text, it is itself a digest of Daniel Gimaret, *Les noms divins*, and Fakhr ad-din Razi, *Traité sur les noms divins*; see http://www.chishti.ru/one.htm (accessed on 11 June 2014). The gist of this detailed history is to underscore the absorption of many gifted, and also sincere, scholars with competitive notions of how Allah came to be the name for the Thing, the Absolute, the One.

12. See Hawting, *Idea of Idolatry*, 130–49, for the academic debate about these three female deities of pre-Islamic Arabia.

13. See step 3 in this Naqshbandi Sufi website: http://nurmuhammad.com/pbuh /?p=2095 (accessed on 11 June 2014), but for the actual image I am indebted to Feyza Burak for locating the son of the magnificent calligrapher Fevzi Günüç, who completed this image in 1314 AH (1998/1999 CE).

14. The reference to Jews may seem strange, but a Jewish Palestinian Ottoman subject, writing from the battle lines of World War I, records: "We see here that we have many enemies who rise up against us, but Allah will save us from them." Yehuda Amon in Abramson, *Soldiers Tales*, 85. For discussion of the contemporary controversy re Christian use of Allah in Malaysia, see conclusion.

15. Yasein Muhammad, University of Western Cape, email (accessed on 6 February 2012). Emphasis added.

16. See chapter 4 for an extended treatment of Hitchens and his riposte to all theisms, but especially the Islamic variety.

17. Cragg, *Call of the Minaret*, 36.

18. I am indebted to Dr. Jim Cross for the metaphor of the diamond. He bears no responsibility for the theological conclusions deduced from it, however; they remain my own.

19. On this as on so many other issues of Christian-Muslim theological engagement, with differences that shout out to be discussed rather than minimized, Kenneth Cragg argues the Christian perspective with bold clarity. See especially Cragg, *Jesus and the Muslim*.

20. Chapter 2, "The Qur'anic Jesus." I am grateful to Peter Gottschalk for the clarification, and the phraseology, of this section; personal communication, 11 July 2013.

21. Murata and Chittick, *Vision of Islam*, 46–47. This is a very popular textbook, and its judgments pertain to many diverse audiences, both Muslim and non-Muslim. Added to their two reasons for confusion re Allah and God is a third: the name Allah becomes *ism-i dhat*, that is, the name, and the only name, that can be said to refer to God's essence.

22. In chapter 5, "Allah Debated," I will take note of Christian polemicists who deride the Qur'an, Islam, and, of course, Allah. One of them, Jack Chick, is allegedly the best-selling polemicist of modern times, having sold over 800 million copies of his several tracts. Not only does he credit Catholicism with having founded Islam, but he also sees Allah as but a variant of the pagan moon god, as in this link: http://www.chick.com/reading/tracts/0042/0042_01.asp (accessed on 11 June 2014).

23. Quoted in Taji-Farouki, *Modern Muslims*, chap. 8, 25.

24. Sells, Michael, *Unsaying*, 11. The fuller quote includes reference to "the mononomic, generic God"; the qualifiers are omitted here for directness and simplicity.

25. This insight comes from a private communication with Carl W. Ernst, UNC-CH, 12 July 2013.

26. Translated by Cleary, The Qur'an, 147, but modified with reference to Abdel Haleem, The Qur'an, 190. Most of the Qur'anic translations that follow come from these two sources or from the privately circulated renditions of Shawkat Toorawa, which he has kindly permitted me to cite.

CHAPTER ONE

1. Concerning Sahih Muslim Hadith 4731, the noted eighteenth-century Sufi master Ahmad Ibn 'Ajibah, in explaining the *hadith*, "Indeed Allah created Adam in His image," writes that "Allah gave Adam attributes that in a way resemble His own attributes. And these attributes are the [seven] attributes of meaning [e.g., life, power, knowledge, will over his actions, hearing, seeing, and speech]. Also He has made Adam a storehouse for many of His names. . . . So some people have the name 'al-Karim' (the Generous) become apparent on them [and thus they engage in acts of generosity]. Some people have the name 'Al-Rahim' (the Merciful) become apparent on them [and thus they show mercy to the creation of Allah]. . . . [al-Mabahith al-Asliyyah, line 22: 'And the reality of the human has a pattern in the Divine.']" Quoted in http://www

.sunniforum.com/forum/showthread.php?10399-God-created-man-in-his-own-image (accessed on 20 February 2014).

2. Ibid. The examples are mine.

3. For the poetics and politics of Eve as unnamed in the Qur'an, Sa'diyya Shaikh has provided a novel interpretation in Shaikh, *Sufi Narratives*, 142–43.

4. http://forums.islamicawakening.com/f40/meaning-inna-lillahi-wa-inna-ilahi-raajioon-30347/, cited in abbreviated and slightly modified form (accessed on 12 February 2013).

5. http://perennialreflection.wordpress.com/2011/05/08/tasbih-the-muslim-rosary/ (accessed but also summarized on 9 January 2013), but Qur'anic citation following the pattern of Cleary's translation, while substituting Allah for God.

6. Muhaiyaddeen, *Resonance of Allah*, 703.

7. See Cornell, *Realm of the Saint*, 137, on the *hizb Allah* of the thirteenth-century Maghribi Sufi exemplar, Abu Madyan.

8. The Ayatollah Khomeini ironically combined two forms of Allah in the fullest form of his own name: Ayatollah Ruhullah Khomeini.

9. The most insightful analysis of this critical handbook of popular meditation throughout the Muslim world is provided in Cornell, *Realm of the Saint*, esp. 175–77.

10. So common, and critical, is this phrase that it has its own name: *talbiya*. Among the many recent discussions of its deep history, marking Muslim pilgrims as distinct from their pagan, or *jahiliya*, precursors, see Seidensticker, "Sources," 293–321.

11. Cited and abbreviated from Gril, "There Is No Word," with detranslation of God to Allah in keeping with the spirit of this commentary and following the pattern of Cleary's translation in format. The author's insight into the complex thought of Ibn 'Arabi is at once lucid and highly original.

12. For this, as for many other insights about Allah, I am indebted to Professor Carl W. Ernst.

13. Its title, *Kitab al-'Abadila*, is a word play on *basmala*, which in its plural form would be *basamila*. See Ibn 'Arabi, *'Abadila*. So, by analogy, if you have many *Abdullahs*, they become *abadila*. This connection of two parts of the name as one orthographically also has another connotation, already noted by Ghazali in *Ninety-Nine Beautiful Names*, 178: "With 'Abdullah (servant of God) we form its plural by a single word (*'abadila*) rather than by two: *'Ibad Allah*, to stress the imposing of a name which is a also a free disposition regarding the one named!"

14. Al-Ruhani, *Fath Allah*, part 1, chap. 18, 139–58.

15. http://www.tumblr.com/tagged/5%20percenters (accessed on 11 June 2014).

16. Knight, "The Taqwacore Version."

17. For a brief popular exposition, see Bakhtiar, *Sufi*, 114–15. For a lengthy, near-exhaustive survey, see Gril, "La Science des lettres."

18. For a chart on how *abjad* works, consult http://www.princeton.edu/~achaney/tmve/wiki100k/docs/Abjad.html (accessed on 3 March 2014).

19. See note 47 below for Ibn Khaldun, *Muqaddimah*, and his discussion of *'ilm al-huruf*. There are also number/letter correspondences in *Rasa'I Ikhwan al-Safa*.

20. The further conceit, that the whole of the *basmala* is summarized in the letter *ba*, and the whole of the *ba* in the dot under the *ba*, has been examined by many de-

vout Muslims. It will be revisited below in chapter 4 with discussion of Ahmed Hulusi and his presence on the World Wide Web. For the longer history of the odyssey of *ba* in Sufism, one can do no better than consult Schimmel, *Mystical Dimensions* (Appendix 1, "Letter Symbolism in Sufi Literature"), 411–25.

21. This practice has been discussed and analyzed in Lawrence, *The Qur'an*, 190–92.

22. Ibn Khaldun, *Muqaddimah*, 87–89. Even in dismissing its authority, however, Ibn Khaldun ascribes the origin of the art of geomancy to ancient Romans such as Ptolemy or to scriptural prophets, whether the biblical Daniel or the Qur'anic Idris, and the practice of using numbers including numbers of the Divine Name has persisted in many Muslim societies till today.

23. www.madisonmorrison.com/topics/pattern-as-cosmology-in-islamic-geometric-art/pattern-4.html (accessed on 11 June 2014), but here reinterpreted by the contemporary American artist Katie Cooke.

CHAPTER TWO

1. There are several versions of this joke, and multiple websites about Mulla Nasruddin Hoca, the "simple" sage. The citation here is from Halman, *The Tales of Nasrettin Hoca*, 92. For a different version of the Hoca's public bath encounter with the feared Tamerlane, see http://salpagarov.narod.ru/kultura/hoca/Jokes.htm (accessed on 11 June 2014).

2. Jonathan Berkey makes a critical observation on the fluidity of the 'ulama ranks: "Religious scholarship could be a channel of social mobility, particularly under the conditions of the Middle Period (1200–1800), when the widespread creation and endowment of institutions such as madrasas provided scholarships to support students who might otherwise have lacked the financial resources to devote themselves to full-time study in preparation for a religious or legal career. It was even possible for individuals to acquire wealth through a career in religious scholarship, for example through a practice common in Mamluk times of particular scholars holding paying professorships at several institutions simultaneously. As a result, the 'ulama never constituted a closed profession, let alone a sacramentally distinct group (i.e., a clergy). Above all, individuals of vastly different socio-economic rank and of professional function participated in diverse ways in the transmission of religious knowledge which, in the end, is the only real marker of those who constituted the 'ulama" (209). As important as is their openness to access from below, the other point to note is that becoming a member of the 'ulama class was also always a mark of upward social mobility, and it also involved the proximity of military and political elites, as Berkey goes on to explain in the same chapter of his masterful overview of medieval Islamic society. See Berkey, *Formation of Islam*, 209–15.

3. For more on this perennial puzzle, see Rubinstein, *Aristotle's Children*.

4. On this point as on many others, al-Kindi was indebted to the sixth-century Christian philosopher John Philoponus. For further reference, see Endress, "The Circle of al-Kindi," 52–58; and also Gutas, *Greek Thought*, 145.

5. That came later with Ibn Sina; see Inati, *Problem of Evil*.

6. Among the numerous other Islamic philosophers who could be considered on

the issue of God's name and the dilemma of calling on the name without fully knowing God is al-Farabi (d. 950), who combines Aristotelian with Neoplatonic approaches when he asserts: "It is very difficult to know what God is because of the limitation of our intellect and its union with matter. Just as light is the principle by which colors become visible, in like manner it would seem logical to say that a perfect light should produce a perfect vision. Instead, the very opposite occurs. A perfect light dazzles the vision. The same is true of God. The imperfect knowledge we have of God is due to the fact that He is infinitely perfect. That explains why His infinitely perfect being bewilders our mind. But if we could strip our nature of all that we call 'matter' then certainly our knowledge of His being would be quite perfect." Yet in another place he says: "God is knowable and unknowable, evident and hidden, and the best knowledge of Him is to know that He is something the human mind cannot thoroughly understand." Cited in http://www.sacred-texts.com/isl/palf/palf07.htm (accessed on 12 January 2014).

7. Moosa, *Ghazali*, 173.

8. Consider the rebuke of Ibn ʿArabi to Ibn Rushd that begins chapter 3, depicting the Sufi way to Allah.

9. Harun Yahya is also cited below in chapter 4. He has been much critiqued on the Internet, most recently at http://www.irtiqa-blog.com/2013/01/the-importance-of-evolution-and-islam.html (accessed on 11 June 2014).

10. Josef van Ess, *Flowering of Muslim Theology*, 184. Fazlur Rahman echoes the same lament: the growth and persistence of "a sharp cleavage between the intellectual oligarchy and the multitude of the stupid" (*Prophecy in Islam*, 45).

11. This point is extensively developed in Sells, *Unsaying* (65, 244–45n8). Sells notes that there were many philosophical and juridical positions, e.g., Ashʿaris and Hanbalis, elided in their resort to *bi la kayfa*. For the Muʿtazilis, by contrast, it was important to know *kayfa*, i.e., how, or more precisely, how did these transpositions of the divine onto the human, the celestial to the terrestrial, actually take place?

12. In the late twentieth and now the twenty-first century, by contrast, Sufi adepts such as Ahmed Hulusi simply trust in the authority of science to validate the claims of revelation. See chapter 5.

13. Rahman, *Prophecy in Islam*, 98–99, though Moosa has qualified that critique in *Ghazali and the Poetics of Imagination*, 261–64.

14. Sells, *Unsaying*, 88–89.

15. Ibn ʿAtaʾ Allah Al-Iskandari, *Book of Illuminations*, 19–20.

16. Sells, *Unsaying*, 105–15. In analyzing the moment (*waqt*), Sells deftly portrays the endless movement from one state to another, so that the two hands of Allah become a metaphor for love-knowledge, *fana-baqa*, as "in each moment, each breath the heart reflects a new manifestation (love/*fana*) and becomes one with the divine in that manifestation (knowledge/*baqa*)" (115).

17. I am grateful to Kenneth L. Honerkamp for permission to quote from his forthcoming essay for *Wiley-Blackwell Companion of Islamic Spirituality*, "The Spirituality of Litanies, Invocations and Devotional Texts in Islam: Gleanings from the Textual Tradition of Sufism," where he elaborates on the outlook and practice of Ibn ʿAbbad of Ronda, along with other Sufi masters from Al-Andalus. For more on this topic, see chapter 3.

18. Schimmel, *Mystical Dimensions*, observes that this later tradition evokes man as the solace of Allah. "God, in His eternal loneliness, wanted to be known, so he created a world in which man is the highest manifestation" (189). That prompt from the Unseen has spurred the mystical quest to know the Treasure, even while protecting and honoring its persistent, insurmountable occlusion.

19. See ibid.

20. Only in the twentieth century, and primarily in the United States, did there appear movements that defined themselves as Sufi rather than Muslim. See Gisela Webb, "Negotiating Boundaries," on both the Sufi Order of the West and the Bawa Muhaiyaddeen Fellowship.

21. Sells, *Unsaying*, 5.

22. *Khoda* is the Persian translation of Allah, and until recently it framed the most familiar greeting among North Indian and Pakistani Muslims: *Khoda hafiz*, "may God protect you." Jamal Elias makes the valuable distinction between monotheism and monolatry. The former led to abolishing idols dedicated to Uzza in seventh-century Arabia, but the latter has caused a shift from the greeting *Khoda hafiz* to *Allah hafiz*. While both greetings stress the idea that the Thing, the Absolute, the One can protect, the recent shift to *Allah hafiz* verges on monolatry, to the extent that its practitioners believe that no other name will protect Muslims except the name Allah. Elias, "God," 178–80.

23. Nasr, *Islamic Cosmological Doctrines*, 52, as cited in Muzaffar Iqbal, *Biological Origins*, http://cis-ca.org/kalam/muzaffar.htm (accessed on 20 May 2013).

24. Marquet, "Quelles furent les relations."

25. Nasr, *Islamic Cosmological Doctrines*, 69. Also see Ikhwan as-Safa in http://www.iep.utm.edu/ikhwan-al-safa/ (accessed on 11 June 2014), and for a full evaluation of their relationship to contemporary philosophical issues, http://plato.stanford.edu/entries/ikhwan-al-safa/ (accessed on 11 June 2014).

26. Hamidullah and Iqbal, *The Emergence of Islam*, 133–34. The best treatment of the Ikhwan remains Nasr, *Islamic Cosmological Doctrines*. But also note other discussions in Martin, *Defenders of Reason*; and Fakhry, "Philosophy and Theology."

27. http://www.asharis.com/creed/ (accessed on 10 May 2013); slightly reworded here.

28. Ibid. (accessed on 1 March 2014).

CHAPTER THREE

1. The narrative here attributed to Omar Khayyam comes from his role as the central character in Yalsizucanlar, *The Thing*, 52–53; while the citation from Ibn ʿArabi is provided in Chittick, "Divine Names," 109.

2. I am indebted to Leela Prasad for this and other insights into the arguments of this chapter.

3. Al-Jerrahi, *Irshad*, 31–33. The four levels or signs in Arabic are *ayat al-aflakiya* (terrestrial), *ayat al-sufliya* (celestial), *ayat al-nafsiya* (psychological), and *ayat al-tanziliya* (revelatory).

4. Ibn ʿAtaʾ Allah Al-Iskandari, *Book of Illuminations*, 210–11.

5. Rinpoche, *Living and Dying*, 41.

6. Kugle, *Sufis and Saints' Bodies*, 142.

7. Quoted from Hujwiri in the classic book Schimmel, *Mystical Dimensions*, 169.

8. Addas, *Red Sulphur*, 37.

9. The real "unlettered" person, Ibn ʿArabi says, is someone who "does not use rational proofs to attain to the knowledge of divine things" (*Meccan Revelations*, I. 644).

10. Addas, *Red Sulphur*, 37, quoting *Meccan Revelations*, I. 154. Karen Armstrong also notes the relationship between Ibn ʿArabi and Ibn Rushd, but primarily stresses their divergent reception in the West and Islam. "Ibn ʿArabi did not influence the West. While western Christendom embraced Ibn Rushd's Aristotelian God, most of Islamdom opted, until relatively recently, for the imaginative God of the mystics (Armstrong, *A History of God*, 234).

11. Ibn ʿArabi, *Bezels*, 62.

12. Ghazali, *Beautiful Names*, 170–76.

13. It can be accessed at his website devoted to this artistic marvel: http://www .thecube ofcubes.com/ (accessed on 14 June 2014).

14. See also the related coffee table book, *Where the Two Oceans Meet*.

15. From Muhammad Asad, as quoted, with modifications, in Safi, *Memories*, 93–94.

16. Haeri, *Calling Allah*, 37.

17. An orally received adaptation from a Sufi master familiar with major mystical theorists, dedicated to the exposition of Shaykh al-Akbar but in daily meditation favoring Al-Ghazali's practice over the speculations of Ibn ʿArabi; Damascus, Syria, 1996. To review Al-Ghazali's effort to include all the names under ten possible categories, see Ghazali, *Beautiful Names*, 159–62.

18. William Chittick, "Divine Names," 111.

19. Ibid., 113.

20. Ibn ʿAtaʾ Allah Al-Iskandari, *Book of Illuminations*, 19–20.

21. Haeri, *Calling Allah*, 37. "According to Islamic cosmology, all existence is based upon a harmonious polarity of the active or male (*jalal*) and the receptive or female (*jamal*) attributes.

22. Sells, *Mystical Languages*, chaps. 3, 4.

23. Böwering, "Allah and His Attributes." I have selected only some names, while omitting others, from the author's list, at the same time modifying the frame categories. He retains Allah throughout the article, as do I in my extensive citation from the foremost reference book, at least in English, on Qurʾanic themes, topics, names, and places.

24. *Gulshan-i Raz*, Rule II, as cited in http://archive.org/stream/gulshanirazmys tiooshabuoft/gulshanirazmystiooshabuoft_djvu.txt (accessed on 24 August 2013).

25. Shabistari's vision, of course, is very close to the cosmology of the Ikhwan as-Safa, outlined at the end of chapter 2. God, intellect, and soul form the apogee in the hierarchical structure of the latter, while Creator, Universal Reason, and the Universal Soul launch Shabistari's descent through several regions till he, too, arrives at the three kingdoms—mineral, plant, and animal, with man, or humankind, becoming the subset of the last or animal kingdom.

26. Ibid.

27. The quote comes from a collection of *hadith* compiled by Sunni scholar ibn Hanbal (d. 855 CE) and is provided in Ibn Qayyim, *Invocation*, 144. Translation is here emended to capture the symbolic meaning of *jaffa al-qalam*, "the pen dried," that is, its ink will only be dry when Allah has writ with it on Judgment Day. I am indebted to Professor Carl W. Ernst for this insight and this correction.

28. Ibid., 146.

29. Ibid., 146–50; the entire set of citations comes from a chapter titled "The Light of Allah's Attributes."

30. Morris, "Spiritual Ascension" in Ibn 'Arabi, *Les illuminations de La Mecque/The Meccan Illuminations*, 363.

31. Muhaiyaddeen, *Resonance of Allah*, 135.

32. Muhaiyaddeen, *Islam and World Peace*, 102–3.

33. It is here translated by Swami Madhavananda; see http://archive.org/stream /Brihadaranyaka.Upanishad.Shankara.Bhashya.by.Swami.Madhavananda#page/n35 /mode/2up (accessed on 25 March 2013).

34. John Donne, *Holy Sonnets* XIV, from http://www.luminarium.org/sevenlit /donne/sonnet14.php (accessed on 30 July 2013).

35. Muhaiyaddeen, *Resonance of Allah*. In two critical passages the *shaykh* outlines his reasoning for these numbers. "A human being takes 15–16 breaths every minute. Thus in twenty four hours, he will take 15 or 16 x 60 x 24 breaths, which works out to 21,621 per day" (113n36). And then later, "If, through the divine analytic wisdom of the *Qutbiyyat*, one can bring this *dhikr* into the soul and make it travel along with the breath, then the *dhikr*, the wisdom, and the soul would ascend and descend as one, in union, 43,242 times a day (the number of breaths a human being takes per day)" (331n17).

36. Ibid., 106–29, abbreviated.

37. Ibid., 133.

38. This deepened sense of recovery is yet another insight that I have gleaned from Leela Prasad in her attentive, and creative, reading of an earlier draft of this manuscript.

39. Cited and abbreviated from Baqli, *The Unveiling*, 5–6.

40. *Divan*, 637:15 as quoted in Keshavarz, *Reading Mystical Lyric*, 113. In this instance, as in many others, Rumi is referring to a *hadith*, here the famous *hadith qudsi* (that is one where Allah Himself is the speaker): "I was a hidden treasure; then I wished to become known. And so I created the creation, that I may be known."

41. *Divan*, 2997:10, in ibid., 57.

42. *Divan*, 33:14–15, in ibid., 86.

43. From the *Divan* of Sa'di, not as famous as his *Gulistan* or *Bustan*, but cited here from a contemporary Iranian edition: *Kulliyat-e Sa'di*, 832.

44. Ibid., 790.

45. Hafez, *Faces of Love*, 148. While the beloved here could be a human or divine form, in another poem the subject/object is clearly Allah:

O God, be kind, and open wide your door,
I don't want others' kindness any more;

And if I've strayed from the right path, I know
That You will guide me where I have to go.
(If He considers me at all, then I
will gladly give my soul for Him, and die);
All powerful God, who needs no human prayer,
Open your door to me, receive me there.

Both these remarkable poems, along with Davis's introduction to Jahan Malek Khatun, are provided in Hafez, *Faces of Love*, xlii–lviii, 148, 161.

46. Rumi, *A Garden beyond Paradise*, 44–45.

47. Faith means, according to James, "faith in the existence of an unseen order of some kind in which the riddles of the natural order may be found explained. William James, "Is Life Worth Living?" 1895:40. Quoted from http://archive.org/stream/islifeworth livinoojameuoft/islifeworthlivinoojameuoft_djvu.txt (accessed on 30 March 2013).

48. Richardson, *William James*, 373, with acknowledgment of the decisive influence that George Fox, founder of Quakerism, had on James's inward turn.

CHAPTER FOUR

1. *The Rubaiyat of Omar Khayyam* (trans., Richard Le Gallienne) is quoted by Hitchens in the middle epigram announcing *god is not Great*; for the preceding quote, see p. 1.

2. Ibid., 124.

3. Lambek, "Certain Knowledge," 23; slightly abbreviated here.

4. Much of what follows has been adapted from Lawrence, "Muslim Engagement," 126–49.

5. For a clear retelling and brilliant exposition of this story, see Cornell, "The Ethiopian's Dilemma," 85–130. Several insights from that book inform and support the arguments of this study. Concerning polemics on the Internet, Cornell notes: "Saint John of Damascus (d. 749) wrote one of the first Christian polemics against Islam in his book *The Fount of Wisdom*. Today the chapter of this book on the 'Heresy of the Ishmaelites' (i.e., the Muslims) can be found on a Christian website called 'e-Sword-Users.org.'" And later, on how theology requires boundaries, he observes: "Every act of interreligious accommodation brings up the question of boundaries. Although the Kathisma of the Virgin [in Jerusalem] was a religious site, the compromise that allowed Muslims and Christians to share it was secular. At this site tolerance could exist only by keeping theology out of the discussion." And finally, on the value of an outsider's perspective, he argues: "the comparative perspective of an outsider would be useful in casting new light on one's own theological tradition." It is my hope that the latter goal can be partially realized in the evidence and arguments of the current book.

6. Donner, *Early Islamic Conquests*, 295–96.

7. Mourad and Lindsay, *Radicalization of Sunni Jihad Ideology*, 3.

8. Hillenbrand, *Crusades*, 243.

9. Quoted in Lawrence, *Shattering the Myth*, 68. The most insightful study of Sayyid

Qutb understands him as both a modernist and a fundamentalist. Like all fundamentalists, Qutb saw the world in binary terms: good vs. evil, Islam vs. the West, good Muslims, that is, Muslim mujahideen, vs. bad Muslims, whether Muslim secularists or compromising ruling elites. At the same time, however, Qutb was a thoroughgoing rationalist who accepted the relationship of knowledge to power in the modern state system and tried to use modern instruments in pursuit of "an overarching moral unity to overcome the fragmentation of knowledge that characterizes the modern world." See Euben, *Enemy in the Mirror*, 165–66.

10. Miller, "On 'The Summit,'" cited by permission of the author.

11. Lawrence, *Messages*, 19:205. The full poem is even more ironic given the circumstance of Bin Laden's actual death in May 2011:

I shall lead my steed
and hurl us both at the target.
Oh Lord, if my end is night,
may my tomb not be draped
in green mantles.
No, let it be the belly of an eagle,
perched up on high with his kin.
So let me be a martyr,
dwelling in a high mountain pass
among a band of knights who,
united in devotion to God,
descend to face armies.
When they leave this world,
they leave trouble behind,
and meet their Day of Judgment,
as told in the scriptures.

12. Miller, "On 'The Summit.'" The added emphases are mine.

13. Lawrence, *Messages*, 11:106–29, 3:23–30.

14. Ibid., 18:179–85.

15. Wilson, *Alif*, 111.

16. Ibid., 112. In addition to all the mainstream reviews of *Gödel, Escher, Bach* (*GEB*), there is a generation of geeks even more attuned to the mysteries of the Internet during the past two decades who see that book as prophetic. One even goes so far as to claim that *GEB* is "the secret nerd bible of my generation." He then adds, "If there's a thread that runs through all this stuff, it's the related ideas of recursion and self-reference—the strange loops that Hofstadter finds in (at the heart of) every system he studies. Recursion is weird. Look for it and you find it everywhere, and everywhere you find it, things that appear to be finite and arid and boring become infinitely, fractally interesting. In fact when I reread the Narnia books after reading *GEB*, I became obsessed with the idea of Narnia as an incomplete, infinitely regressing system. If the Pevensies die into Narnia in The Last Battle, and Narnia then collapses into Aslan's Country, how do we know that Aslan's Country won't then collapse into some still higher

reality, and so on, and so on, worlds without end? You could never be sure." http://levgrossman.com/2010/07/douglas-hofstadter-me-an-effing-great-book/ (accessed on 28 August 2013).

17. Wilson, *Alif*, 112.

CHAPTER FIVE

1. A recent effort to survey the options for translating the Arabic Qur'an into several languages is provided in Taji-Farouki, *Modern Muslims*. Enormous in scope, it covers almost all the vernacular linguistic traditions within the large arc of Muslim observance across Africa and Asia. It also has substantial chapters on Turkish, Persian, Arabic, Bosnian, German, and Chinese exegetes and/or translators. It further includes both a summary of English translations of the Qur'an as well as a long chapter on a controversial but little studied Arab-American commentator from the late twentieth to the early twenty-first century, Muhammad al-'Asi; see introduction, above.

2. For the quotation from Hulusi, see "on the names of Allah" at http://www.ahmedhulusi.org/en/ (accessed on 3 January 2013). So much has been written about Islam on the Internet that one has to select from multiple websites both in the Muslim world and Euro-America. The four best books in English are: Eickelman and Anderson, *New Media in the Muslim World*; Bunt, *iMuslims*, with special attention to Muslim bloggers and cyber environments; El-Nawawy and Khamis, *Islam dot com*, which discusses the most frequented Islamic websites; and Howard, *Digital Origins*, which looks at the political role of media ownership and technology use. Since 2006 there has also been an excellent online journal, *CyberOrient*, edited by Daniel Varisco, which tracks the representation of Islam in cyberspace, though mainly with reference to the impact of the Internet and new media in Middle Eastern contexts. None of these sources deals directly or explicitly with the multifaceted Muslim approach to Allah.

3. Jalees Rehman is a Pakistani-born American doctor, pharmacologist, and professor, who is also an addicted blogger. See, for example, his postings on http://fragments-of-truth.blogspot.com. While I do not agree with all his arguments, causes, or judgments, I applaud his honesty about the limits of Arabic language as an unassailable religious authority.

4. Like many Kingdom of Saudi Arabia sites, this has almost no religious theme, or message, focusing instead on commercial options, products, and services with a global reach; and it is projected in both Arabic and English. See www.awalnet.com/en/ (accessed on 11 June 2014).

5. Bunt, *iMuslims*, 81–85. The quote is a paraphrase of the query posed by the author on p. 81. Bunt explores the multiple ways that Muslim cybernauts, especially college students, tried to make use of digital formats for exploration of scripture and expansion of Muslim advocacy online.

6. The site is Alexa.com, a web information company founded in 1996; it provides updated monthly analytics on a wide range of virtual products and commercial as well as noncommercial websites. The html cited here is http://www.alexa.com/topsites/category/Top/Society/Religion_and_Spirituality/Islam (accessed on 30 May 2013).

7. See Blank, *Mullahs*.

8. Bunt, *iMuslims*, 283, abbreviated and edited here to fit the context of discussing website competition among Muslim website managers and users.

9. Himmelfarb, "A Neo-Luddite," A56.

10. Bunt, *iMuslims*, 80.

11. See http://islam.uga.edu/, but also note how quickly some of these hyperlinks change or are discarded. There are, of course, many other sites that could be noted. For a comprehensive list, as of 2003, see Bunt, *Islam in the Digital Age*, 223–26, and then for a further set of references, as of 2008, see Bunt, *iMuslims*, as well as his blog (virtuallyislamic.blogspot.com) and a further site in progress: http://islamicstudies .tumblr.com/.

12. Lawrence, "Allah On-Line," 237. I have changed the quote slightly to conform to the argument of this chapter.

13. Sardar, *Reading the Qur'an*, xiv.

14. Ibid., xv.

15. Ibid., 23, 35, 373.

16. See a particularly trenchant critique of Harun Yahya's views at http://www .irtiqa-blog.com/2013/01/the-importance-of-evolution-and-islam.html (accessed on 12 June 2014).

17. Not surprisingly, followers of Rashad Khalifa saw in these events, and numbers, confirmation of his special apostolic status (see http://masjidtucson.org/current /Khalifa_trial_sentencing.html). They viewed him as "a messenger of the Covenant," with a special apostolic relationship to Allah. Other Muslims, however, saw him as perhaps a Coptic decoy trying to subvert "true" Islam. The query spurred yet another of the many vacuous exchanges that, alas, also characterize part of the virtual culture of Internet communications, but also see a serious effort to refute Khalifa's views at http:// www.islamawareness.net/Deviant/Submitters/rashad_khalifa_purifier_or_pretender .html (accessed on 12 June 2014).

18. For in-depth consideration of Nursi, his thought, his writings, and his movement, see Mardin, *Religion and Social Change*. Though many other books have been written on Nursi, none has the thoroughness or subtlety of Mardin's classic study.

19. The author or translator here takes further license to add the commentary "in accord with the meaning signified by the letter B," as though it were part of the original text, which, of course, it is not. Ibid., 7. For another effort in the same direction, also from a Turkish source, see Kenan-Rifai, *Listen*.

20. www.ahmedhulusi.org/en/ (accessed on 3 January 2013).

21. See www.ahmedhulusi.org/en/quran/names-of-allah.html (accessed on 12 June 2014), where all of the *asma'(A)llah husna* are also examined, though without the same detail or import as is focused on Allah.

22. Two other major Muslim thinkers, both from late nineteenth- or early twentieth-century British India, struggled to reconcile the claims of science with the authority of scripture, specifically the Qur'an. They were Sayyid Ahmad Khan of Aligarh and Muhammad Iqbal of Lahore. For a more detailed exposition of their life story—activities, writings, and enduring impact, see Lawrence, *The Qur'an*, chaps. 11, 12.

23. El Saadawi, *The Innocence of the Devil*, 200–204. These are the so-called Satanic Verses, made even more scandalous by the Salman Rushdie novel of that title, *The*

Satanic Verses (1989); so blasphemous was its narrative that the Ayatollah Khomeini felt provoked to issue a *fatwa* against the author.

24. Hubal, their alleged son, is reckoned to be a third "pagan" deity, and when Osama bin Laden wants to excoriate President George W. Bush he labels him, and all America, as "the Hubal of the modern age." Lawrence, *Messages*, 10:205 and 14:149.

25. Of the many sources that could be consulted, one that comes up frequently is WikiIslam. See http://wikiislam.net/wiki/Hubal, itself parallel to the site in Wikipedia on Allat: http://en.wikipedia.org/wiki/Al-1 %C4%81t (accessed on 12 June 2014).

26. The argument that Patricia Crone makes about Hubal may also apply to Allat, namely that these deities were imported into a pagan cultic shrine practice where Allah was given a degree of preference, though not enough to qualify him as a "High God," the thesis argued by Wellhausen and later Watt. See Crone, *Meccan Trade*, 193–94.

27. For much of this information, see http://al-muqaddasarabianblog.blogspot.ca /2012/03/deity-allat.html (accessed on 11 January 2013).

28. http://www.metrolyrics.com/allah-hoo-allah-hoo-lyrics-nusrat-fateh-ali-khan .html (accessed on 12 July 2014). For more on Nusrat Fateh Ali Khan and the role of music or *sama'* in Chishti spirituality, see Ernst and Lawrence, *Sufi Martyrs*, 134–39.

29. The play on "*hu*," "*hu*," "*hu*" has a long tradition in Sufism, and it was cited by Rumi in the *Masnavi* as the key exchange between "The Policeman and the Drunkard" illustrating the benefit of spiritual intoxication. See Kritzeck, *Anthology*, 245–46.

30. Excerpted from the long, detailed commentary of a Chishti master trying to explicate the many options for the origin of the name Allah; http://www.chishti.ru/d _name.htm (accessed on 30 May 2013).

CONCLUSION

1. I am here echoing without fully engaging the project of Mohammed Arkoun, an Algerian semiotician. Steeped in Francophone culture and a longtime professor at the Sorbonne, Arkoun elaborated in numerous writings what he called applied Islamology. At its heart was the task of critiquing "the ideological function of orthodoxy" in search of the unthought/unthinkable as a historical, and not merely philosophical, project. See Arkoun, *Rethinking Islam*, 47, and for a magisterial analysis of Arkoun, comparing his legacy with that of other Muslim modernists, see Kersten, *Cosmopolitans and Heretics*, esp. 198–209.

2. See introduction.

3. George, "No Ethics without Things," but see also his "Ethics, Iconoclasm," 589–621. In both essays George quotes from Langenbach, "Iconoclash," 176–81.

4. George, *Picturing Islam*, on the inset between pp. 46–47, includes these two Qur'anic chapters, along with other calligraphic representations, done in marble paste, gold leaf, and acrylic on canvas. There are few other critical works on Islamic art, but especially calligraphy as a newly created kind of mass market art, that approach the subtlety and insight of George's monograph on the Achinese artist Abdul Djalil Pirous.

5. The commentary here is excepted from the artist's statement that accompanied a group exhibit of exiled Iranian women artists, titled Labyrinth of Exile, and shown

at the UCLA Fowler Museum of Cultural History (25 June–18 September 1994). I have paraphrased the syntax slightly in order to underscore the point about connecting literature to art.

6. See National Public Radio, 12 June 2013, http://www.npr.org/blogs/thetwo-way/2013/06/12/191091018/egyptian-author-sentenced-to-prison-for-book-where-is-god (accessed on 12 June 2014).

7. On the censorship issue surrounding the play, see http://wiki.ncac.org/God_Resigns_in_the_Summit_Meeting (accessed on 12 June 2014); for the book itself, see El Saadawi, *God Resigns and Isis*.

8. For more on this painting and the artist's cosmopolitan creativity, see Lawrence, "The Fuzzy Logic of M. F. Husain," 269–74. I also wrote about my own association with the author soon after his death on 9 June 2011. See article at https://today.duke.edu/2011/06/husain (accessed on 12 June 2014).

9. Ummah Defense, IslamGames, 2001, CD-ROM. Islam Fun, Innovative Minds, 2002, CD-ROM (accessed via Google search on 10 January 2013). After the 7 July 2005 attacks on London, the videogame world was scoured for possible incendiary suggestions that might have influenced the attackers. Responding to an article in the *Wall Street Journal*, *New York Times* columnist Thomas Friedman on 22 July 2005 flagged the *Journal* reports and quoted this tidbit: "One game, 'Ummah Defense I,' has the world 'finally united under the Banner of Islam' in 2114, until a revolt by disbelievers. The player's goal is to seek out and destroy the disbelievers." See www.nytimes.com/2005/07/22/opinion/22friedman.html (accessed on 12 June 2014).

10. PC CD-ROM Maze of Destiny, copyright 2004 Islamgames.com, back cover (slightly paraphrased).

11. Sardar, in *Reading the Qur'an*, decries the influence of *madrasa* straitjacket teaching of the Qur'an, even as he argues insistently and repeatedly for new readings that "delineate the pluralistic and humane message of the Qur'an" (51).

12. Seierstad, *The Bookseller of Kabul*, 194–96. I am indebted to her for insight into the background of her book, and also into the contest to understand Allah in current Afghanistan, both of which she shared with me at a 2012 Oslo conference. Organized by the Literaturhuset, with funding from the Norwegian Ministry of Foreign Affairs, the 4th International Saladin Days was designed to probe the mindset of Islamophobia, and to offset the horror of the sequential bombing and mass murders committed by Anders Breivik on 22 July 2011. See http://www.litteraturhuset.no/nyheter/2012/saladin 2012.html (accessed on 12 June 2012).

13. To explore more about the Malaysian controversy on Christian use of Allah, see the recent *Wall Street Journal* article, http://online.wsj.com/news/articles/SB100014 24052702303848104579308180235121604 (accessed on 12 June 2014). Especially disturbing is the survey cited in the last paragraph of this article: "On the specific use of the word 'Allah,' a recent survey by the University of Malaya's Centre for Democracy and Elections showed that 77% of 1,676 citizens surveyed in peninsular Malaysia believe that Muslims should have exclusive right to use the word 'Allah,' while only 11% supported non-Muslims using the word." What is not said here is that all those surveyed were Malay Muslims, not Chinese or Indians or Malay Christians, so politicians loyal to Malay Muslim constituents will continue to feel justified using Allah as a

moniker for Islamic loyalty rather than the Name of the Thing, the Absolute, the One beyond knowing or claiming or limiting.

14. ʿAli, *The Holy Qurʾan*.

15. See Imad-ad-Dean Ahmad, http://theamericanmuslim.org/tam.php/features /articles/book_review_on_the_new_revised_edition_of_yusuf_alis_quran_translation (accessed on 4 December 2012).

16. Excerpted from the preface to Yusuf Ali at http://www.institutealislam.com/the -holy-quran/preface-to-the-first-edition-1934/ (accessed on 4 December 2012). Though many references to the Yusuf Ali edition, recycled and modified by Amana, have now disappeared from the Internet, it is still available on the following site: http://www .sacred-texts.com/isl/quran/00101.htm (accessed on 11 June 2014).

17. See Sardar, *Reading the Qurʾan*, 49.

18. Muhaiyaddeen, *Islam and World Peace*, 146.

19. Kugle, *Sufis and Saints' Bodies*, 222.

20. Ibid., 238.

21. Ibid., 258.

22. Ibid., 287.

23. Ibid., 287–88.

24. Ibid., 290.

Bibliography

Abramson, Glenda. *Soldiers' Tales: Two Palestinian Jewish Soldiers in the Ottoman Army during the First World War*. London and Portland, Ore.: Vallentine Mitchell, 2013.

Abdel Haleem, M. A. S. *The Qur'an: A New Translation*. Oxford: Oxford University Press, 2004.

Addas, Claude. *The Quest for Red Sulphur: The Life of Ibn 'Arabi*. Translated by Peter Kingsley. Cambridge: The Islamic Texts Society, 1993.

Ali, Abdullah Yusuf. *The Holy Qur'an: English Translation and Commentary (with Arabic Text)*. 1st ed. Kashmiri Bazar, Lahore: Shaikh Muhammad Ashraf, 1934.

Arkoun, Muhammad. *Rethinking Islam: Common Questions/Uncommon Answers*. Translated by Robert Lee. Boulder, Colo.: Westview Press, 1994.

Armstrong, Karen. *A History of God: The 4,000-year Quest of Judaism, Christianity, and Islam*. New York: Ballantine Books, 1993.

Bakhtiar, Laleh. *Sufi: Expressions of the Mystic Quest*. 1976. London: Thames & Hudson, 2004.

Baqli, Ruzbihan. *The Unveiling of Secrets: Diary of a Sufi Master*. Translated by Carl W. Ernst. Chapel Hill, NC: Parvardigar Press, 1997.

Berkey, Jonathan. *The Formation of Islam: Religion and Society in the Near East, 600–1800*. Cambridge: Cambridge University Press, 2003.

Blank, Jonah. *Mullahs on the Mainframe*. Chicago: University of Chicago Press, 2001.

Böwering, Gerhard. "Allah and His Attributes." In *Encyclopaedia of the Qur'an*, Edited by Jane Dammen McAuliffe. Brill Online (accessed on 25 March 2014).

Bunt, Gary R. *iMuslims: Rewiring the House of Islam*. Chapel Hill: University of North Carolina Press, 2009.

———. *Islam in the Digital Age: E-Jihad, Online Fatwas and Cyber Islamic Environments*. London: Pluto Press, 2003.

Chittick, William C. "Divine Names and Theopteries." In *Les illuminations de La Mecque/The Meccan Illuminations* by Ibn 'Arabi, 75–116. Textes choisis/Selected texts. Paris: Sindbad, 1988.

Cleary, Thomas. *The Qur'an: A New Translation*. Chicago: Starlatch Press, 2004.

Cornell, Vincent J. "The Ethiopian's Dilemma: Islam, Religious Boundaries, and the Identity of God." In *Do Jews, Christians, and Muslims Worship the Same God?* by Jacob Neusner, Baruch A. Levine, Bruce D. Chilton, and Vincent J. Cornell, 85–130. Nashville, TN: Abingdon Press, 2012.

———. *The Realm of the Saint: Power and Authority in Moroccan Sufism*. Austin: University of Texas Press, 1998.

Cragg, Kenneth. *The Call of the Minaret*. 1956. Oxford: Oneworld Press, 2000.

———. *Jesus and the Muslim: An Exploration*. 1985. Oxford: Oneworld Press, 1999.

Crone, Patricia. *Meccan Trade and The Rise of Islam*. Oxford: Basil Blackwell, 1987.

Donner, Fred M. *The Early Islamic Conquests*. Princeton: Princeton University Press. 1981.

———. *Muhammad and the Believers: At the Origins of Islam*. Cambridge: Harvard University Press, 2010.

Eickelman, Dale, and Jon W. Anderson, eds. *New Media in the Muslim World: The Emerging Public Sphere*. 2nd ed. Bloomington: Indiana University Press, 2003.

Elias, Jamal J. "God." In *Key Themes for the Study of Islam*, edited by Jamal J. Elias, 161–81. Oxford: Oneworld Publications, 2010.

Endress, G. "The Circle of al-Kindi." In *The Ancient Tradition in Christian and Islamic Hellenism*, edited by G. Endress and R. Kruk, 52–58. Leiden: Research School CNWS, 1997.

Ernst, Carl W., and Bruce B. Lawrence. *Sufi Martyrs of Love: The Chishti Brotherhood in South Asia and Beyond*. New York: Palgrave, 2002.

Euben, Roxanne. *Enemy in the Mirror: Islamic Fundamentalism and the Limits of Modern Rationalism: A Work of Comparative Political Theory*. Princeton: Princeton University Press, 1999.

Fakhry, Majid. "Philosophy and Theology: From the 8th Century to the Present." In *The Oxford History of Islam*, edited by John L. Esposito, 269–304. New York: Oxford University Press, 1999.

George, Kenneth M. "No Ethics without Things." *Journal of Religious Ethics*, forthcoming.

———. "Ethics, Iconoclasm, and Qur'anic Art in Indonesia." *Cultural Anthropology* 24, no. 4 (2009): 589–621.

———. *Picturing Islam: Art and Ethics in a Muslim Lifeworld*. Oxford: Wiley-Blackwell, 2010.

Ghazali, Abu Hamid Muhammad ibn Muhammad al-. *The Ninety-nine Beautiful Names of Allah*. Translated by David Burrell and Nazih Daher. Cambridge: Islamic Texts Society, 1992.

Gimaret, Daniel. *Les noms divins en Islam: Exégèse lexicographique et théologique*. Paris: Les éditions du Cerf, 1988.

Gril, Denis. "There Is No Word in the World That Does Not Indicate His Praise." Translated by Lakshmi Pachenick. *Journal of the Muhyiddin Ibn 'Arabi Society*, special issue *Praise*, 21 (1997): 31–43. http://www.ibnarabisociety.org/articles/indicatehispraise.html (accessed on 3 January 2013).

———. "La science des lettres." In Ibn al-'Arabi, Muhyi al-din, *The Meccan Illuminations: Selected Texts*, translated by William C. Chittick, Michel Chodkiewicz, Denis Gril, and James W. Morris, 383–487. Paris: Sindbad, 1988.

Gutas, Dimitri. *Greek Thought, Arabic Culture: The Graeco-Arabic Translation Movement in Baghdad and Early 'Abbasid Society (2nd–4th/8th–10th Centuries)*. London: Routledge, 1998.

Haeri, Fadhlalla. *Calling Allah by His Most Beautiful Names*. Wierda Park, Centurion, South Africa: Zahra Trust, 2002.

Hafez Shirazi. *Faces of Love: Hafez and the Poets of Shiraz*. Translated by Dick Davis. New York: Penguin, 2013.

Halman, Talat, trans. *The Tales of Nasrettin Hoca*. Istanbul: Silk Road Publications, n.d.

Hamidullah, Muhammad, and Afzal Iqbal. *The Emergence of Islam: Lectures on the Development of Islamic World-view, Intellectual Tradition and Polity*. Islamabad: Islamic Research Institute, 1993.

Hamner, Juliane, and Omid Safi, eds. *The Cambridge Companion to American Islam*. New York: Cambridge University Press, 2013.

Hawting, G. R. *The Idea of Idolatry and the Emergence of Islam: From Polemic to History*. Cambridge: Cambridge University Press, 1999.

Hillenbrand, Carole. *The Crusades: Islamic Perspectives*. Edinburgh: Edinburgh University Press, 1999.

Himmelfarb, Gertrude. "A Neo-Luddite Reflects on the Internet." *Chronicle of Higher Education* 43, no. 10 (November 1, 1996). http://chronicle.com/article/A-Neo -Luddite-Reflects-on-the/74797/.

Hitchens, Christopher. *God Is Not Great: How Religion Poisons Everything*. New York: Atlantic Books, 2007.

Hofstader, Douglas R. *Gödel, Escher, Bach: An Eternal Golden Braid*. 1979. New York: Basic Books, 1999.

Howard, Phillip N. *The Digital Origins of Dictatorship and Democracy: Information Technology and Political Islam*. Oxford: Oxford University Press, 2010.

Hulusi, Ahmed. *Prologue to Decoding the Quran: A Sufi Perspective in Light of the Letter B*. www.ahmedhulusi.org/en (accessed on 12 August 2013).

Ibn 'Arabi, Muhyiddin, *Kitab al-'Abadila*. Cairo: Maktaba al-Qahira, 1993.

———. Les illuminations de La Mecque/*The Meccan Illuminations: Textes choisis/ Selected Texts*. Translated by William C. Chittick, Michel Chodkiewicz, Denis Gril, and James W. Morris. Paris: Sindbad, 1989.

———. *Bezels of Wisdom*. Translated by R. W. J. Austin. New York: Paulist Press, 1980.

Ibn 'Ata' Allah al-Iskandari. *The Book of Illuminations* (*Kitab al-tanwir fi isqat al-tadbir*). Translated by Scott A. Kugle. Louisville, Ky.: Fons Vitae, 2005.

Ibn Khaldun, 'Abd ar-Rahman. *The Muqaddimah*. Translated by Franz Rosenthal. Abridged by N. J. Dawood. Introduced by Bruce B. Lawrence. Princeton: Princeton University Press, 2005.

Ibn Qayyim al-Jawziyya. *The Invocation of Allah (Al-Wabil al-sayyib min al-kalim at-tayyib)*. Translated by M. A. Qasmi. Delhi: Adam Publishers, 2008.

Inati, Shams C. *The Problem of Evil: Ibn Sina's Theodicy*. Binghamton, N.Y.: Global Publications, 2000.

Al-Jerrahi, Sheikh Muzaffar Ozak. *Irshad: Wisdom of a Sufi Master*. Translated by Muhtar Holland. Warwick, N.Y: Amity House, 1988.

Kenan-Rifai. *Listen: Commentary on the Spiritual Couplets of Mevlana Rumi*. Translated by Victoria Holbrook. Louisville, Ky: Fons Vitae, 2011.

Kersten, Carool. *Cosmopolitans and Heretics: New Muslim Intellectuals and the Study of Islam*. New York: Columbia University Press, 2011.

Keshavarz, Fatemeh. *Reading Mystical Lyric: The Case of Jalal al-Din Rumi*. Columbia: University of South Carolina Press, 1998.

Khayyam, Omar. *The Rubaiyat of Omar Khayyam*. Translated by Richard Le Gallienne. New York: John Lane Company, 1916.

Knight, Michael Muhammad. "The Taqwacore Version (of Allah and Islam)." *Critical Muslim* 2 (2012): 78–84.

———. *The Taqwacores*. New York: SoftSkullPress, 2004.

Kritzeck, James, ed. *Anthology of Islamic Literature*. New York: Mentor, 1964.

Kugle, Scott. *Sufis and Saints' Bodies*. Chapel Hill: University of North Carolina Press, 2007.

Lambek, Michael. "Certain Knowledge, Contestable Authority: Power and Practice on the Islamic Periphery." *American Ethnologist* 17, no. 1 (February 1990): 23–40.

Langenbach, Ray, with Arahmaiani. "Iconoclash." *Broadsheet* 36, no. 3 (2007): 176–81.

Lawrence, Bruce B. "All Distinctions Are Political, Artificial: The Fuzzy Logic of M. F. Husain." *Common Knowledge* 19, no. 2 (April 2013): 269–74.

———. "Muslim Engagement with Injustice and Violence." In *The Oxford Handbook on Religious Violence*, edited by Mark Juergensmeyer et al., 126–52. New York: Oxford University Press, 2013.

———. "Osama bin Laden—The Man and the Myth." In *The Leader: Psychohistorical Essays*, 2nd ed., edited by Charles B. Strozier, 119–34. New York: Springer, 2011.

———. *The Qur'an: A Biography*. London: Atlantic Books, 2007.

———, ed. *Messages to the World: The Statements of Osama bin Laden*. London and New York: Verso, 2005.

———. "Allah On-Line: The Practice of Global Islam in the Information Age." In *Practicing Religion in the Age of the Media: Explorations in Media, Religion, and Culture*, edited by Stewart M. Hoover and Lynn Schofield Clark, 237–53. New York: Columbia University Press, 2002.

———. *Shattering the Myth: Islam beyond Violence*. Princeton: Princeton University Press, 1998.

Mardin, Serif. *Religion and Social Change in Modern Turkey: The Case of Bediuzzaman Said Nursi*. Albany: State University of New York Press, 1989.

Marquet, Yves. "Quelles furent les relations entre Jabir ibn Hayyan et les Ihwan as-Safa?" *Studia Islamica* 1, no. 64 (1986): 39–51.

Martin, Richard C. *Defenders of Reason in Islam*. Oxford: Oneworld, 1997.

Miller, W. Flagg, "On 'The Summit of the Hindu Kush': Osama Bin Laden's 1996 Declaration of War Reconsidered." Unpublished talk, University of Michigan, March 2005.

Montaigne, Michel de. *Essays*. Translated by Charles Cotton. Illustrated by Salvador Dali. New York: Doubleday, 1947.

Moosa, Ebrahim. *Ghazali and the Poetics of Imagination*. Chapel Hill: University of North Carolina Press, 2005.

Morris, James W. "Ibn al-ʿArabi's Spiritual Ascension." In Ibn al-ʿArabi, Muhyi al-din, *The Meccan Illuminations: Selected Texts*, translated by William C. Chittick, Michel Chodkiewicz, Denis Gril, and James W. Morris, 351–81. Paris: Sindbad, 1989.

Mourad, Suleiman, with James E. Lindsay. *The Radicalization of Sunni Jihad Ideology in the Crusader Period*. Aldershot: Ashgate, 2011.

Moustafa, Ahmed. *Where the Two Oceans Meet: The Art of Ahmed Moustafa*. Fe-Noon Ahmed Moustafa UK Ltd., 1998.

———. *The Attributes of Divine Perfection: The Concept of God in Islam*. Jeddah: The Book Foundation, 1998.

Muhaiyaddeen, Muhammad Raheeem Bawa. *Islam and World Peace: Explanations of a Sufi*. Philadelphia: Fellowship Press, 1987.

———. *The Resonance of Allah: Resplendent Explanations Arising from the Nur, Allah's Wisdom of Grace*. Philadelphia: Fellowship Press, 1981.

Murata, Sachiko, and William C. Chittick. *The Vision of Islam*. St. Paul: Paragon House, 1994.

Nasr, Seyyed Hossein. *An Introduction to Islamic Cosmological Doctrines: Conceptions of Nature and Methods Used for Its Study by the Ikhwan Al-Safa, Al-Biruni, and Ibn Sina*. Albany: State University of New York Press, 1992.

El- Nawawy, Mohammed, and Sahar Khamis. *Islam dot com: Contemporary Islamic Discourses in Cyberspace*. New York: Palgrave Macmillan, 2009.

Neuwirth, Angelika et al. *The Qur'an in Context: Historical and Literary Investigations into the Qur'anic Milieu*. Leiden: E. J. Brill, 2011.

Rahman, Fazlur. *Prophecy in Islam: Philosophy and Orthodoxy*. Chicago: University of Chicago Press, 1958.

Razi, Fakhr ad-din. *Traite sur les noms divins*. 2 vols. Translated by Maurice Gloton. Paris: Dervy, 1986.

Richardson, Robert D. *William James: In the Maelstrom of American Modernism*. New York: Houghton Mifflin, 2006.

Rinpoche, Sogyal. *The Tibetan Book of Living and Dying*. San Francisco: HarperSanFrancisco, 1999.

Rubinstein, Richard. *Aristotle's Children: How Christians, Muslims, and Jews Rediscovered Ancient Wisdom and Illuminated the Dark Ages*. New York: Harcourt, 2003.

Ruhani, Maulana Bazi. *The Conquest of Allah through the Special Qualities of the Name Allah (Al-Fath Allah fi Khasa'is al-Ism Allah)*. Lahore: Idarah Tasnif al-Adab, 2000.

Rumi, Jalal ad-din. *A Garden beyond Paradise: The Mystical Poetry of Rumi*. Translated by Jonathan Star and Shahram Shiva. New York: Bantam Books, 1992.

El Saadawi, Nawal. *The Dramatic Literature of Nawal El Saadawi: God Resigns and Isis*. London: Saqi Books (Kindle edition), 2012.

———. *The Innocence of the Devil (Jannat wal-Iblis)*. Translated by Sherif Hetata. Berkeley: University of California Press, 1994.

Sa'di, Muslih ad-din. *Kulliyat-e Sa'di*. Edited by Zaka al-Mulk Furughi. 1354. Teheran, 1975.

Safi, Omid. *Memories of Muhammad*. San Francisco: HarperOne, 2009.

Sardar, Ziauddin. *Reading the Qur'an: The Contemporary Relevance of the Sacred Text of Islam*. London: Hurst & Co., 2011.

Schimmel, Annemarie. *Mystical Dimensions of Islam*. Chapel Hill: University of North Carolina Press, 1975.

Seidensticker, Tilman. "Sources for the History of Pre-Islamic Religion." In Angelika

Neuwirth et al., *The Qur'an in Context: Historical and Literary Investigations into the Qur'anic Milieu*, 293–321. Leiden: E. J. Brill, 2011.

Seierstaad, Asne. *The Bookseller of Kabul*. New York: Little, Brown and Company, 2011.

Sells, Michael A. *Mystical Languages of Unsaying*. Chicago: University of Chicago Press, 1994.

Shahrastani, Muhammad Ibn 'Abd al-Karim al-. *Keys to the Arcana: Shahrastani's Esoteric Commentary on the Qur'an*. Translated by Toby Meyer. Oxford: Oxford University Press, 2009.

Shaikh, Sa'diyya. *Sufi Narratives of Intimacy: Ibn 'Arabi, Gender, and Sexuality*. Chapel Hill: University of North Carolina Press, 2012.

Taji-Farouki, Suha, ed. *Modern Muslims Reading the Qur'an*. Oxford: Oxford University Press, forthcoming.

Van Ess, Josef. *The Flowering of Muslim Theology*. Translated by Jane Marie Todd. Cambridge: Harvard University Press, 2006.

Varisco, Daniel M., ed. *CyberOrient: Online Journal of the Virtual Middle East*. 2006.

Webb, Gisela. "Negotiating Boundaries: American Sufis." In *The Cambridge Companion to American Islam*, edited by Juliane Hamner and Omid Safi, 190–207. New York: Cambridge University Press, 2013.

Wilson, G. Willow. *Alif the Unseen*. New York: Grove Press, 2012.

Yalsizucanlar, Sadik. *The Thing*. Istanbul: Timas Publishing, 2009.

Acknowledgments

Acknowledgments are the easiest and the hardest part of any book project. They are the easiest because they do not involve research, evidence, or arguments. Nor do they set forth agendas for reflection or action. Yet they do require a level of exactitude that is at once unconscious and pervasive. How many people have helped at what levels in what ways to make this book a near reality? If I had to provide the most inclusive calculus of gratitude, it would extend back to Professor Khaliq Ahmad Nizami, who hosted me and my family in Aligarh from 1974 to 1976. Professor Nizami's generosity of time and spirit introduced me to an engagement with South Asian Islam, and especially institutional Sufism, that has informed all my subsequent academic labor, including this book. It was another Indian exemplar, Maqbool Fida Husain, also known as M. F. Husain, who spurred me to rethink categories of visual and verbal truth. My wife and I were privileged to meet Maqbool, as we called him, at the opening of the Museum of Islamic Art in Doha in 2008. Two years later when we returned to Doha as the first scholars-in-residence at this same museum, we spent many hours with Maqbool. We also hosted what turned out to be his last birthday party in a symposium dedicated to him in September 2010. (He died in June 2011 at the age of ninety-five.) Five of the people attending that Doha symposium also contributed to this book: Kristine Stiles, by her vigorous insistence on performing, not just viewing, art; Ken George, by his wondrous engagement with Indonesian artists, including Arahmaiani, whose work is also examined in this book; Carl and Judy Ernst, who together have provided some of the most lively, and informed, discussions of art and society that I have ever had; and Ahmed Moustafa, the Egyptian calligrapher, whose Ka'ba cube redefines the nature of Allah's Ninety-nine Names as also the *barzakh* realm of the human imagination. Now Owais Husain, M. F. Husain's son, has kindly agreed to let me include images of two of his father's paintings in this book. While I have many others to thank, I could not have conceived or written this book without the catalyst and creativity of M. F. Husain, and so it is to him that I dedicate my own quest to understand, and to help others understand, who is Allah.

Duke University has provided me an institution from which to work, with a library and office that made many forays into discrete subtopics not only possible but actually enjoyable. Two other institutions have contributed to the emergence and reshaping of the central themes of my project. One was Literaturhuset (Literature House) in Oslo, Norway, where I was invited to be a guest speaker in March 2012 and also had the privilege of sharing a public forum with author Asne Seierstaad as we together explored the meaning of Allah in contemporary Afghanistan. The other institution that assisted me was the Centre for the Comparative Study of Muslim Societies at Simon Fraser University in British Columbia. There, my friend and colleague Derryl McLean invited me, along with my spouse, miriam cooke, to lead a summer seminar, which I did while at the same time offering a public lecture entitled "Who is Allah?" Both the Vancouver venue and its lively audience provided insight into the multiple dimensions of my topic.

Many others were instrumental in making this book not just possible but also more capacious and accessible to a broad readership. It was Elaine Maisner of UNC Press who insisted that I make a stab at this topic for the subcluster of whos and whats that she oversees in the press's series Islamic Civilization and Muslim Networks, which I coedit with Carl Ernst. It was during a conversation at the annual American Academy of Religion meeting in Fall 2011 in San Francisco that the seed was planted. It has continued to grow under her watchful, critical, but also friendly eye. I am indebted to her, as I am to others at UNC Press, including anonymous readers of an early version, who made me work harder to sharpen arguments, refine evidence, and also provide both summaries and sidebars for future readers.

In making the actual manuscript into a book, no one stands ahead of miriam cooke. She is my spouse but much more. She has read and commented on nearly every word. She also provided the Montaigne epigraph that defines not just the first chapter but also the entire book. Also generous with time and insight about my arguments has been Dr. Jim Cross. The father of one of my prized former students, Jonathan Cross, Dr. Cross volunteered to read a bit of what I was writing in Fall 2013, and then ended up reading, correcting, and commenting on the entire manuscript. I have mentioned Dr. Cross's thoughtful provocations at particular points in some endnotes, but he did much more than any endnote could satisfactorily register. Also reading an early version of the manuscript was Samara Holub-Moorman, a 2009 graduate of Reed College, who had helped me edit an earlier book and once again provided assistance in reshaping this manuscript into a better book. Numerous others read all or part of the manuscript and offered constructive suggestions about both its content and its exposition. They include colleagues Leela Prasad, Melvin Peters, Peter Gottschalk, Richard Martin, Omid Safi, Scott Kugle, Vince and Rkia Cornell, Abdullahi an-Naʿim, Ken George, and SherAli Tareen. Shawkat Torowa at Cornell University, a gifted linguist and close friend, has been especially generous in allowing me to cite lyrical renditions of the Qurʾan that he has privately circulated.

The final push to make images part of this book was a parallel endeavor to editing its content. It was also an unexpected challenge. I would not have reached the goal line in tracing sources, securing permissions, and organizing a file of photos had it not been for the assistance of Peter Cooke, my nephew and an Honors Carolina student. Peter did forensic labor that helped make the images possible, and his sister, my niece Katie Cooke, a senior at Wake Forest University, provided a service I could scarcely have imagined, and one for which I am indebted to her: two of the images that could not be captured from virtual sources she re-created as new images, and then made photos of them that I could, and did, include in the book. I owe both Peter and Katie Cooke a huge debt of gratitude for their role in adding a visual breadth as well as depth to what I have written.

Lastly I must say that I have often experienced what is known as *baraka*, or divine blessing, in the stages that led up to the making and finalizing of this book. There are countless artists and supporters of art who have helped me: I had given up on contacting the son of Fevzi Gunuc when my friend Feyza Burak Adli secured the necessary permission for his spectacular calligraphy of Allah/Muhammad and then, through her sister, Sena Celik Burak, helped obtain a clearer resolution copy of this same image in Istanbul. On another set of photos related to the marvelous *pir* of Philadelphia, Shaykh Bawa Muhaiyaddeen, I was connected to his inner fellowship by Gisela Webb of Seton Hall and then aided immensely by Kelly Hayden of the Bawa Muhaiyaddeen Fellowship. For the photo of Indonesian artist Arahmaiani the artist herself helped me track down the elusive permission needed from a Chinese photographer.

One crucial element, though, seemed to elude me. In early January 2014, as the manuscript was nearing completion, it became clear that I could not locate anywhere on the World Wide Web the calligraphic expression of Allah that I hoped would grace each section of the book. I had assumed that I could, and would, find it, as I had so many other visual elements that had inspired me, for the eventual production of the book. I was close to despair about this gaping void when I had to visit Washington, D.C., for a late January conference at George Washington University. While there, I contacted the calligrapher Mohamed Zakariya. I had never met him. He invited me to tea in his Arlington, Virginia, home. We talked for almost three hours. They felt like thirty minutes. As we parted, Mohamed said: "I'll make you a *lafz-e celal*, the calligraphic element that features Allah, and send it to you in North Carolina." And he did. As a result, the same American artist who provided the popular Eid U.S. postage stamp has now graced my book with his masterful lines and strokes and signature (on the bottom left side of the opening element of each chapter).

Also *baraka*, from another era, is the cover of the book. Moroccan artist Mohamed Melehi provided this acrylic painting of *hu*, the pronoun that stands for A-l-l-a-hu in Arabic. He had done the painting while at Duke in the late 1980s, then gifted it to me and my wife, miriam cooke, before leaving North Carolina to return to Asila, his home in Morocco. Mohamed graciously allowed us to use a photo of this same painting for the cover of the book.

I have no words to thank the diverse cluster of high-minded, generous people who have assisted me with the idea, the prospect, the process, and now the near reality of a book tracing Allah through myriad times, places, and circumstances. What I have done with all their labor is no fault of theirs. Whatever remains in the *barzakh*, a liminal space between certainty and uncertainty, clarity and obscurity, is my burden, and mine alone, to bear.

Index

(n. 4). See also *Dhikr*; Divine Names; Invocations; *Jihad*

Allah ta'ala (Allah the Lofty the Exalted): as invocation, 25, 29–30, 34, 51, 52, 108, 114; and science, 151, 153

Allahu Akbar (Allah is Greater): as call to prayer, 7, 8, 29–30, 31, 32, 34, 147, 169; media on, 7–8; Hitchens on, 119–20; and radical religious activists, 140; and paintings, 167, 169

Allat, 11, 154–56, 200 (n. 26)

Al-Qaida, 134, 136, 140, 178

Amana Publications, 174, 202 (n. 16)

Amon, Yehuda, 188 (n. 14)

Amulets, 50, 51

al-Andalus, 70, 192 (n. 17)

Anderson, Jon W., 198 (n. 2)

An-Nur (Radiant, Unending Light), 101

Apophatic language, 76–77

Aquinas, Thomas, 64

Arab Christians, 2, 13

Arabia, polytheism in, 10–11

Arabic Bible, 2

Arabic language: as liturgical language, 13; as language of final divine revelation, 15, 18, 86; linguistics of, 19; and numerology, 50; and *'ulama*, 56; and Qur'an, 118–19, 120, 141–42; Hitchens on, 120; as sacred language of Islam, 141; in twenty-first century, 142; translation of, 142, 198 (n. 1); and Internet, 142, 198 (n. 2); limits of, 142, 198 (n. 3); and orthography, 164; lack of neutral pronoun in, 187 (n. 5)

Arahmaiani, 164–66, 169, 179

Aramaic Christianity, 3

Aristotle, 59–61, 63, 82, 89, 192 (n. 6), 194 (n. 10)

Arkan (pillars), 11, 130

Arkoun, Mohammed, 200 (n. 1)

Armstrong, Karen, 20, 194 (n. 10)

Armstrong, Neil, 7–8

Ar-Rahman, 11

Art and artists: and Islamic creativity, 20, 163–64; and video games, 164, 169–71, 173, 175, 201 (n. 9); and performance art, 164–66; and women, 164–66, 200–201 (n. 5); and photography, 166; and Qur'an, 166, 200 (n. 4); and literature, 166–67, 171–72; and paintings, 167, 169; and invocation of Allah, 179–80

Ash'ari, Abu Hasan, 82

Ash'arites, 71, 81–82

'Asi, Muhammad al-, 18

Asma Allah al-husna (Most Beautiful Names of Allah), 26, 175–76. *See also* Divine Names

As-salamu 'alaykum, 35

Astrology, 52

Atheism, 118, 119–20

A'udhu bi(A)llahi min ash-shaitan ar rajim (I take refuge in Allah from the accursed Satan), 155

Augustine, Saint, 62, 187 (n. 3)

Avicenna. *See* Ibn Sina

AwalNet, 143

Ayat al-Kursi, 34–35, 126

Ayat(A)llah (verse of sign of Allah), 36

Ayatollahs, 36

Baqli, Ruzbihan, 112–13, 114

Barzakh (barrier and bridge), 40–41, 97, 137, 139, 177, 181

Basmala: practice of, 37, 38, 41, 91–92, 158, 161; and numerology, 50–51, 54; meaning of letter *b* in, 151, 153

Battle of Badr, 125

Battle of Hunain, 127–28

Battle of the Trench, 126

Battle of Uhud, 126

Bawa Muhaiyaddeen, Muhammad Raheem, 104–9, 111, 112, 114, 175–76, 195 (n. 35)

Beautiful Names of Allah, 45, 50, 53, 67, 93. *See also* Divine Names

Bedouin tribes, 127

Berkey, Jonathan, 191 (n. 2)

Bible: Arabic, 2; English translations of,

17, 121; Book of Revelation, 46; Genesis, 46; Gospels, 87; Hebrew Bible, 87, 120, 139; New Testament, 87, 120, 139
Big bang theory, 63
Bi la kayfa (acceptance of Allah's creation), 64
Bilal al-Habshi, 169
Bin Laden, Osama, 22, 119, 132–36, 140, 197 (n. 11), 200 (n. 24)
Bismi(A)llah (in the name of Allah): and Blondy, 4–5; as invocation, 7, 19, 23, 37, 38, 41; numerology of, 50–51, 52, 54, 190–91 (n. 20); Hulusi on, 153
Bistami, 40
Blogspot, 143
Blondy, Alpha, 4–5, 14, 24
Bodily perfection, 85–86
Bohras, 145
Böwering, Gerhard, 194 (n. 23)
Breivik, Anders, 201 (n. 12)
Brethren of Purity (Ikhwan as-Safa), 77–82, 179, 194 (n. 25)
Buddhism, 2, 88, 164
Bunt, Gary, 146–47, 198 (nn. 2, 5), 199 (n. 11)
Bush, George W., 136, 200 (n. 24)
Buyids, 69–70

Catholics, 32, 140
Chick, Jack, 20, 120, 121, 189 (n. 22)
Children: female infanticide, 121–22; and care of orphans, 122–23
Chishti order, 158–60, 177–78, 188 (n. 11)
Chittick, William, 173, 189 (n. 21)
Christians and Christianity: Arab, 2, 13; Aramaic, 3; refutations of Islam, 14, 17, 189 (n. 22); dialogical readings of Allah, 14–15, 189 (n. 19); and Catholics, 32, 140; on creation, 61; and scriptural perfection, 86; and violence, 140; Malay, 173, 201–2 (n. 13); polemics against Islam, 196 (n. 5)
Cleary, Thomas, 189 (n. 26), 190 (nn. 5, 11)
Cognitive knowledge, 73, 75

Cooke, Katie, 191 (n. 23)
Cornell, Vincent J., 196 (n. 5)
Cosmic perfection, 85
Cragg, Kenneth, 14–15, 20, 189 (n. 19)
Creatio ex nihilo, 60–61, 63, 64
Crone, Patricia, 200 (n. 26)
Cross, Jim, 189 (n. 18)
Crusades, 131, 140
Cyber-Islamic environments (CIES), 146
CyberOrient, 198 (n. 2)

Dala'il al-Khayrat, 36
Damad, Mir, 63, 64
Dar al-Islam, 132
Darwin, Charles, 63, 78, 80
Dervishes, 48, 73, 75
Descartes, René, 178
Dhat (essence of Allah), 34, 104
Dhikr (remembrance): in workplace, 32; and Sufism, 77, 85–88, 107, 117; introspective labor of, 83, 85; invocations distinguished from, 84–85; and observation, 85; and true seeker, 88–89; and *basmala*, 91–92; and Divine Names, 92–93, 95–100, 114; and Allah embodied as light, 100–102; and Allah as directive light, 102–4; and Allah as Nur/Light, 104–6, 175; and heart and stomach of faith, 106–9, 111, 195 (n. 35); and calligraphic piety, 111; and Prophet Muhammad, 111–12; from Divine Other to Divine Beloved, 112–14; and poison of separation, 114–15; and tavern of love, 116–17; and Bin Laden, 133–34
Digital Islam, 170
Divans (Persian poetry), 112, 113
Divination, 52
Divine Names: Ninety-Nine Names, 26, 32, 45, 67, 68, 87, 92, 93, 95, 98, 129, 181; and 'AbdAllah, 42–43, 44, 53–54; Ibn 'Arabi on, 42–43, 53–54, 65, 96–98, 101–2, 103, 194 (n. 17); Beautiful Names of Allah, 45, 50, 53, 67, 95–97, 146, 149, 158, 175–76; and

numerology, 50, 191 (n. 22); mystery of, 68; and language, 76–77, 83; as nontrivial, 77; Ghazali on, 92, 194 (n. 17); basic questions on, 92–93; and *dhikr*, 92–93, 95–100, 114; artistic renditions of, 93; Qur'an on, 93, 95–100, 152; and strategy of one plus three, 96–98; and intervention, 99; as paired epithets, 99; and oversight, 99–100; and forgiveness, 100; and mercy and forgiveness, 100; in relation to creatures and the universe, 100; and idolatry, 101; and science, 149–51; and *hu*, 156, 158; and Sufism, 175–76

Doctrine of the Incarnation, 15
Donne, John, 106
Duns Scotus, 64

Egypt, 166–67
Eickelman, Dale, 198 (n. 2)
Elias, Jamal, 193 (n. 22)
Elijah, Prophet, 43–44
Elites: intellectual approaches of, 54, 55; and Hoca, 56; hierarchy of, 58, 82; and translation movement, 60. See also *'Ulama*
Ernst, Carl W., 20
Eve, 190 (n. 4)
Evil eye, 51
Evolution, 77–81

Facebook, 143, 144, 148
Falasifa (philosophers): audience of, 57; and Aristotle, 60–61; and rationalism, 64–65, 90; and Qur'an, 67–68; role of, 69; and *shari'a*, 71; and Qushayri, 98. *See also specific philosophers*
Faqih (consensus seeker), 71, 72
Farabi, al-, 192 (n. 6)
Farid, Baba, 158–60
Female infanticide, 121, 122
Feminist advocates, 153–56

Five Percenters, 47–48, 49
Foda, Farag, 167
Fort Hood, Tex., 7
Fox, George, 139, 196 (n. 48)
Friedman, Thomas, 201 (n. 9)
Fuqaha (jurists): audience of, 57, 58; and Qur'an, 58, 67–68; as surrogates of Divine Judgment, 59; role of, 69, 71; and Sufism, 75

Gabriel (archangel), and Muhammad's revelations, 9, 10, 19, 20, 120, 121, 124, 125, 140
Gandhi, Mahatma, 139
Gematria, 45, 46
Gender: Allah as beyond, 3–4, 161; as marker of context for dwelling on name of Allah, 55; and translation, 187–88 (n. 5). *See also* Women
Geomancy, 52, 54, 191 (n. 22)
George, Kenneth M., 200 (n. 4)
Ghadir Khumm, 70
Ghazali, Abu Hamid Muhammad ibn Muhammad al-: on temporal origination of the world, 6; as scholar, 57, 64; audience of, 65, 192 (n. 13); and Sufism, 75, 76–77; on Divine Names, 92, 194 (n. 17); as champion of Allah, 179; on 'Abdullah, 190 (n. 13)
Gimaret, Daniel, 188 (n. 11)
God: as absolute, 2; naming of, 2–3; of Abraham, 12; distinctions in names for, 15, 16; relationship of Allah to, 16–18, 189 (n. 21)
Godlas, Alan, 147
Gospels, 87
Gottschalk, Peter, 189 (n. 20)
Gril, Denis, 20, 190 (n. 11)
Gulen, Fetullah, 149, 150
Gulen movement, 148, 149
Gulf War of 1991, 133

Habib Allah (the beloved of God), 36
Hadi (guide or leader), 145

HADI (Human Assistance and Development International), 145, 198 (n. 6)

Hadith (traditions): as Muhammad's words and actions, 20; and *'ulama*, 56, 71, 73; on knowledge, 74; and Divine Light, 102–3; and *jinn*, 137; and Internet, 144; and Adam, 189 (n. 1); and hidden treasure, 195 (n. 40)

Haeri, Fadhlalla, 97

Hafez Shirazi, 113, 115, 195–96 (n. 45)

Hagar, 12, 13, 123

Hajj (pilgrimage), 13, 34, 177

Hajji (pilgrim), 37, 190 (n. 10)

Haleem, Abdel, 189 (n. 26)

Hallaj, 40

Halman, Talat, 191 (n. 1)

Haqiqa (truth), 74, 75

Harun Yahya, 148

Hasan, Nidal, 7

Hawazin, 127

Hawting, G. R., 188 (n. 9)

Healing rituals, and magic squares, 50, 51

Hezb Allah, 36, 190 (n. 7)

Hidden Imam, 69

Hijra (exodus), 123–25

Hilali, al-, 174, 175

Himmelfarb, Gertrude, 146

Hinduism, 2, 105, 106

Hitchens, Christopher, 14, 20, 118, 119–20, 196 (n. 1)

Hoca, Nasruddin, 56, 58, 59, 76, 82, 191 (n. 1)

Hofstadter, Douglas: *Gödel, Escher, Bach*, 138–39, 197–98 (n. 16)

Holographic principle, 152

Homeland (TV series), 7

Honerkamp, Kenneth L., 192 (n. 17)

Howard, Phillip N., 198 (n. 2)

Hu, and Allah, 156, 158, 200 (n. 29)

Hubal, 200 (nn. 24, 26)

Hulusi, Ahmed, 142, 148–49, 151–53, 191 (n. 20), 192 (n. 12)

Husain, M. F., 79, 167, 169, 179

Iblis, 98

Ibn 'Abbad of Ronda, 67, 192 (n. 17)

Ibn 'Abd al-Wahhab, 178

Ibn 'Ajibah, Ahmad, 189 (n. 1)

Ibn al-Walid, Khalid, 126

Ibn 'Arabi, Muhyiddin: on attributes of Allah, 25; mystical meditation by, 38–39; and *barzakh*, 40; on Divine Names, 42–43, 53–54, 65, 96–98, 101–2, 103, 194 (n. 17); *Kitab al'Abadila*, 42–44; treatises of, 65; on metaphors, 65–66; literary legacy of, 76; on *dhikr*, 84, 193 (n. 1); and Ibn Rushd, 89–91, 192 (n. 8), 194 (n. 10); *Fusus al-Hikam*, 91, 92; on Seth, 91–92; as champion of Allah, 179; Gril on, 190 (n. 11); on "unlettered" person, 194 (n. 9)

Ibn 'Ata' Allah al-Iskandari, 65, 66–67, 97, 188 (n. 5)

Ibn Buwayh, Ahmad, 69–70

Ibn Buwayh, 'Ali, 69, 70

Ibn Buwayh, Husayn, 69

Ibn Hanbal, 195 (n. 27)

Ibn Hayyan, Jabir, 49, 79

Ibn Hayyan, Ja'far, 80

Ibn Hazm, 78–79

Ibn Ibrahim, Qasim, 78

Ibn Ja'far, Isma'il, 69

Ibn Khaldun, 'Abd ar-Rahman, 52, 191 (n. 22)

Ibn Qayyim al-Jawziyya, 102–3, 195 (n. 27)

Ibn Rushd, and Ibn 'Arabi, 89–91, 192 (n. 8), 194 (n. 10)

Ibn Sina: on causation, 61–62, 63, 64; and Allah as First Cause, 61–62, 191 (n. 5); role of, 61–63; background of, 62; challenges to, 63–64; Ghazali on, 65

Ibn Taymiyya, 102, 103, 131, 133

'Id al-Adha, 134

Idolatry, 101, 130

Idris, Prophet, 44–45

Ijtihads (interpretations of foundational texts), 144

Ikhwan as-Safa (Brethren of Purity), 77–82, 179, 194 (n. 25)

Ilyas (Elias), 42–43, 44, 45

Imdadullah, Hajji, 177–78

Indo-European languages, 142

Injil, 87

Inquisitions, 140

Insha'(A)llah, as invocation, 34–35

International Institute of Islamic Thought, 174

Internet: and cyberspace practices, 22, 146–47, 198 (n. 2); and numerology, 52–53, 54, 149; and Ash'rites, 82; and Bin Laden, 119, 133, 135, 140; and Arabic language, 142, 198 (n. 2); and Information Revolution, 142–43; and knowledge management, 143; and Allah, 144–46, 148–51, 153–56, 160–62; and website names, 145, 199 (n. 8); and interpretation of Qur'an, 147–48; and Sufism, 148–49, 158–60; and science, 149–53; and feminist advocates, 153–56; and Chishti website, 158–60, 188 (n. 11); limitations of, 161–62; Cornell on, 196 (n. 5)

Intuitive knowledge, 73–74

Invocations: bismi(A)llah as, 7, 19, 23, 37, 38, 41; approaches to, 20, 24, 25–26, 53–54, 67, 179–80; Allah ta'ala as, 25, 29–30, 34, 51, 52, 108, 114; mystical approach, 25, 38–39; magical approach, 26, 45–47; mainstream approach, 26–32, 34–35; and charity, 27–28; and Adam as successor to Allah, 28–29, 36; and performing the name, 29–31; in workplace, 32, 34–35; and praise for Allah, 36–37; and barzakh, 40–41; and numerology, 45–53, 54; 'ulama related to, 56, 57; intellectual approach compared to, 67–68; dhikr distinguished from, 84–85; and total reliance on Allah, 90

Iqbal, Muhammad, 199 (n. 22)

Iran, 166

Iranian Revolution of 1978, 140

Iraq, 120, 166

Isaac, 13

Ishmael, 12–13, 123

Islam: Allah as name embodying all that defines life, 2; as conduit of Allah, 6; Allah as name of God, 13; and daily prayers, 13, 32, 34, 42, 75; diversity within, 13–14; and cyberspace practices, 22, 198 (n. 2); surrender as literal meaning of, 29; prophets in, 36; numerology in, 46–47, 48, 49, 50, 52, 149; on creation, 61; and Sufism, 74, 193 (n. 20); Hitchens on, 118, 120; role of violence in, 119, 120, 121–22, 123, 124, 128–29, 140; and exodus from Arabia to Africa, 123–24; and exodus from Mecca to Medina, 124–25; and conversion, 126–27; and Ridda wars, 128; and fundamentalism, 131, 140, 197 (n. 9); and Internet, 143, 144–48, 149; and rival orthodoxies, 146; negative stereotypes of, 175; Christian polemics against, 196 (n. 5). See also Muslims; Shi'i Islam; Sunni Islam; Umma

Islam Games, 170

Islamic expansion, 59, 128, 129, 130–31

IslamiCity website, 145

Islamic speculative theology (kalam), 78, 187 (n. 4)

Islamophobia, 201 (n. 12)

Isma'ilis, 145, 160

Ism akbar (secret name of Allah), 50

Jahliyya (period of ignorance), 123, 131

Jalal (majesty), 97, 194 (n. 21)

Jamal (beauty), 97, 194 (n. 21)

James, William, 116–17, 160, 196 (n. 48)

Jerrahi, Muzaffar Ozak al-, 85–87

Jerusalem, Crusader conquest of, 131

Jesus Christ, 2, 15, 36, 44

Jews and Judaism: repetition of name

Moosa, Ebrahim, 192 (n. 13)

Moses, as *kalimu(A)llah*, 36

Moustafa, Ahmed, 40, 93, 167

Moza, Sheikha, 169

M-theory, 152

Mufti (advisory judge), 71

Muhammad, Prophet: dates in life of, 6;
revelations of, 6, 9, 10–11, 15, 19–20,
45, 87, 120, 121, 123–24, 125, 140, 153,
188 (n. 9); theological distinctions
with Allah, 11–13; as final prophet, 12,
15, 36, 141; on *sadaqa*, 27; laudatory
names of, 36; final revelation of, 39,
153; tribal background of, 59, 121; and
sunnah, 66; descendants of, 70; and
Sufism, 72, 73; and Divine Names,
92; and *dhikr*, 111–12; and violence,
119, 123, 124, 126; Hitchens on, 120;
and sanctified war, 125–26; as com-
promiser and peace maker, 126–28;
death of, 128–29, 130; and *jihad*, 131–
32; quotes attributed to, 151. See also
Hadith; *Sunnah*

Muhasibi, 78

Muʿin ad-din, 177

Mujtahid (investigating judge), 71

Murata, Sachiko, 189 (n. 21)

Muslim Brotherhood, 131, 140

Muslims: Allah as name beyond names
for, 2; population of, 6; Allah domi-
nating mindset of, 9; markers for self-
identity, 11, 14; Allah as name of God
for, 13, 18; diversity within, 13–14;
and invocation of Allah, 19; *shariʿa*
as central to identity, 69; and Arabic
language, 141. See also *Umma*

Mutakallimun (theologians): audience of, 57; and philosophers, 63;
and Qurʾan, 67–68; role of, 69; and
shariʿa, 71; and Qushayri, 98

Muʿtazilites, 64–65, 71, 82, 192 (n. 11)

Nafs (single self), 28, 30–31, 91

Nasser, Gamal Abdel, 131

Nawawi, an-, 187 (n. 1)

Nayan (Tamil), 108, 114

Neoplatonism, 62, 104, 192 (n. 6)

Neshat, Shirin, 166, 169, 179

Ninety-Nine Names. *See* Divine Names

Numerology, 45–53, 54, 149, 190–91
(n. 20), 191 (n. 22)

Nurcu Movement, 150

Nursi, Bediuzzaman Said, 148, 149–51,
179, 199 (n. 18)

Nursi movement, 148

Obama, Barack, 169

Occultation, 69

Officializing strategies, 144

One (*ahad*): Allah as, 3, 6, 23, 24, 187
(n. 4); Jesus Christ as, 15

Operation Desert Fox, 132

Oxford Islamic Studies Online, 154

Parochialism, and universalism, 16

Perfection and four perfections, 85–86

Performance art, 164–66

Philoponus, John, 191 (n. 4)

Pir (master), 109

Pirous, Abdul Djalil, 166, 200 (n. 4)

Platonic thought, 62

Polytheism, 10–11, 62, 130

Popular culture, magic squares in, 49–51

Prasad, Leela, 193 (n. 2), 195 (n. 38)

Psalms, 87

Ptolemy, 191 (n. 22)

Qadi (court judge), 71–72

Qalandars, 48

Qaradawi, Yusuf al-, 146

Qibla (point of orientation), 13

Quantum mechanics, 152, 153

Qurʾan: Allah as God of, 2, 16–17; description of Allah in, 8; citing of, 9;
and use of name Allah, 9, 10; and
Muhammad as final prophet, 12,
15; and Muhammad's revelations,
19–20, 34, 45, 87, 120, 121, 123–24,
125, 140, 153, 188 (n. 9); Most Beautiful Names of Allah in, 26; on four

Bruce B. Lawrence, *Who Is Allah?* (2015).

Ebrahim Moosa, *What Is a Madrasa?* (2015).

Edward E. Curtis IV, *The Call of Bilal: Islam in the African Diaspora* (2014).

Sahar Amer, *What Is Veiling?* (2014).

Rudolph T. Ware III, *The Walking Qur'an: Islamic Education, Embodied Knowledge, and History in West Africa* (2014).

Sa'diyya Shaikh, *Sufi Narratives of Intimacy: Ibn 'Arabī, Gender, and Sexuality* (2012).

Karen G. Ruffle, *Gender, Sainthood, and Everyday Practice in South Asian Shi'ism* (2011).

Jonah Steinberg, *Isma'ili Modern: Globalization and Identity in a Muslim Community* (2011).

Iftikhar Dadi, *Modernism and the Art of Muslim South Asia* (2010).

Gary R. Bunt, *iMuslims: Rewiring the House of Islam* (2009).

Fatemeh Keshavarz, *Jasmine and Stars: Reading More than "Lolita" in Tehran* (2007).

Scott A. Kugle, *Sufis and Saints' Bodies: Mysticism, Corporeality, and Sacred Power in Islam* (2007).

Roxani Eleni Margariti, *Aden and the Indian Ocean Trade: 150 Years in the Life of a Medieval Arabian Port* (2007).

Sufia M. Uddin, *Constructing Bangladesh: Religion, Ethnicity, and Language in an Islamic Nation* (2006).

Omid Safi, *The Politics of Knowledge in Premodern Islam: Negotiating Ideology and Religious Inquiry* (2006).

Ebrahim Moosa, *Ghazālī and the Poetics of Imagination* (2005).

miriam cooke and Bruce B. Lawrence, eds., *Muslim Networks from Hajj to Hip Hop* (2005).

Carl W. Ernst, *Following Muhammad: Rethinking Islam in the Contemporary World* (2003).